BOOKS ABOUT DESIGN AND PROGR

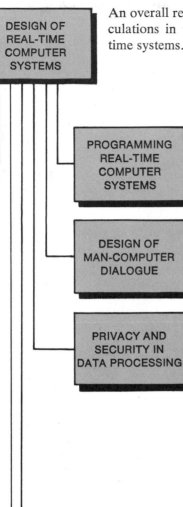

DESIGN OF REAL-TIME COMPUTER SYSTEMS

An overall review of tech culations in the design time systems.

PROGRAMMING REAL-TIME COMPUTER SYSTEMS

Programming mechanisms, program testing tools and techniques, problems encountered, implementation considerations, project management.

DESIGN OF MAN-COMPUTER DIALOGUE

A guide to the design of man-machine dialogues; detailed examination of the many types of real-time man-computer interface, especially for commercial and management-information systems.

PRIVACY AND SECURITY IN DATA PROCESSING

About the prevention of unauthorized access to computers and data banks, embezzlement, crime, sabotage and invasion of privacy.

A BOOK ABOUT USERS OF SUCH SYSTEMS
(CO-AUTHOR ADRIAN NORMAN)

THE COMPUTERIZED SOCIETY

Euphoria; Alarm; Protection Action. An appraisal of the impact of computers on society over the next fifteen years, and the steps that can be taken to direct it into the most beneficial channels.

PROGRAMMING
REAL-TIME COMPUTER SYSTEMS

Prentice-Hall Series in Automatic Computation

George Forsythe, editor

ARBIB, *Theories of Abstract Automata*

BATES AND DOUGLAS, *Programming Language/One*

BAUMANN, FELICIANO, BAUER, AND SAMELSON, *Introduction to ALGOL*

BLUMENTHAL, *Management Information Systems*

BOBROW AND SCHWARTZ, editors, *Computers and the Policy-Making Community: Applications to International Relations*

BOWLES, editor, *Computers in Humanistic Research*

CESCHINO AND KUNTZMANN, *Numerical Solution of Initial Value Problems*

CRESS, DIRKSEN, AND GRAHAM, *Fortran IV with Watfor*

DESMONDE, *A Conversational Graphic Data Processing System: The IBM 1130/2250*

DESMONDE, *Computers and Their Uses*

DESMONDE, *Real-Time Data Processing Systems: Introductory Concepts*

EVANS, WALLACE, AND SUTHERLAND, *Simulation Using Digital Computers*

FIKE, *Computer Evaluation of Mathematical Functions*

FORSYTHE AND MOLER, *Computer Solution of Linear Algebraic Systems*

GOLDEN, *Fortran IV: Programming and Computing*

GOLDEN AND LEICHUS, *IBM 360: Programming and Computing*

GORDON, *System Simulation*

GREENSPAN, *Lectures on the Numerical Solution of Linear, Singular and Nonlinear Differential Equations*

GRISWOLD, POAGE, AND POLONSKY, *The SNOBOL4 Programming Language*

GRUENBERGER, editor, *Computers and Communications—Toward a Computer Utility*

GRUENBERGER, editor, *Critical Factors in Data Management*

HARTMANIS AND STEARNS, *Algebraic Structure Theory of Sequential Machines*

HULL, *Introduction to Computing*

LOUDEN, *Programming the IBM 1130 and 1800*

MARTIN, *Design of Real-Time Computer Systems*

MARTIN, *Programming Real-Time Computer Systems*

MARTIN, *Telecommunications and the Computer*

MARTIN, *Teleprocessing Network Organization*

MINSKY, *Computation: Finite and Infinite Machines*

MOORE, *Interval Analysis*

SAMMET, *Programming Languages: History and Fundamentals*

SCHULTZ, *Digital Processing: A System Orientation*

SNYDER, *Chebyshev Methods in Numerical Approximation*

STERLING AND POLLACK, *Introduction to Statistical Data Processing*

STROUD AND SECREST, *Gaussian Quadrature Formulas*

TRAUB, *Iterative Methods for the Solution of Equations*

VARGA, *Matrix Iterative Analysis*

VAZSONYI, *Problem Solving by Digital Computers with PL/1 Programming*

WILKINSON, *Rounding Errors in Algebraic Processes*

ZIEGLER, *Time-Sharing Data Processing Systems*

Frontispiece. Ninety separate pieces of equipment making up American Airlines' SABRE reservations system are shown in this photograph made at the airline's electronic reservations center at Briarcliff Manor, N. Y., with a Nikon Fisheye lens.

PROGRAMMING

REAL-TIME COMPUTER SYSTEMS

JAMES MARTIN

Staff Member
IBM Systems Research Institute

PRENTICE-HALL, INC.

ENGLEWOOD CLIFFS, N.J.

© 1965 by
Prentice-Hall, Inc.
Englewood Cliffs, N.J.

Printed in the United States of America
73050-C

Library of Congress Catalog Card No. 65-24603

Current printing (last digit):
13   12   11   10

PRENTICE-HALL INTERNATIONAL, INC., *London*
PRENTICE-HALL OF AUSTRALIA, PTY., LTD., *Sydney*
PRENTICE-HALL OF CANADA, LTD., *Toronto*
PRENTICE-HALL OF INDIA (PRIVATE) LTD., *New Delhi*
PRENTICE-HALL OF JAPAN, INC., *Tokyo*

PREFACE

The trend in the use of data processing is towards larger, more integrated systems. The hardware now available is enabling many companies to combine functions that were previously done separately. Scientific, commercial, and real-time processing are being handled on one machine or network of machines. Data transmission links are speeding the flow of business and technical information, and remote enquiry stations are becoming an increasingly common facility.

Scientists and others are finding that time-sharing techniques can vastly increase the availability and usefulness of their computers, while massive random-access storage devices are today part of the solution to many file management problems in business and government. Computers are being used on-line to chemical plants, jet-engine test beds, classrooms, and the shop floor in factories. Man is acquiring a new relationship with the machines through the use of distant displays and console devices.

As these trends spread, programmers and systems analysts are faced with an increasingly difficult task. Many programs may be in the computer at one time. Different operations interrupt each other in a complex fashion. Events no longer fit into predetermined timing patterns, and elaborate Supervisory Programs are needed for coordinating these events and allocating priorities. Data has to be located in and read from large files without holding up other processing. Errors and emergencies have become more difficult to deal with.

This book describes the methods used in programming complex systems of this type. While many of the techniques described apply to non-real-time systems, emphasis is given to real-time with its special problems and dangers.

The state of this art is changing rapidly and by the time a book is edited and published there are already new ideas, new methods, and new machines. It is hoped that, although the details change, the principles set out in this book will remain true long enough for the work to be of value.

J.M.

ACKNOWLEDGEMENTS

There are many acknowledgements that should accompany a book of this nature. The development of the techniques it describes has been the result of the creativity and labor of a very large number of persons. Most of the techniques are now coming into common computer usage, but the work that has led to these methods was originated on certain pioneering installations which include:

SAGE

Project Mercury

American Airlines SABRE System

Pan American Airways PANAMAC System

New York Stock Exchange System

First National Bank of Chicago

IBM's Internal Teleprocessing System

To the many Systems Engineers and Programmers who worked on these and other projects, the author is indebted.

Some material is taken from a report on system testing prepared for the PANAMAC System by Messrs. J. Egglezos, C. Barbel, T. P. Taylor, and the author.

The manuscript was read and valuable criticisms made by Messrs. C. Vince and P. Neall in London, and by Mr. W. B. Elmore in New York.

Generous help was given in the preparation of this book by various members of the International Business Machines Corporation in London, Paris, and the United States.

CONTENTS

ix

BASIC CONCEPTS

There are certain basic concepts, principles, and terms which are defined and explained in this work. The following index lists these, along with the page on which a definition or introductory explanation of them is given. Fig. 1 serves as a guide for the readers of varying interests who will be concerned with the use of the book.

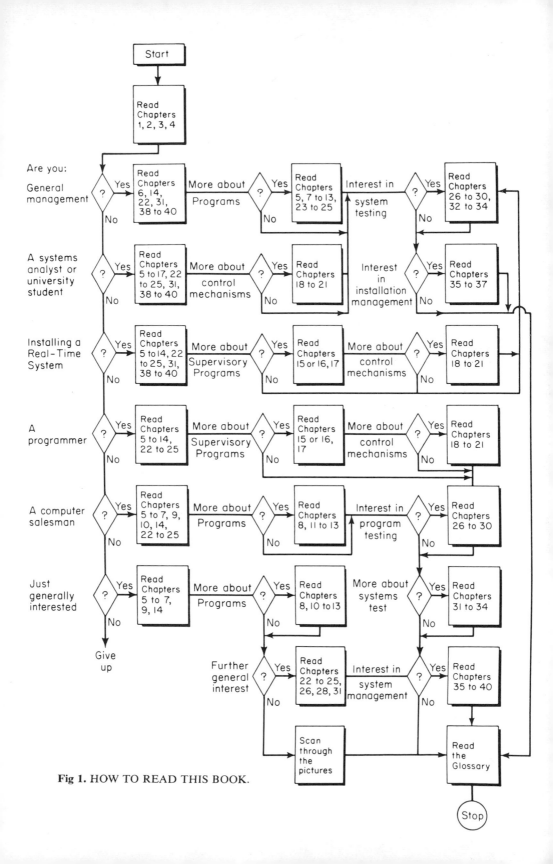

Fig 1. HOW TO READ THIS BOOK.

SECTION **I**

THE GENERAL PICTURE

1 A REAL-TIME INTRODUCTION

A revolution is taking place in the world of data processing.

The introduction of the electronic computer, a little more than a decade ago, fundamentally changed the techniques of data processing. Punched card installations, accounting machines and calculators were replaced by computers, slowly and cautiously at first, and later more rapidly. The potentialities of data processing expanded enormously. Work previously undreamed of soon became possible on the new machines.

By now computers are a familiar sight in industry and commerce, in laboratories and government departments. They chew through vast files of card or tape, do calculations and make logical decisions. Reams and reams of paper flow from their high speed printers. Whole floors of churning card punches and reproducers, sorters and collators, clanking accounting machines and girls pushing trolley loads of cards, have been replaced by the grey and blue computers flickering their lights and spinning their tape reels.

Today, a second revolution is in progress, and its effect will ultimately be more rewarding than the first.

Systems described as "on-line" and "real-time" are now being installed and planned. In these, data may be entered directly into the computer system from the environment it works with, and information is sent back there. The wide variety of devices which feed data into the computer and which receive the processed information are referred to in this book as *terminals*.

The terminals may be in the computer room or they may be far away, connected to the computer by telephone line or other forms of telecommunication links.

A batch of data travels from the terminal to the computer. It is processed and another batch of data is sent back to the terminal in reply.

3

These batches of data are referred to throughout the book as *messages* or *transactions*.

Messages arriving at the computer from its terminals are not stored in serial files on tapes or on cards to be sorted and batch-processed; they are processed immediately so that a reply may go back to the requisite terminals within seconds or fractions of seconds. The terminals may be many miles from the computer. For example, in the Pan American Airline Reservation System they are all over the world. A message originating in a travel agent's office in Rome would have a reply from the on-line real-time computer in New York within five seconds.

The terminals in such a system may be designed for entering commercial data or they may be technical equipment such as thermocouples, strain gauges and so on. A very wide variety of devices is possible for collecting data at their source and for delivering the results of the computation at the place where they are needed (Fig. 2). The network of terminals marks the system as "on-line."

An on-line system may be defined as one in which the input data enter the computer directly from their point of origin and/or in which output data are transmitted directly to where they are used.

The intermediate stages of punching data on cards or paper tape, or of writing magnetic tape, or off-line printing, are largely avoided.

The computer system, then, instead of doing a piece of work, the results of which will be used at a later time, can now enter directly into a minute-by-minute *control* of an environment. It can operate a reservation network for hotels or airlines. It can control a steel mill and optimize its efficiency. It can monitor a manned space flight. It can give bank customers up-to-the-minute details of their accounts. It can schedule work through a factory and re-schedule it whenever new requirements occur or when the situation on the shop floor changes. It can speed up the flow of traffic in a city by detecting the positions of vehicles and changing the traffic lights in the optimum manner.

This is "real-time."

A real-time computer system may be defined as one which controls an environment by receiving data, processing them and returning the results sufficiently quickly to affect the functioning of the environment at that time.

"Real-time" is a term that is defined differently by different authorities. The question of "response time" may enter into the definition.

Response time is the time the system takes to react to a given input. If a message is keyed into a terminal by an operator and the reply from the computer is typed at the same terminal, *"response time" may be defined as the time interval between the operator pressing the last key and the terminal typing the first letter of the reply.* For different kinds of terminals response time may be defined similarly as the interval between an event and the system's response to the event.

In order to control an environment a short response time from the computer is necessary. The speed of response differs from one type of system to another according to their needs. In a system for radar scanning a response time of milliseconds is needed. Airline reservation systems in

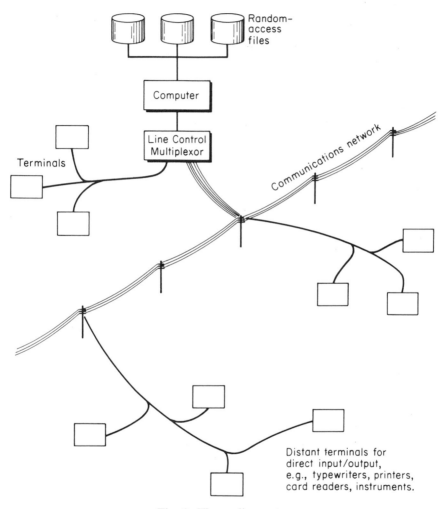

Random-access files

Computer

Line Control Multiplexor

Terminals

Communications network

Distant terminals for direct input/output, e.g., typewriters, printers, card readers, instruments.

Fig. 2. The on-line system.

America have been programmed to give a maximum response time of about three seconds. A warehousing control system may have a response time of thirty seconds. In a system used for controlling a paper mill a five minute response time may be adequate. On some systems the response time is longer than this, perhaps half an hour or more; but above this it becomes arguable whether the system should still be described as "real-time."

In order to bring about this major advance in computer usage, four technological developments were required.

First, the computer had to be directly linked to a telecommunications network. Data have to pass from remote points, over telephone or telegraph links, or possibly microwave links, to the computer. As they travel over the lines in the form of pulses they must be converted into bits in the computer. The bits are stored in the computer memory to form characters or words ready for processing. Similarly, characters or words fom the computer may be transmitted to the far-away locations. In this way, computers may "talk" to computers, or a man may communicate with a distant machine. In a similar way, a computer may read instruments in a plant or operate controlling devices such as valves or speed regulators, or even traffic lights in a city street. In some applications many communication lines will be attached to one computer and each line may have more than one terminal. An elaborate *multiplexor* or line control unit is required for scanning the lines and accepting or transmitting messages in parallel.

Second, it was necessary to devise terminals which could be attached to the communications network. The terminal is the interface between the computer system and the outside world: the man-machine link, or the final link between the computer and the environment it is controlling. In a commercial system the terminals may be devices such as teleprinters or perhaps small card readers or paper tape readers. In the SAGE air defence network radar units form the input, and cathode ray tubes are used as terminals for the operators to inspect maps of selected areas.

At Cape Kennedy, large sets of indicator lights form a terminal to a system monitoring manned space flights. The board-room of the future is likely to have a display screen and controls for interrogating a "Total Information System."

The terminals in a process-control application are the measuring instruments and regulating devices, along with typewriters, display screens and other means of communicating with operators. A very wide variety of terminals are possible, and it is certain that applications of the future will give rise to an almost infinite array of devices that may be hooked up to a computer in this manner. In some applications many terminals will be hooked up to one communication line. Control units will translate the action of the terminals into pulses suitable for transmission over the lines, and conversely, they will convert the reply message into a form which will operate the terminal. It may be necessary for the control unit to recognize codes. For example, a message may be sent down a line from the computer, requesting a terminal with a certain address to transmit if it has a message. This is called *polling*.

Third, large files are a development of computer technology and have made possible many of the real-time applications. The system must have quick access to a large store of information in order to provide the data necessary for control.

Computers of the past have had large files of data on magnetic tape. To find an item at random on a magnetic tape, however, may take a minute or even longer, depending upon the length of the tape. The computer has to scan through the tape searching for the item. This time is too long for most real-time systems in which items must be located in a fraction of a second. Therefore, rather than scanning a tape serially, it is necessary to have a file from which the computer can quickly pick out an item at random. Large *random-access files* have been developed in which any of a very large number of items can be located and read in a fraction of a second.

A booking system for airlines, for example, must have almost immediate access to details of seat availability on all segments of all its flights for some time in the future. This will need several million characters of random-access storage. Larger airline reservation systems also keep details of all the passengers and much other information. This needs several hundred million characters randomly accessible.

In a similar manner, a banking system will keep the records of all customer accounts in its memory. A credit-checking system will keep a blacklist of persons with bad debts. A production control system may keep records of orders to be manufactured, machine tool loadings, schedules or work to be routed through the factory, and other information. A large information retrieval system may need a memory running into billions of characters.

The main forms of random-access memory are drums with an access time of about 5 to 30 milliseconds, disk files which have much greater capacity but access times ranging from about 30 to 600 milliseconds, and magnetic strip or card files with access times of about 50 to 800 milliseconds and the possibility of very large volumes. Several of these, or combinations of them, may be attached to one system. Generally speaking, the larger the volume, the more expensive it is to build a system with a quick access time.

Finally, in order to implement these real-time and on-line applications and to give them a fast enough response time and sufficient reliability, an advance in programming techniques is required. Many of the hardware problems have been solved. A new real-time application today is likely to use standard off-the-shelf equipment. The programming, however, will not be standard except in a very minor degree. For most future systems the programming will need to be thought out afresh, and for some of the systems that are operating, the problems connected with the programming have been very severe.

It is intended in the following pages to illustrate the problems that are likely to face a real-time programming team and to indicate solutions that have been found to these so far. The art of programming real-time systems is still in its infancy. Many developments are likely to be seen in the years to come. This book cannot, then, pretend to provide final answers to the problems it raises, but by highlighting the difficulties and presenting a variety of suggestions and techniques it is hoped that it will do much to further the cross-pollination of ideas that is essential in the development of computer usage. It is hoped that the following pages will help stimulate the thinking and discussion of the teams implementing these systems.

If the salesman or the potential buyers of a real-time system understand the mechanics and functions of the proposed system without knowing the programming aspects that go with it, they are likely to end up with a system that is unable to do the job for which it was intended. In an alarmingly high proportion of systems in the past the programming complexities were much greater than originally anticipated. The core size was too small or the speed was not fast enough. Sometimes the queues building up in the system became too long. It is only with an understanding of the techniques involved that such things can be avoided.

In general, the programming for a real-time system is more complex than on an equivalent batch-processing or "conventional" system. The new data processing techniques bringing the change from batch-processing systems to real-time systems are a change to a higher degree of automation. Transactions flow to the system, are processed and flow back without any punching of cards or any action by the computer operator. There is little or no changing of tape reels or setting of switches. The complete cycle of control happens automatically, without human intervention. At the same time, the programs have become more complicated because they handle functions over which there was manual control before. For example, the system will handle almost all error conditions automatically without requesting help from the operator. Random-access processing is used, and there are no interruptions for sorting. There are no end-of-reel conditions or card decks to be loaded.

This change is, in a sense, the computer "growing up". It is no longer one machine in one room, with an operator making it perform a succession of functions. It is now an autonomous system carrying out all, or almost all, of its functions by itself. It can load its own core with programs when it requires them, and gain access to all the data it requires from its on-line files. It can check its own work and its input and, to a large extent, deal with errors. It may be one computer or many computers talking to each other. By means of tele-communication links it spreads its tentacles into the environment it is controlling, and its nerve endings may be anywhere in a factory, or anywhere in a city, or, with the largest systems, all around the world. An airline agent in London asks a computer in New York a question and gets his reply in London in two seconds. A bank customer withdraws some cash, and his account record is up-dated in the computer files immediately. A rocket carrying an astronaut fails to reach orbital velocity, and the monitoring computer gives instructions to bring him down immediately before he crash-lands in Africa.

But to achieve this, new problems in programming must be overcome. New techniques must be developed. It is essential that these are understood at the time the system is planned as well as later when it is being implemented. That is the purpose of this book.

2 WHY REAL-TIME?

Before discussing the techniques involved in real-time systems, it will help to keep the subject in better perspective if the reasons for real-time are examined. Why is "real-time" needed? What are its economic justifications? When is a real-time system preferable to a batch-processing system? Should all of the system be on-line or could part of it be off-line? How rapidly must the system respond to various inputs? Can a slow response be tolerated?

If the programmers and designers have these questions in mind the cost and complexity may be considerably reduced. There is a great temptation to over-engineer these systems, to build sophistications into the programs, to give the system a very fast response time, to make the system even slicker than it need be. Programmers are apt to build in fascinating, but economically unnecessary, routines for making the system give a highly polished performance. Some of the first commercial systems were programmed to have a response time of two or three seconds. This gave rise to a very elaborate degree of multi-programming which caused severe problems, as will be described in the pages to follow. It might be economically justifiable, in some cases, to have a system which gives a response within twenty seconds or so, and this would ease many of the subsequent troubles.

On most computers it pays to program for simplicity. With real-time machines this principle is even more true. If the reasons for having a real-time system are fully understood, then it is possible to plan the programming from the start to be as simple as possible.

What, then, are the economic justifications for real-time systems?

In looking at the uses for these new techniques, it is possible to split them into two categories. First, work which has been done in the past either manually or by machines, might be done more economically or more efficiently, which ultimately means the same, by on-line real-time systems. Second, and far more excitingly, the new systems open up potentialities for doing work which it was quite impossible to do before. The computer industry as a whole has been faced with these two phases of its operation, initially the mechanization of work already being done and, later, the achievement of new types of work unthinkable before such machines came into existence.

The second phase uses the machines to truly extend man's capabilities, to push forward new frontiers in science and business. This phase is more difficult to evaluate and much more difficult to implement. In considering the operation of a company, it is easy for the accountant, for example, to understand ways of mechanizing his present procedures; but it is much more difficult for him to appreciate the benefits of new procedures that were previously undreamed of.

Let us consider first the use of real-time and random-access systems in mechanizing present-day work.

It is pleasant, now that the world of computers has become so complex, to let one's imagination drift back to the days of Dickens. In those days data-processing was done by a clerk with a quill pen, perched on a high stool and perhaps wearing a top hat. In front of him he had a set of thick and well-bound ledgers. If an order was made for a certain quantity of goods, a clerk would deal with this transaction in its entirety. He might look at his stock sheets to see whether the order could be fulfilled from stock or whether some of it had to be manufactured. He would update the order book and if any goods were sent he would modify the stock sheets to make out a bill for the customer, and make an entry on the appropriate page of a customer ledger; a simple process which was easy to understand. If anyone had any query about the state of the business, about a certain item of stock, or about the debt outstanding of a customer, the clerk could turn to the appropriate pages of his ledgers and immediately produce the answer. One can imagine such a clerk today taking orders by telephone and answering queries over the telephone. He would balance his books at the end of each day, and if costing figures were required he could maintain these in a similar way so that they were as up-to-date as required.

However, admirable as the methods of the Dickensian clerk were, they could only work in a fairly small company. As the company grew, the sizes of the ledgers increased until several clerks were needed to maintain them. Division of labor made the job easier, and one clerk would maintain the stock sheets while another did the billing, and so on. Earlier in this century various means for mechanization were introduced and, to make efficient use of these, the work was split up into batches. For example, several hundred transactions may be grouped into a batch. One accounting function would be carried out on all of these by one clerk or one machine, and then the next function would be performed by another clerk or another machine. When punched card accounting was introduced it became economical to have very large batches. Many trays of cards would be fed through one machine before the set-up of that machine was changed for the next function it would perform. Similarly, with the use of magnetic tape on computers, large tape files would be processed with one program before the file was sorted ready for the next operation.

In working this way the flexibility of the old clerical methods was lost. It was no longer possible to give one transaction individual treatment. It was no longer possible to give quick answers to inquiries about the status of an account, or the credit-worthiness of a customer, or the amount of an item in stock. Or, at least, if such an enquiry was made, the answer might be one week out-of-date or more than that. When items were to be posted it was necessary for the computer to read every item in the file as it scanned its way to the ones to be updated, and every item had often to be written out afresh on a new tape, whether it was updated or not.

Batch-processing, then, was not the ideal way to operate. It would have been much more convenient for management to have all the information about running their organization up-to-date and at their finger tips. However, the volumes had become such that computers had to be used, and computers using magnetic tape or card files read information serially. It could be shown that the larger the batch size handled by the machine, the more efficient it was from the machine point of view. Because of the nature of this equipment, management was living with a compromise. Today that compromise has been in existence for so long that it has become the accepted method of operation, and little thought is given to its desirability.

The use of random-access files and on-line real-time systems for accounting is, surprisingly enough, rather like a return to the old clerical methods. The computer now, rather like the clerk on the high stool, has quick access to any part of any of the ledgers. Inquiries can be made at any time and they receive a quick answer that is up-to-date. Special customers can have fast treatment. It is possible in certain cases to deviate from the ordered sequence of events.

The cost of operating this way is sometimes—but not always—higher than the serial approach of conventional computer systems. The serial approach often requires the reading of an entire file when the activity of that file is only 5 per cent or less. In other words, 95 per cent of the items or more are read into the computer from magnetic tape, inspected and written on another tape, without being processed at all. This reading and writing is a complete waste, but it is necessitated by the nature of magnetic

A new device developed by International Business Machines Corporation to simplify and speed store-to-warehouse ordering. The IBM 1094 line entry terminal—designed for use wherever order forms are filled out—enables store personnel to order from a central point in seconds. The store manager surveys shelf stock (left), notes items that need replacement in a 1094 order entry book (with each item of inventory listed by number on a separate line) and then places the book alongside the 1094 (right) and presses keys to indicate the items to be ordered. The order information is transmitted to the warehouse where it automatically is punched into cards and processed prior to being assembled for shipping.

tape. With a random-access approach only the required records need be read into the computer. Inactive records, although instantly available, are not referred to.

It is possible, though not always desirable, to complete at one time all the actions connected with a transaction. The transaction enters the system and is processed almost immediately. All the appropriate "ledgers" are updated, and the reply or output document, if any, is produced at that time. With telecommunication links the input can originate wherever an appropriate terminal is situated, and the output document can also be produced anywhere. The system contains up-to-the-minute information and can be interrogated from any point on the communication network. If it is possible to dial the machine on the public telephone lines, it may be interrogated from anywhere in the country. Computers have been devised that can speak with a human voice in answer to telephone inquiries, though teleprinters or other terminals could be used. Almost any type of interrogation may be possible in such a real-time business system.

An NCR Window Posting Machine being used at a bank counter. It is connected directly to a distant computer by telephone lines. Customer accounts are kept on random-access files attached to the computer.

It was possible to ask a Dickensian clerk to do some calculations or to extract statistics from his books. He would interrupt his routine work and, perhaps on a pad of scrap paper, would work out the answers to the request. In a similar manner a computer could interrupt its present work, load itself with the appropriate program from the random-access file, clear a working area in its storage and answer the query, referring to whatever files it may need.

It may be desirable not to have too many such queries because they slow down the system, and the Supervisory Program needed may become complex, as will be described later. However, some systems spend almost all their time answering queries.

There is normally a large card punch room or possibly paper tape punch room associated with a commercial computer installation. Documents are punched into cards which serve as input to the machine. An on-line system avoids much of this. Transactions are keyed directly into the operator sets of the system. Sometimes the output may be on the originating document itself. This may be inserted into a terminal as if this were a typewriter. The input data are keyed in, and the reply comes from the computer in a second or so, to be typed on the document. A good example of this is the on-line savings bank systems that have been installed. The bank teller inserts a savings pass-book into his operator set. Details of the transaction, normally a deposit or a withdrawal of cash, are keyed in, being printed on the pass-book at the same time. A second or so later the reply from the computer is printed, giving the customer's new balance. The process is very quick and secure. If the customer does not have a sufficient amount in his account this is known immediately. This type of system has greatly reduced clerical errors, and the staff needed by the bank is cut down because there is no intermediate preparation of documents or punched cards. Furthermore, the customer will be able to withdraw cash from any branch of the bank that is connected to the on-line system.

In a manufacturing plant much of the input to the costing and accounting system will come from the shop floor. This will include information such as machine set-up times, the times at which jobs are started and completed, scrap values, etc. A data collection system may be used for obtaining this information. Terminals such as key-board-type devices can be placed on the shop floor where a foreman or workman can enter the required information. There may be machines for reading the numbers on badges of the workman entering information or, possibly, time-recording devices attached to the machine tools themselves. By collecting this information with an on-line system much clerical work is eliminated, errors are reduced, and the computer has a truly up-to-date picture of the situation on the shop floor. This information may be used to produce cost figures that are up-to-date. In a more advanced system it may be used for controlling hour-by-hour what is happening on the shop floor of a factory.

To achieve its objective of maximizing profit, the management of a

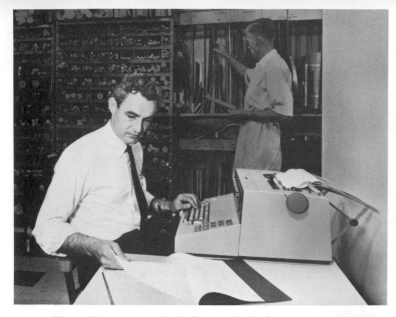

Three illustrations of real-time terminals in use in a factory. Up-to-the-minute data collection from the shop floor makes possible dynamic scheduling of the flow of work through the factory. The current inventory status is always known. The objectives of such a system are to minimize inventory and maximize the amount of work the factory can handle.

manufacturing concern must establish a plan, execute it and then evaluate it. In order to control and minimize costs these must be evaluated continuously, and any of them that become too high may then be dealt with quickly. Similarly, production plans should be reevaluated continuously as new orders arrive in the factory. Any change in the work to be done, or the resources to do it, should give rise to a new assessment of the work schedule. If the firm is to stay ahead of competition, its decisions must be made as quickly as possible, and these decisions must be based upon the latest facts. A real-time system which contains all these facts, and which may be interrogated quickly by management at any time, will enable management to make the necessary decisions quickly and accurately.

Attempts have been made in the past to use tape computers for production scheduling. The computer produces a net break-down of the parts that have to be manufactured in order to fulfill the orders on hand. It then might attempt to work out how these parts shall be manufactured. It might schedule the routing of the parts through the shop floor of the factory, specifying, for example, the quantity of a particular item to be manufactured, and on which machine; this batch will then go to another machine for the next operation, and so on. In this way it might be possible to work out a detailed time-table for all the operations to be done on machine tools in a job shop. But this type of scheduling rarely works in practice because it is not flexible enough. Unforeseen events occur; a machine tool breaks down. A new and urgent order comes in, which has to have priority. A certain type of material runs out or is not up to standard and cannot be used. A foreman needs to put an apprentice on a certain machine who cannot perform a particular operation on the schedule. Any such event, of which there are many in practice, starts off a chain reaction affecting subsequent events, and soon the schedule becomes meaningless and impossible to adhere to. The only solution to this is to make up a new schedule every time an unforeseen event throws it out of gear. To make up the schedule afresh would not be a difficult task even for a small computer, provided it had access to all the necessary information. It would need access to records giving information about the loading on all the various machine tools and about the queues of items waiting for processing on these machine tools. It would need access to records saying which operations have to be done on each item and in what sequence. To re-schedule the work it would need to refer to these records many times and at random. Furthermore, it would be necessary for the records themselves to be up-to-date. An on-line computer with random-access files would have the facilities to do this.

In attempting to do this one is attempting to increase the efficiency of the factory. Many job shops today have their machine tools loaded less than 50 per cent. This is obviously wasteful but it has proved almost impossible to correct the methods of the past. If a computer system can be devised which improves the routing of work through the job-shop it will increase the loading of the machines. To increase the loading of the machines by 5 per cent in the moderate sized factory would pay for a more than adequate computer.

Operating in this way, the computer has taken on a *control* function. Instead of its old function of processing a batch of data or doing a set of calculations, which may be done independently of time, it is now controlling an environment, and time is vital. It takes up-to-the-minute data from the shop floor, forms an image of the situation, applies a set of decision rules to it, and sends back instructions for the foreman and operators. In this way it controls what is happening in the optimum manner (Fig. 3).

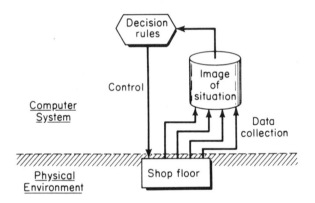

Fig. 3. Real-time control of an environment.

A data processing system in practice could control much more than the dispatching on the shop floor. It would be likely to deal with many functions involved in the running of the factory. These may include inventory control and purchasing, planning of parts, materials and manpower, operations evaluation, costing, billing, and so on. Figure 4 illustrates some of these functions.

Figure 4, like Fig. 3 is grossly oversimplified. If it were drawn in detail it could show the various manufacturing and assembly stages that products pass through. It would contain images of the loading on the various machines, work in progress, manpower assignment to different departments, process plans and assembly plans, and so on. These images will be on random-access files which could be interrogated by management as required and referred to quickly by the computer when applying its decision-making rules.

We have now arrived at the concept of a *Total Information System* in

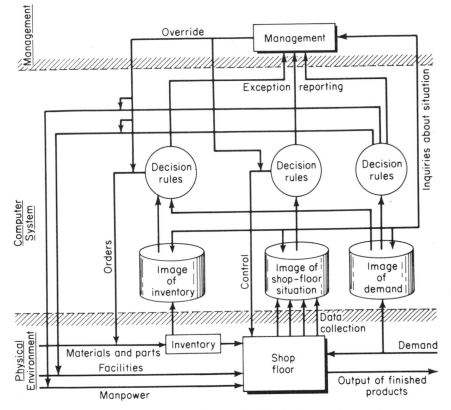

Fig. 4. Further elements in control of a factory environment.

which all the possible data processing within an organization is integrated. All the pertinent facts and figures are contained in random-access files and are immediately available to management or computer alike. Data for the system are recorded directly at their source and so are up-to-date and error free as far as possible. Decisions made by the computer are conveyed directly to where they are used in the organization. Any exceptional state of affairs or any situation not in the computer's rule-book is reported directly to the appropriate management.

Not all the processing of the system need be real-time or on-line. If it is economical to do some of it in a batch-processing manner, then this may be combined with the real-time work. This is going to be the case in many types of systems. One of the problems that this book must deal with is that of combining real-time work with batch-processing in the same system. In discussing the use of the computer for control purposes in this manner we are no longer talking about the mechanization of work that is already being done in another way. Continuous optimization of the flow of work through a factory could only be done by hand in a very small factory. In a factory other than the smallest, the flow of work cannot be continuously optimized by manual methods because the number of decisions and calculations that would have to be made is too great. It can only be done by a computer system working on a real-time basis.

This may be more obvious to the reader when discussing the flow of traffic through a city. If the traffic lights could change at the optimum moments considering *all* the vehicles in the streets, this would substantially improve the traffic flow. A policeman could certainly change the lights at one intersection at the optimum times. If he had some device for telling him what traffic was there he might change the lights at four intersections in an optimum manner. But he could certainly not do so for a hundred intersections. Furthermore, a large number of human traffic light changers dotted throughout the city would not be of much use. However, an on-line computer would be fast enough to take all the traffic and all the lights into consideration. It might attempt to batch the vehicles into "platoons" and manoeuvre these through the streets with the minimum interference between each other and with the minimum stopping and starting.

Similar arguments apply to the use of computers in other control applications, for example, computers used to optimize the performance of chemical plants and electricity power stations. Here again, readings are taken to provide an image of the current status on the plant. Calculations are made from the readings, and decision rules are applied, so that the computer may control a plant or send instructions to its operator. The same results cannot be achieved by unaided human effort due to the speed at which calculations and logical decisions must be made. One man could control a very small chemical plant or a small power station with simple instrumentation, but as the plant becomes larger he will no longer be able to optimize its performance.

If manual control is used for a larger plant, as indeed it is for many, the results will not be as good as when a computer is used. A man will control performance or processes by experience or intuition and will obtain acceptable working results but not the maximum possible efficiency. To justify the computer the economic decision must be made: does the increase in efficiency it produces pay for the cost of the computer and its control instrumentation?

Indeed, for any computer used in industry or commerce the ultimate answer to this question "why?" should be the economic answer: "it lowers the cost of operating or increases the profitability." If a real-time system gives up-to-the-minute costing figures, are these of sufficient value to pay for the increase in cost of the computer? If a system gives management up-to-date information or decreases the management planning cycle, what value can be placed upon this? If a real-time system gives speedier action or better customer service, will this pay for the increase in cost of the computer? In some cases these may be difficult questions to answer.

A British European Airways reservation clerk in London, operating a Uniset, part of an automatic seat reservation system controlled by two Univac 490 real-time computers. The clerk speaking to a potential passenger on the telephone can obtain immediate information as to the availability of seats on any flight. Passenger names and details are to be stored in the computer's files.

The evaluation of data processing systems has traditionally rested upon the notion of cost displacement, but now significant economic benefits of many systems accrue from the so-called intangible benefits to management. Computer systems can no longer be viewed as essentially productive. A real-time system is usually not justified merely by the staff it displaces. It must also be justified by an increase in efficiency of operation. It may be an information system to help in maintaining control of a business operating in a changing environment. For example, a firm may operate in a period of changing demand. A dynamic control system would enable it to respond to this change in an economically efficient manner. However, it may be very difficult to place an economic value on this facility. Often, the economics of a real-time system are clearly justified, for example, a 5 per cent increase in the loading of planes due to an airline booking system, 5 per cent increase in the output of a paper mill, a 6 per cent scrap saving in the steel rolling mill; but in other applications intangibles have to be assessed, such as increased customer service or better management information.

The aims of a real-time system, then, are likely to be the tying together of different decisions or actions so that some process can be carried out more efficiently. Functions that were formerly done on separate computer runs may be linked, for example, doing stock control at the same time as pre-billing. The system may couple together elements of an operation that are separated by distance, such as the allocation of trucks to jobs on a railroad. It may collect data from many different points and correlate them in sufficient time to control some process. This may be a business process, like the selling of airline seats, an operational process such as the flow of work through a factory, or a technical process such as the testing of a jet-engine with many instruments.

It may disseminate information from its files to persons making enquiries, or carry out processing of various types to give quick answers to questions. It may enable state and local governments to integrate their record keeping. It may be installed to give speedier action in some situation, for example, bank customers queuing to draw cash in their lunch hour, or two airplanes on a possible collision course. It may be installed simply because it is the cheapest way of handling data transmission links. It may enable companies too small to own a computer to share the cost of a distant machine and rent the terminals for their work.

Perhaps most important of all, real-time processing is becoming a part, sometimes a small part, of information-handling systems in numerous types of organizations.

The work in a company is likely to be divided among commercial batch processing, scientific calculations, and real-time, but everywhere the trend is towards a computer or network of computers that integrate these different types of processing. This is likely to involve large direct-access files and multi-programming techniques. It will be a complex system, with the programming problems discussed in this book.

It will be designed to decrease management planning cycles, maximize turnover, make the best use of an organization's facilities and provide information where and when it is wanted. It will enable an organization to deal with urgent orders rapidly, or dispatch spare parts at the time

The IBM 7770 audio response unit obtains information from a computer in response to a dialed telephone inquiry and provides an answer in the form of spoken words. It makes the millions of business facts stored in a computer available over the telephone and is used in companies where immediate information is required for efficient transaction of business. To answer an inquiry, the 7770 assembles the proper words from a recorded vocabulary stored on a magnetic recording drum (shown in uncovered panel at left), amplifies them and transmits them back over the dialing phone. In the picture above, an IBM engineer uses a nearby telephone to communicate with the unit.

they are requested. A company with a well-planned information handling system will be able to react quickly in changing business circumstances. In carrying out the system analysis and planning the programs, the cost of giving the system different reaction times must be considered. Where a system carries out several different functions, some of these may need a response in seconds, some in minutes, some in hours or days. When a salesgirl has a customer on the telephone, she will want a very quick reply from the terminal she uses. When a message asking about machine loadings is sent, a reply may be needed in minutes.

On some systems there will be little difference on cost between giving a fast response and a slow one, but often this does make a difference. The difficulties of programming and program testing may increase because more transactions must be handled simultaneously if a fast response is needed, or programs must be interrupted a greater number of times.

The question of priorities also affects the programming. Do certain functions always need high priority? Should some operations always interrupt others? Is especially high reliability needed for certain functions? Should specified files be duplicated? What expansion will be needed in the future? Careful attention to the reasons behind these questions will enable the programming to be as effective as possible without being over-complicated or more expensive than necessary.

3 THE RANGE OF REAL-TIME SYSTEMS

The real-time systems that have been installed to date vary from very small single computers with relatively simple programs, to the largest and most expensive multi-computer systems in the world. This chapter describes this range and indicates in it various common types of systems. Chapter 5 picks out seven points in the spectrum which are used as reference points throughout the book to help the reader fit the remaining chapters into perspective.

Fortunately, not all real-time systems have the same problems and therefore it is important that the reader maintain a sense of perspective. It would be quite wrong, for example, to associate all the problems of a multi-programmed airline reservation system with a small real-time savings bank application.

When discussing the complexity, and hence the problems, of these systems, six aspects of the subject may be considered:

1. *The complexity of the equipment.* How many computers are used? How many communication lines and terminals? How many random-access files, and do they operate in parallel? Is back-up or standby equipment used to give added reliability?

2. *The response time.* That is the elapsed time between a transaction entering the computer system and the completion of its processing, or the sending of a message in reply.

3. *The average interarrival time.* The average time between the arrival at the computer of separate transactions ready for processing.

4. *The total number of instructions* in the real-time Application Programs. Non-real-time or off-line programs have not been included in

this count because they do not substantially affect the complexity or problems of the real-time system. Supervisory or Control Programs have not been included either. A person with no knowledge of these can still assess the Application of data-processing programs.

5. *The complexity of individual Application Programs.* How complex would be the program for processing one message by itself? On some large and complex systems, certain individual Application Programs can be quite small and uncomplicated. At the other extreme, on some small systems such as a computer for optimizing the performance of a petroleum plant or job shop, the individual Application Programs may be relatively complex.

6. *The complexity of the Supervisory Programs.* This is the Control or Executive program which schedules the work, organizes input and output operations, and so on. On small systems it can be a fairly simple program and may involve only a small addition to the standard program packages provided by the computer manufacturers. On large and complex systems it can be a very sophisticated and intricate group of programs. It is discussed at length in Sections III and IV of this book. Its complexity is determined to a large extent by:

(a) The complexity of the equipment.

(b) The degree of multi-programming, i.e., the simultaneous processing of transactions.

(c) The complexity of the priority structure. On some systems all transactions have the same priority, but on others there are differences in priorities between different messages or different functions.

1. *The Complexity of the Equipment*

The simplest form of real-time system might have one device such as a typewriter which can send a message to the computer. The computer interrupts its processing, handles the message, perhaps sends a reply, and then continues its processing. The computer may have a random-access file attached, and the typewriter may update or interrogate this. Slightly more complicated would be a system with several terminals or typewriters. These may be attached to a buffer or they may be all on one communication

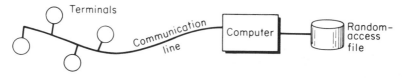

Fig. 5. A system with one communication line.

line (Fig. 5). Only one terminal can send a message at one time. The next step up in complexity would be to have more than one communications line (Fig. 6).

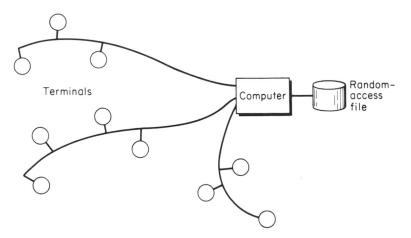

Fig. 6. A system with several communication lines.

With two or more lines, message handling may or may not overlap in the computer. This depends upon the size and throughput of the system. Systems with a high throughput will process messages in parallel.

With some makes of equipment the communication line is able to go directly into the computer. The computer assembles the bits and characters from the line and compiles the messages under program control. With other systems the communication lines do not go into the computer but into a separate programmed *Multiplexor* or Line Control Computer. This is in effect a small special purpose computer for controlling communication line input and output. To it can be attached any general purpose computer which reads data from it and sends data to it in the same way that it would to any input/output unit (Fig. 7).

In some systems more than one computer has been used because one computer is not big enough or fast enough. In a two-computer system, one may handle the input and output to the Line Control device and files, while the other does the processing. A good reason for this could be

Fig. 7. A system with a separate Line Control Computer.

that the processing computer is doing non-real-time work, but is interrupted occasionally by the other which has assembled some real-time messages ready for processing (Fig. 8).

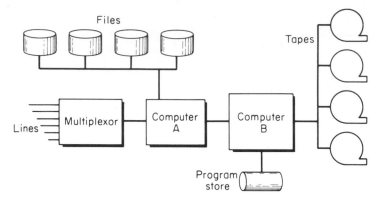

Fig. 8. A multi-computer system.

Computer B in Fig. 8 may be a much more powerful machine than A. Computer A may handle some simple real-time transactions itself, such as requests for interrogation of the files. When a transaction requires more complex processing it interrupts computer B. This prepares a reply for A to send and then continues its other work. Computer A may queue the messages so that it does not interrupt computer B very often. Computer B may have a program store on a disk file or drum so that it can load itself with the necessary real-time programs.

Because of the nature of the real-time work a very high degree of reliability may be needed in the system. This may be achieved by duplicating the components of the system. If one computer has a breakdown-time of 2 per cent, two similar machines backing each other up will have a breakdown-time of approximately 0.04 per cent. "Duplexing" in this manner increases the equipment complexity, especially if switch-

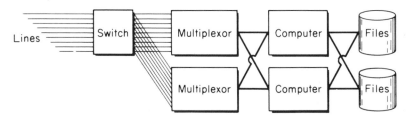

Fig. 9. A duplexed system.

over on failure is to be automatic. A duplexed version of the system in Fig. 7 is shown in Fig. 9. Many systems of this type have been installed.

It will be seen here that if a Line Control Unit, computer or file fails, the system can be switched so that the duplicate takes over.

The cost of this may not be as prohibitive as it seems at first sight if the standby computer can be doing other work while standing by. The complexity of the Supervisory Programs, however, is increased. Every time a file is updated, for example, it is necessary to update both files. If a file breaks down and then later is returned to use, it must be quickly updated with all that it has missed, and this updating must not interfere with current work using the files.

Triplexing the equipment would, of course, give even higher reliability but would be even more expensive. On certain special systems, however, very high reliability is essential, whatever the cost. On the American moon shots, for example, the monitoring computer is to be quadruplexed.

The configurations illustrated above are the types in common usage. It is possible to have systems that are much more complex than these, often with more than two interconnected computers. In systems where the interval between message arrivals is short and the file access time long, one computer cannot cope without multi-programming, i.e., handling two or more transactions at once. In this case, it has been suggested that several small computers should be used instead and the work split between them. The programming techniques described in this book relate to systems such as those above. However, the principles and conclusions that emerge would be applicable to any configuration, not only to these more common ones.

2. *The Response Time*

The response time, in this discussion, is the total time a transaction remains in the computer system, i.e., from the time at which it is completely received to the time at which a reply starts to be transmitted, or, if there is no reply, the time at which processing is completed.

In a simple case, then, the response time is the time the computer takes to interrupt what it was doing and to process the transaction. There may, however, be certain delays involved in the response time. First, there may be several transactions contending for the computer's time, so that the transaction may have to wait in various queues, like a customer going to the Motor Vehicle Licencing Office at a peak period. Second, the computer may, in some applications, be doing another job and the trans-action will have to wait until it is convenient to process it.

In some types of systems a high speed response time is necessary because of the nature of the work. The computer has to be programmed to react quickly. In others it does not matter—a response time of twenty seconds may be adequate.

The range of response times in some existing applications is shown in Fig. 10. A bank teller or an airline reservation clerk may desire a response time of three seconds or less, so as to give customers or telephone enquirers the best possible service. A warehouseman making stock inquiries may be content with a reply in twenty seconds. For controlling a petroleum plant, five minutes may be adequate, and for sending instructions to the

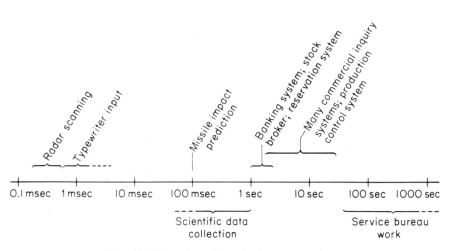

Fig. 10. Examples of required response times.

shop floor of a factory perhaps half an hour is soon enough. Some scientific control and data logging applications require very much shorter response times than these. Examples are data logging on a jet engine or rocket motor test bed, scanning radar read-outs or tracking a missile to predict its impact point. The interval between events may be only a few milliseconds, and the response must be programmed not to exceed this brief period. A clock or similar device in a computer is used to prevent the computer from being tied up on one transaction so that it cannot provide this response time when required.

3. *The Interval Between Events*

The interval between the arrival of transactions at the computer may be random and determined by external events such as a clerk pressing a key; or it may be cyclical and governed by a clock or scanning device in the computer.

As with the response time, it may vary from a fraction of a millisecond to half an hour or more. The range of inter-arrival times is shown in Fig. 11 for some existing applications.

An airline reservation system with a thousand terminals may have transactions pouring into it from all over a country at a rate that will be as high as twenty per second at peak periods. On the other hand, some inquiry systems may only have an occasional inquiry now and then. A savings bank with a steady stream of customers into each of its branches at lunchtime might average about one transaction every two seconds. In

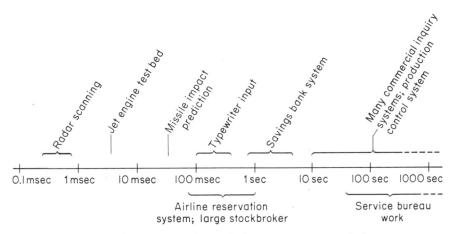

Fig. 11. Examples of intervals between message arrivals.

a European bank with a large number of branches this could be much higher. A typist keying characters into an on-line terminal may send them at a rate of five to ten per second.

When considering transaction rates for random systems like these, it is necessary to examine the times of maximum traffic because the system must be built to handle these peaks. Indeed, it must in some way or other cater for the very rare circumstance of all the terminal operators pressing their buttons at the same instant. It will not attempt to process a flood of messages of this magnitude at once, but, on the other hand, if a momentary transaction peak reaches the computer, none of these messages must be lost.

In radar scanning or data logging applications the inputs are scanned with a fixed cycle time. This will probably be of the same order as the response time quoted above.

4. *The Number of Instructions in the Application Programs*

The variation in the number of instructions in the real-time Application Programs gives a good indication of the range of complexity of these systems. Some small systems have less than a thousand instructions but the big ones exceed 200,000. Figure 12 illustrates this spread.

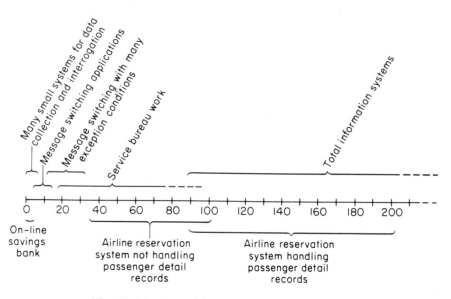

Fig. 12. Number of instructions for on-line work.

These figures are for the real-time programs only. In other words, this mass of coding is in the system ready for use at any one time. The programs must all fit together like cogs in a machine. Many non-real-time systems have a similar quantity of programming, but there it is not so significant because their work is done at different times, independently of one another. A new non-real-time program can be written without any knowledge of those that already exist. A new real-time program must fit in with the others and conform to the rules they obey. Non-real-time programs are soloists, doing their acts individually. Real-time programs are members of an orchestra and must work together, obeying the conductor.

There is, therefore, a big difference in system complexity between a system with a small number of program instructions and one with a large number. It is not merely a difference in quantity as it may be with non-real-time programs. Much better *organization* is needed to put together the bigger system. A savings bank application with 2000 lines of code is like a sonata for a string quartet, and a reservation system with 200,000 lines of code is like an oratorio for full orchestra and massed choruses. The players in the string quartet may be as good as those in the oratorio or better, but the oratorio needs professional stage management.

In systems with a large amount of programming, only a portion of this will be in the core, or immediately accessible portion of the computer memory, at one time. The system with 200,000 instructions may have room for only 40,000, or less, in core. Indeed, even the system with only 2,000 instructions may keep those not frequently used in a backing file.

In some systems it will be necessary to continuously select and read segments of a program into the computer core. A large system may call these in at as high a rate as 20 or more per second, and an elaborate mechanism is needed to handle this. A small system will call in external programs only to handle an exceptional condition—perhaps once every half minute or less frequently than that.

5. The Complexity of the Programs

The number of instructions is not directly related to the complexity of the programs. A large commercial system with many files to update for different purposes may have a large number of fairly simple programs. On the other hand, a system for tracking a missile and predicting its impact point, or for optimizing a chemical process, may have one or two programs only, but these are complex and involve elaborate mathematics.

The complexity of the Supervisory Programs will be more directly related to the size of the system. If there are multiple computers, or elaborate input/output devices, or a large number of random-access files, this will complicate the Supervisory Programs as the later chapters illustrate. If there are many Application Programs to be selected and called in from a backing file, an elaborate mechanism will be needed to organize this. The complexity of the priority structure will also have an effect. In some systems the transactions all have the same priority, like customers joining a cafeteria queue. Imagine how much more difficult it would be to organize a cafeteria queue if various customers had different priorities. This situation would be even worse if certain high-priority customers were in a raging hurry; so much so, that the actual serving of other customers had to be interrupted to serve them. In some real-time systems the messages to be processed have different priorities, and certain messages may be in a raging hurry. For example, in a system used for monitoring space flights from Cape Kennedy the priority structure is complex, and often the processing of one message is interrupted to process another more urgent one.

The Supervisory Program and the system testing will be more difficult if multi-programming is involved, i.e., the concurrent processing of more than one message. Where work on one message is stopped to work on another, either for reasons of timing or priority, sufficient details must be stored about the situation on the first message to ensure that work on it can be taken up again as though no interruption had occurred. Some Supervisory Programs have to control the situation where processing is constantly switching back and forth between one message and another.

One reason for this can be seen by inspecting Figs. 10 and 11. In some systems the response time is less than the average time between the arrivals of messages, but in others new messages will arrive before the processing of the last one. In an airline reservation system during the peak period, the messages may flood in as fast as twenty per second or more, and it may take a second to process each message, including all the references to random-access files which take a relatively long time. While the file references are going on, the computer may have no more processing to complete on that message. It has to wait until its file request is satisfied. Therefore, it is quite practical for it to be working on another transaction. In fact, twenty or more transactions may be under way at the same time, but this considerably complicates the programming and particularly the testing of the system when the programs are fitted together.

It will be seen that the range of real-time systems is a wide one. There is a big difference in the effort required to implement a large, duplexed, multi-programmed system and a small, single, real-time computer with serial processing. Some of the techniques needed for the big system are also necessary for the small one, but not all of them.

It would be a mistake for potential users of a small system, such as a savings bank, to let themselves be influenced by reports of the problems and set-backs on some of the very large, complex systems. This, unfortunately, has tended to happen, and in some people's minds the mere term 'real-time' conjures up horrific images of programming problems, regardless of system size. On the other hand, a firm that has installed successfully a small non-multi-programmed real-time system may be tempted to move upwards to a more complex system without sufficient regard for the dangers that lie ahead.

The ocean of real-time systems is wide; and it is necessary to know whereabouts in these waters the systems discussed lie. To this end Chapter 5 picks out seven reference points on the chart. These seven systems are used to help the reader place the arguments of the book into perspective.

4 DIFFICULTIES OF REAL-TIME PROGRAMMING

There are many problems associated with the programming of real-time systems. This chapter attempts to describe these.

Fortunately not all of the problems catalogued below apply to all types of real-time systems. However, many of the more complex systems do have to face up to all of these difficulties. This chapter attempts to associate the type of system with the problems that are likely to arise.

DYNAMIC SCHEDULING   A computer used for a conventional data processing application normally follows a repetitive cycle which may be planned and timed in detail by the programmer. Input and output operations are normally of a known length and time and may be balanced with each other and against the processing that is to be done. *The pattern of events is constant.*

In an on-line system this is unlikely to be true. Messages arrive at *random times* and are probably *varied in their length and nature.* For example, enquiries enter a credit checking system or an inventory system at unplanned times. When a clerk requires information he sends a message to the computer. Transactions enter a real-time banking system at times when customers pay in or withdraw cash at a bank counter. This occurs at random.

In addition to being random with respect to time, it is probable that different messages reaching the computer of a real-time system will require different programs. *Different functions will be executed in an unplanned sequence.* Because of this, dynamic scheduling of the work may be needed;

35

that is, scheduling which changes with the changing requirements instead of being fixed as it would be on a conventional computer application. Unlike a conventional application, the timing pattern can constantly change from second to second. It is, therefore, necessary to schedule this unpredictable sequence of operations so that the data are still handled in the minimum time and the computer facilities are used to their best. This will be a function of a Control or *Supervisory Program*. The Supervisory Program is often complex and much more difficult to plan and write than normal data processing programs. It is discussed at length in the chapters to follow.

DYNAMIC CORE ALLOCATION In the system that varies continuously in the manner described, it is possible that the requirements for computer core storage will change from transaction to transaction. An area of storage needed at one time for one type of program may be needed shortly afterwards for a different type of program. For this reason a *dynamic allocation of computer memory* is required. The use to which an area of core is put may change from second to second. Core is allocated to different functions as required.

If the system uses dynamic core allocation in this way, the continuously changing assignment of core to its various functions will be the work of the Supervisory Program. It may be necessary to write the Application Programs so that they can operate in different areas of core at different moments of time. In other words, programs would be *relocatable*.

New segments of program may have to be called into the memory of a complex computer from a backing file, second-by-second. The organization needed to call in programs when required, to branch to them, and branch from one segment of program to another, can become very complex. Again, this organization is carried out continuously by a Supervisory Program.

ALLOCATION OF PRIORITIES Different clerks operating the terminals of a real-time system are quite likely to send in messages to the computer at the same instant in time. For example, in an airline reservation system, attempts to book seats or to carry out other functions may be made in various agents' offices at the same instant in time. In fact, the system may have many messages contending for the use of the central processing unit at one time, and these messages may be of different types.

Some means of *allocating priority between the various messages* may be necessary. In some systems all messages have the same priority, but in others high priority messages must jump the queue and be processed quickly. The latter is likely to be the case in some commercial data processing systems or in technical systems such as those which control a chemical plant or monitor a defense network. Some systems utilize many different priority levels.

It will be seen, then, that the processing in a moderately complex real-time system does not follow a constant predictable routine. Rather, the pattern changes moment by moment, like the patterns of the sand on the seashore being washed by the waves. This means that the planning of the processing and the selection of the computer with appropriate memory size and speed may become more complex than in a system in which the events are repetitive and predictable.

MULTI-PROGRAMMING Another factor that adds to the difficulties of real-time is multi-programming, that is, the concurrent operation of more than one program. In a simple system only one transaction or message at a time will be processed. Work will not start on the next message until the preceding message is completed. In this type of system it may be necessary to jump from one program to another program when different types of messages are received, but transactions will not be processed *in parallel*. However, in more complex systems it becomes necessary to process transactions in parallel, because the time taken to handle one transaction is greater than the interval of time between the arrivals of transactions. When two or more transactions have to be processed simultaneously in this manner, this is referred to as multi-programming. *The degree of multi-programming* varies considerably from one type of system to another, but always it adds complications to the program writing and particularly to the program testing.

A system with a computer handling several messages at the same time is like a juggler trying to keep several balls in the air at once. The more balls he keeps in the air, the more difficult it becomes. Similarly, the higher the degree of multi-programming, the more complex is the Supervisory Program, and the more difficult. the program testing.

A system designer may be forced to use multi-programming because the time taken to read data from the files or to update them is long. Imagine, for example, a system with clerks sending messages from several hundred terminals at various locations. Messages may arrive at the average rate of one every half second. Each message requires, say, six references to random-access files and these references take an average time of a quarter of a second each. This will mean that the computer will on the average be processing three or maybe more transactions at the same time. In the large airline reservation systems as many as 20 transactions may be handled in parallel by the computer.

The random-access file references are not themselves of a predictable time. They might vary from 30 milliseconds up to 600 milliseconds and because of this the timing pattern of the processing changes constantly.

The computer may have allocated priorities between different messages. It may now also be necessary to *allocate priorities between different functions of the system*. The functions such as file references that are taking place at any one instant are unpredictable and constantly variable. Just as the programs in the computer may differ from one instant to another, so also is the timing pattern in the system continually changing, and there are almost an infinite number of variations of this.

INTERRUPTS   It is necessary on computers used in real-time work to have some form of *interrupt* mechanism. When messages reach the computer their arrival may trigger an interrupt in the processing, so that the computer can read them into the appropriate part of its storage and hold them until it is ready for work on them. Similarly, if a real-time clock is used it may be necessary for the clock to interrupt the computer every minute or so, so that the time stored in the computer memory is updated. Events which have to occur at a specific time may be triggered off in this way. In a multi-programmed system it is desirable that there should be an interrupt associated with all input-output operations. For example, when reference to random-access files is made, this reference will take an unpredictable amount of time. When the file reference is complete the computer should be interrupted so that it can read this item from the file into the appropriate place in its memory, and take action on it as soon as is convenient. The structure of the interrupts and interrupt routines may be simple or complex depending upon the application. Large multi-programmed applications may have many interrupts per second. When a program is interrupted, control must later be returned to that program at the point at which it broke off. To do this, sufficient information must be sorted about the program status at the moment of interrupt. This can become complicated, especially as the program that was interrupted may have been using input or output devices at the moment the interrupt occurred. This is rather like comparing an office worker who is able to complete one job at a time, with one for whom the telephones are constantly ringing with urgent work, and who has to be switching back and forth from one vital job to another.

QUEUES   In most real-time systems the rate at which messages arrive varies from one moment to another. If a hundred clerks all decide to use their separate terminal sets at the same instant it may be possible that a hundred messages arrive at the computer all at the same instant. These cannot all be processed at once and therefore *queues* will develop. There are various methods for handling queues that must be available to the real-time programmer. It may also be necessary to queue the output messages. On a multi-programmed system where there are several partially completed messages, these will also be queued; and thus several queues may be waiting for the attention of the processing unit. A complex system may make several references in parallel to its random-access files. Under such conditions, items from the files which are waiting to be used may also have to be put into queues.

The queues build up and are depleted in a probabilistic manner; at one time they will contain many items, but at another time they may be small. This further complicates the work of designing the system and planning the layout of those parts of the memory in which queues are handled. The queues are commonly in the core storage of the computer. In other words, they are programmed queues. Some means must be programmed of *scanning the queues* and taking appropriate items from them for processing. It is the work of a Supervisory Program to decide which item in which queue to process next.

OVERLOADS   Because the transactions or messages arrive at random *the system will occasionally become overloaded.* If all the clerks happen to use their terminals at one moment, the queues of new transactions may grow too great. The computer will be in danger of running out of core storage, or possibly running out of processing time. An input or output channel or an access arm on a disk file may be given too much work, and when this happens excessive queues of items waiting for this facility may build up. It is possible that the computer may begin the processing of several transactions in parallel and be unable to complete them, because in attempting to do so it causes an overload. Such overloads are a normal, but exceptional, state of affairs in many real-time data-processing systems. The sudden flood of messages that produces such overloads will, in a well designed system, only be a short-lived state of affairs. However, programs must be available to handle it. In the multi-programmed system it may be necessary for the computer to detect a potential overload before it actually occurs, in other words before the computer starts processing all the messages that would cause the overload.

There are various methods of handling overloads in real-time systems and these are discussed in Chapter 23.

MULTI-PROCESSING Sometimes more than one computer is used. These are normally interconnected by a data channel which enables one computer to read from, or write in, the memory of the other computer. This use of coupled computers is referred to as *multi-processing*. It may, for example, be used as an alternative to multi-programming. Instead of having one computer do two jobs at once, two computers are used, each doing one job at a time. It may be used to increase the reliability of the system. If one computer breaks down the other one takes over. In some systems the computers execute different functions. For example, one computer may do all the reading and writing on files, and the other computer may process the transaction. Sometimes one computer handles all the input and output on the communication lines, and the other computer does the remainder of the work. In this way it may be possible to use a small or a specialized computer for line control, and a large or conventional computer for the rest of the work. The machine handling all the input and output on the communication lines may also be able to handle the queuing of the messages. Where multi-processing is used, additional control problems are added. One computer may be the "master" and the other the "slave." It will be the job of the Supervisory Program to coordinate the operations of processing units connected together in this way. It may be necessary to have a different Supervisory Program in each of the computers used.

COMMUNICATION LINES Many of the problems outlined above are connected with the difficulties of handling data that arrive at random and which vary in their nature. Other problems in real-time programming are caused by the new types of hardware that are used on this kind of computer system. The use of large random-access files and the use of telecommunication lines and terminals, the use of special equipment and the real-time clock, all introduce new complications into the programming.

Where a computer has attached to it a network of communication lines and each of these communication lines may have one terminal or more, and possibly a very large number of terminals, a program must scan the lines and accept data from them in parallel. One bit is read from one line and then one bit is read from the next line and so on. All of these bits must be assembled into messages. The words and messages must be carefully checked for errors because on communication lines many more errors are likely to occur than in normal computing hardware. Similarly, output messages have to be transmitted bit by bit in parallel. When a terminal has a message to transmit, this may cause an interrupt of the computer. Alternatively, a terminal may have to wait until the computer requests it to transmit.

The computer may compose instructions which tell the terminal to send data. These instructions may be passed down the line from one terminal to another until a terminal has a message to transmit, or the computer may address individual terminals. The computer would scan all the lines in this manner. Some lines or some terminals may be "polled" more often than others because they have higher priority. Line control is a subject which will be discussed in detail in Chapter 11.

RANDOM-ACCESS FILES   Large random-access files also present a whole family of new problems in programming and *data organization*. Where should data be placed on the files in order that they may be located in the minimum time? How can additions and deletions be made to random files in such a way that the information may still be readily found, and the packing of the file is not too low? And perhaps the most difficult problem of all: how can the file addressing be organized?

The basic problem of file addressing is the following: records in the files are identified by a number or key which is characteristic of the application. This may, for example, be an account number in a bank, a part number in a factory, a flight number and date in an airline reservation scheme or perhaps a passenger name. A clerk or a factory hand will key this number or name into his terminal; it is this number which will reach the central processing unit in the input transaction. From this the machine address of the record, that is, its precise location in the files, must be determined so that the record can be read. To convert the original number into the required machine address can be a difficult problem. There are various possible techniques for generating the required file address. These are discussed in Chapter 10.

SUPERVISORY PROGRAMS   In considering all these problems, it becomes apparent that the Supervisory Programs in a large real-time system have much work to do. They are indeed complex programs, and in some systems that have been installed, they have taken as many as 20 man-years to write. It is very important that the Supervisory Programs should be planned well and written correctly. Much of the performance of the system depends upon the skill with which these programs are written.

The Supervisory Program may be compared to the Production Manager in a small engineering company. Imagine a factory machining metal parts. There is no mass production or batch production. Each part is a one-off item to be made individually, just as messages in a real-time computer are processed individually. Orders for parts to be made arrive at the factory continuously but at random, and the nature of the parts varies considerably. Some parts will have a high priority attached to them, but others need not be made immediately. The shop floor of the factory has various groups of machine tools: lathes, milling machines, drills and so on. These may be compared with the input/output units and files on a real-time system or possibly with the programs for carrying out specific tasks. The work of the Production Manager is to route the parts being made through the factory in such a way that the necessary operations are performed in the correct sequence and with as little delay as possible. He must optimize the utilization of the machine tools.

Each group of machine tools may have its own foreman who supervises the work on this section. The Production Manager coordinates the work of these foremen, and they organize the movements of the parts from one section to another. In a similar way an *Input/Output Control Program* may be used for certain input/output units of the computer system. Each input/output channel may have a *Channel Scheduler*. A Supervisory routine coordinates the work of these programs. They may perhaps be regarded as subroutines of this Supervisory routine. When exceptional conditions arise or when emergencies occur, the Supervisory routine should be able to take the necessary action, just as the Production Manager in the factory.

APPLICATION PROGRAMS

Important though the Production Manager is, the actual manufacturing is done by the workers. Similarly, in the computer the processing of transactions, the calculations and the assembly of output messages are done by Application Programs—the programs which correspond, broadly, to the data-processing programs of conventional computer systems.

The Application Programs will normally be written quite separately from the Supervisory Program. The question, therefore, arises: how do the Application Programs interface with the Supervisory Program? What are the connecting links?

Application Programs will normally be written in a language of the level of *Autocoder* or FAP, in which one line of code may result in one machine instruction, or sometimes a macro-instruction, in which case it generates a complete subroutine. To connect the Application Programs to the Supervisory Program, macro-instructions would be written which provide these links. These macro-instructions would normally form part of the Supervisory Program Package.

The Application Programmer would write his programs for a machine which is provided with a clearly defined Supervisory Program and its associated macro-instructions. If the Supervisory Package is written well, he would be able to think about the processing of one message and ignore the relationship of this with any other messages that may be in the system at the same time. He would not have to consider the input/output timing of this program, as this will have been taken care of by the Supervisory Program. The relationship between an Application Program and the other programs with which it is connected is discussed in detail in Chapter 13.

COMMUNICATION WITH THE COMPUTER OPERATOR The person operating the computer on the real-time system has a comparatively easy job, although his status as an operator may be high because he is in charge of a roomful of complex and sophisticated computers and mature judgment is required in times of trouble. For a conventional application the operator is constantly loading up the computer with punched cards or changing magnetic types. A real-time system is designed to be as automatic and as independent of its operator as possible. However, situations will arise when the computer needs the assistance of its operator, and this must be obtained as promptly and efficiently as possible. It will be another job for the Supervisory Program to detect when operator intervention is necessary. The Supervisory Program must ask for help, telling the operator exactly what is wrong or what is required. Similarly, if the operator wishes to communicate with the system, to change its action in some way, or to monitor its performance, this action will also be via the Supervisory Program.

HIGH RELIABILITY Real-time systems need to be much more reliable in general than conventional computers. There are two reason for this:

First: the system is more automatic. Because of the nature of their job, most real-time systems are planned not to stop if it is possible to avoid stopping. Messages entering the system are processed and are returned to the appropriate terminals without any human intervention. If an error occurs during this cycle it may not be detected unless it is obvious to the person operating the terminal. If an error occurs which damages the files, this could be particularly disastrous because it might go undetected. The system would continue in operation with damaged or incorrect file records.

It has often been said that the computer is a moron. Its advantage lies in the fact that it is a high speed moron. If it should deviate from its planned program it is likely to take action that is wildly irrational or produce results that are stupid. If it is doing scientific calculations or batch-processing, this does not matter too much because its wild errors can be detected. If a check total on a batch does not agree the matter is investigated, and the batch is processed again. If a set of equations are solved incorrectly, this too can be detected and put right. However, if a computer goes wrong on a real-time run this may not be detected. A clerk at the terminals may ignore the rubbish that he gets in reply and merely repeat his last message. Unless steps are taken to prevent it, it is quite possible for a real-time computer to over-write the file records. It is as though the Dickensian clerk went berserk and scribbled all over his ledgers and ripped out pages. A high degree of system reliability is necessary to rule out the possibility of this happening.

Mistakes of the type described are more likely to happen because of faults in the programming than because of faults in the electronic circuitry. Good quality computing equipment today is of such a reliability that undetected errors caused by the hardware are very rare indeed. It is interesting to note that when errors occur on the large and complex real-time systems that have come into operation, these are usually programming errors and not hardware errors. Reliability is thus another programming problem of real-time systems. *Reasonableness checks* must be built into the programs. *Means of protecting the files* must be devised and *memory protection aids* must be used. In a system with a high degree of multi-programming it is especially difficult to achieve high reliability in the programs. The program testing needed to ensure this reliability is particularly complex because there are an almost infinite number of combinations of circumstances that must be tested.

The second reason why high reliability is needed in a real-time system is that, because of the nature of the system, it is usually very inconvenient when it ceases to function. For example, the system used by a firm of stockbrokers to maintain immediate contact with brokers on the floor of the stock exchange would impede the business if it failed to function. When a computer controlling a chemical plant fails the plant must be operated manually until the computer is back in operation, and for this period the process cannot be optimized. When an information retrieval system goes down, its users cannot obtain the information they require. An extreme example for the need for reliability is the use of computers in the manned space flight. In the critical seconds after launching a computer makes a decision whether or not the missile is going to go into orbit. If it is not, it must be brought down immediately into a safe landing area. Similarly, a Ballistic Missile Early Warning System and other defense networks need very trustworthy computers.

DUPLEXING AND SWITCHOVER   One way to improve reliability in a real-time system is to duplicate all of the critical components, so that when one computer fails a stand-by computer takes over automatically. Whenever information is written on the files, it is written twice on separate files. Duplexing is, of course, expensive, and whether or not it is used depends upon the need for very high reliability. When duplexing is used, the Supervisory Program must detect the need for a switchover of any of the components, including the computer itself, and must initiate the switchover, whether it is to be done manually by the operator or whether it is to be automatic. There are many programming problems associated with switchover because the need for it may occur when an Application Program is half-completed, when a file has been read but not completely updated, or when a message has been half-received, or when several messages in the system are half-processed. All this half-completed work must be sorted out and, in particular, caution is needed in updating the files; otherwise it may be possible that a file is updated twice and so becomes incorrect. Switchover is discussed in Chapter 25.

FALL-BACK   If it can be achieved, it is desirable that a failure of part of the system should not knock out the entire system. If one communication line fails the computer continues to operate with the other lines. If one file fails, then, as far as possible, work goes on without this file. If one computer fails in a system with more than one computer, those remaining may do a portion of the job. This technique of making the most of a bad situation and continuing to do a portion of the job, is referred to as "graceful degradation." If possible, the system must "fail softly," rather than failing suddenly and perhaps catastrophically. The Supervisory Program initiates a *fall-back*. The system may continue to limp along in the "fall-back" mode until the component that caused the trouble has been put right. The Supervisory Program must then initiate a *recovery*. "Fall-back" and "recovery" may become complex. For example, it may be necessary to change the file on which the data are written. If this is done, all the file addresses referred to by an Application Program must be modified by a Supervisory Program before the file in question is written on. Again, this is a specialized subject and is treated in detail in Chapter 24.

Not all real-time systems need duplexing, or elaborate fall-back procedures. This depends upon the application. However, the designers of any application must always have in their minds the thought: What will happen if the computer or any other part of the hardware fails? In many types of application it will be possible to devise some form of manual by-pass procedure by means of which a very limited but tolerable service can be given until the computer system is fully working again.

PROGRAM TESTING

Because of the high degree of reliability that is needed on real-time programs, thorough program testing is very important. However, program testing on real-time systems presents far more problems than program testing on conventional computer applications. On some of the large systems that have been installed to date it has proved extremely difficult. The crises and delays associated with testing have been considerable. It is apparent that this is one of the fundamental problems of real-time and that techniques more advanced than those for conventional systems are required.

The difficulties of real-time program testing are caused by several factors not found in conventional systems. First, there is the use of terminals and lines for input and output.

It will normally be impractical to use actual terminals and lines for the testing as this would be too slow. Therefore the input and output devices must be simulated. Other special equipment may be needed. If a Supervisory Program is not completed at the time when it is necessary to test the Application Programs, and similarly, if some of the Application Programs are not available at the time they are required to interface with other Application Programs, this gap must somehow be bridged.

Multi-programming introduces additional difficulties, because a wide variety of different combinations of circumstances must be investigated in the testing. When errors occur it may be difficult to say which of the programs in a multi-programmed system caused the error. If more than one computer is used the problems of testing are multiplied, especially if overload and switchover conditions have to be investigated. The complexity of large real-time systems also adds to the difficulties. Where so many programs tie together to make a tightly integrated whole it is necessary to test them working in cooperation with one another. This needs much organization.

Solutions to these problems have been worked out, and they are discussed in Section IV of the book. In general, they involve writing programs which are designed to assist only in the testing of the system. These programs must be available at the time when they are needed for the testing;

they may take several man-years to write. To neglect the planning of these testing aids early in the implementation schedule could prove disastrous.

PROBLEM OF PROGRAMMER COORDINATION   This chapter has described some of the details of a real-time system that make its programming difficult. However, none of the problems so far mentioned are beyond the ingenuity of a reasonably inventive and skilled programmer. There is one problem, however, that needs more than just good programming to solve it. Some of the more ambitious systems have become immensely complex. Some of them have taken as many as a hundred programmers writing routines which must eventually tie together to form one tightly integrated system. If the hundred programmers had been writing separate routines to run on the computer at separate times, this would have presented no problem for a conventional installation. But here the routines must all be capable of working together in the same real-time system. If any programmer makes a change in his programs this may affect the work of many of the other programmers.

Here is the main source of many problems. Programmers constantly find a need to change what they are writing. In fact, the writing of a program is a process of evolution. The first idea crystallizes into the first block diagram. This is elaborated upon and grows. As it grows, it changes constantly. Intricacies are added, and procedures are modified. Almost like the growth of a city over the years, so a program is built up stage by stage. But now a hundred programmers are all building a part of a complex machine. Eventually all these parts have to be put together and mesh smoothly with one another. When this constant evolution is taking place, how can the programming management be sure that all the parts are developing in such a way that they will all fit precisely together to form the integrated system? This is a problem of a new order in programming management. More rigorous techniques are needed than those in common use in the computer world today.

DESIGN PROBLEMS   The *design* of a real-time system can also be very complex. When planning a magnetic tape installation for batch-processing, the program sizes and core requirements can be estimated and the time taken to do the job calculated with sufficient accuracy to enable the selection of the right computer. On the larger real-time installation it has proved much more difficult to make accurate estimates of the program size, and because the contents of the core storage are continually varying, it is difficult to predict how much core storage is needed. The size to which the queues may grow in the memory of the computer is uncertain. The time that will be taken to deplete these queues cannot be stated exactly. Indeed, even the input to the computer is not certain, and on many installations it will vary from moment to moment. Ascertaining the time and core requirements of the computer now involves *probability and queuing theory*. To assist in this design work the technique of *simulation* is frequently used. A model is built of the system and its programs. Into this model input can be fed which corresponds to the input of the actual system when it will be in operation. This input can be varied easily. The delays and the size of the queues can be measured. The model may be adjusted to make these conform with the requirements. If a multi-programmed system is simulated in this way the model itself can become quite complicated, but it is the only sure way to estimate the computer requirements.

MONITORING THE PROGRAMMING PROGRESS   Unfortunately, when a real-time system is being planned, there are many unknowns, especially connected with the programming. When eventually a program is being done, many justifiable decisions may have been taken by the programmers which cause the system to drift away from the original design concepts. It has commonly been the experience on complex real-time systems that a large drift away from the original design has been experienced when a system is being implemented. This drift can have catastrophic results. It may be found that the equipment ordered is no longer able to do the job. An expenditure which cannot be justified is needed to put matters right, or else the programming must be thought out afresh, which may delay the implementation of the system by a year or more. This again is a problem in programming management. How can management be sure that, as these complex programs are being written, they are not drifting away from the original specifications? Again, simulation techniques may be needed. The development of the programs is monitored by adjusting or elaborating the simulation model of the system whenever programming decisions are made or whenever the sizes or timings of programs become more clearly known.

In general, the management problems on a large real-time system are much more complex than on previous types of computer installation. New techniques are needed for monitoring and control. Good documentation techniques are needed, and there must be intricate coordination between the work of different programmers. These and other management problems are discussed later in the book.

SUMMARY   To summarize, the following reasons can make real-time programming more difficult than conventional programming:

(a) Control of communication lines and terminals.

(b) Control of multiple input/output devices.

(c) Organization and addressing of random-access files.

(d) Variable message types and variable processing requirements.

(e) Dynamic program read-in and memory allocation.

(f) Fluctuating message input rate.

(g) Handling of occasional overloads.

(h) Input messages of different priorities.

(i) Handling of queues.

(j) Multi-programming: Processing two or more transactions at once.

(k) Handling of multiple processor interrupts.

(l) Multi-processing: Control of multiple processing units.

(m) Switchover of faulty units, including the central processing unit while work is in progress.

(n) Fall-back to a limited mode of operation, and recovery from fall-back.

(o) Error control.

(p) An intricate Supervisory or Control Program.

(q) The relationship between the Supervisory and the Application Programs.

(r) The relationship between associated Application Programs.

(s) The fitting together of a complex integrated system written by many different programmers.

(t) Many new difficulties in program testing.

(u) Increased reliability requirements.

(v) Design problems and the use of simulation.

(w) New difficulties in programming management.

THE TYPES OF PROGRAM

5 SEVEN REFERENCE SYSTEMS

Chapter 3 illustrated real-time systems ranging from small and relatively simple computers to large and very complex multi-computer systems. Some of the characteristics of real-time apply to all of these systems, but in general the descriptions, suggestions and principles in the remainder of the book apply to specific sections of this wide spectrum. Different techniques are used for different parts of the range.

In order to impose a sense of perspective on the remainder of this book, seven reference systems are used. These are landmarks from which the reader may take his bearings. When a technique or a program is being discussed in the remaining chapters it will be related to these seven typical systems.

Small Commercial System, e.g., a Savings Bank

Commercial records are referred to and updated, and decisions made. Input from terminals by human operators at random times.

Input rate 500 to 5000 transactions or enquiries per hour.

Number of file references 2000 to 20,000 per hour.

Required response time: 10 seconds or less.

Processing is strictly serial, i.e., processing a transaction does not begin until the previous transaction is completed.

All frequently used programs are in core. Exceptionally used ones are on the files.

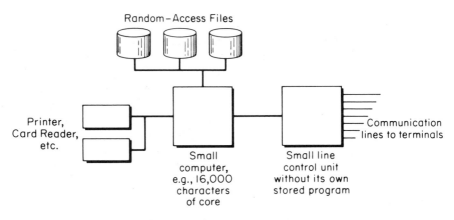

Fig. 13. Reference System No. 1.

Small Process Control System, e.g., Petroleum or Chemical Plant Control

Inputs are pressure and temperature readings and other plant data read under program control. Calculations are made using this, and the output is used to set valves, heaters and other plant controls, or to instruct the plant operator how to set these.

Input rate: Quick scan of 100 or so instruments approximately every minute.

Number of file references: very few, if any.

Required response time: 1 to 5 minutes or more.

All or most of the Application Programs are in core.

One Application Program may be much more complex than one segment of a commercial program.

No multi-programming except for interrupts by high-priority data.

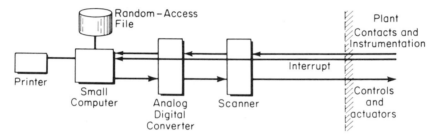

Fig. 14. Reference System No. 2.

Hybrid System, e.g., Warehouse Control, Insurance Company

The main computer does any form of non-real-time work. The small satellite computer collects and stores, on its file, messages arriving on the communication network. It interrupts the main computer at preset intervals or when it has a certain number of messages. The interruptions may take place, perhaps once every half minute, perhaps once every half hour. When they occur, the main computer removes its non-real-time work from core and processes the messages. The replies are sent by the small machine while the large computer continues its other work.

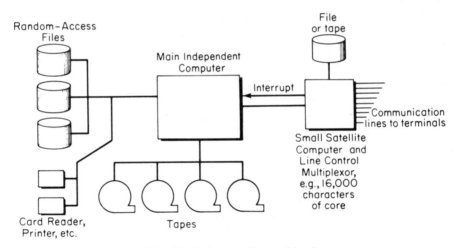

Fig. 15. Reference System No. 3.

Medium-Sized Commercial System, e.g., Warehouse Control

Commercial records are updated and referred to and decisions made.

Input from terminals by human operators at random times.

A portion of the file data must be available at all times, so this is duplicated. A hierarchy of fall-back procedures are used rather than the expense of a fully duplexed system. The vital files are still accessible if any one unit fails.

The large computer may at times do off-line work while the small one does on-line real-time work.

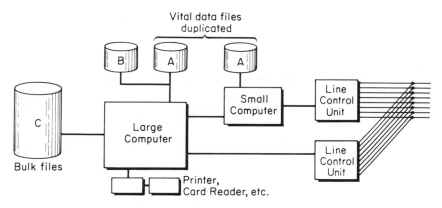

Fig. 16. Reference System No. 4.

Medium-Sized Commercial System, e.g., a Large Stockbroker

Commercial records are referred to and updated, and decisions made.

Input from terminals by human operators at random times.

Input rate: 2000 to 20,000 transactions or enquiries per hour.

Number of file references: 12,000 to 120,000 per hour.

Required response time: 10 seconds or less.

Small degree of multi-programming: 2 or 3 messages may be processed in parallel.

Not all the frequently used programs can be held in core.

Extreme reliability is required; therefore, the system is duplexed.

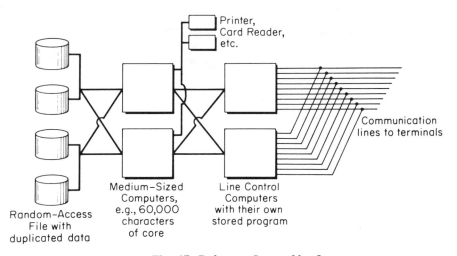

Fig. 17. Reference System No. 5.

Large Commercial System, e.g., Airline Reservation System

Commercial records are referred to and updated, and decisions made.

Input from terminals by human operators at random times.

Input rate: 6,000 to 60,000 transactions or enquiries per hour.

Number of file references: 40,000 to 400,000 per hour.

Required response time: 3 seconds or less.

High degree of multi-programming: 3 or more transactions are processed in parallel.

The majority of the programs are held on the files as there is not room for them in core.

Extreme reliability is required; therefore, the system is duplexed.

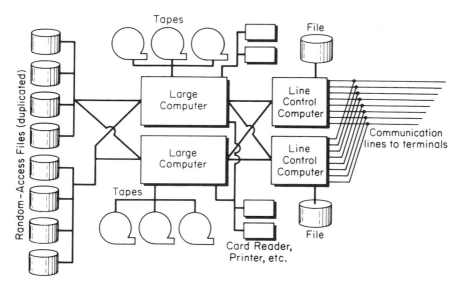

Fig. 18. Reference System No. 6.

A Multi-computer System, e.g., for Information Retrieval

Several small computers are used in one system where no complex processing is required. This avoids the complications of multi-programming and gives added reliability. However, it is expensive and can give logic difficulties if the files are updated by real-time transactions.

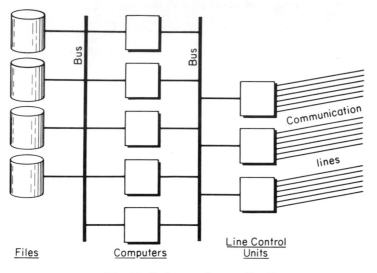

Fig. 19. Reference System No. 7

6 THE THREE KINDS OF PROGRAM

In programming a real-time system three kinds of program are needed. A clean-cut distinction between the three types should be made from the outset. In systems which have not established this division from the start confusion has often resulted. The three kinds of program are:

1. *Application Programs*

These are the programs that carry out the processing of transactions or messages. They correspond to the data-processing programs of conventional applications and are unique to each system. They contain no input-output coding except in the form of macro-instructions which transfer control to an input/output control routine or monitor, which, in a real-time system, is part of the Supervisory Programs.

2. *Supervisory Programs*

These programs coordinate and schedule the work of the Application Programs and carry out service functions for them. It is possible to consider the many Application Programs as sub-routines of the main Supervisory Program. The Supervisory Programs handle input and output operations and the queuing of messages and data. They are designed to coordinate and optimize the machine functions under varying loads. They process interrupts and deal with error or emergency conditions.

3. *Support Programs*

The ultimate working system consists of Application Programs and Supervisory Programs. However, a third set of programs are needed to

61

install the system and to keep it running smoothly. These are referred to as Support Programs and include testing aids, data generator programs, terminal simulators, diagnostics and so on.

The Application Programs are like the workers and plant in a factory, while the Supervisory Programs are like the office staff, management and foremen. The Support Programs are like the maintenance crew, helping to install new plant and to keep the machinery working.

Different terms are used by different organizations to describe these programs. The Application Programs are called "Operational Programs," "Processors," "Ordinary Processors," and so on. The Supervisory Programs are called "Control Programs," "Executive," "Monitors," and other names. A variety of terms are used for the Support Programs. In order to avoid confusion the terms Application, Supervisory and Support Programs are used exclusively throughout this book.

SUPERVISORY SYSTEM

The Supervisory Programs may be written by one team, and classed together as the *Supervisory System*. A manual should be written for this package which the writers of the Application Programs must study. These programmers are then faced with the task, not of programming a computer in the normal way, but of programming a computer-plus-Supervisory-System. In some ways this simplifies their work, but in other ways it restricts it. It gives them tools to use but imposes rules upon them. For example, the programmers are limited in their use of index registers and core storage, but input-output operations are done for them, and they do not have to time these as on a conventional system.

The Supervisory Programs may be provided by a computer manufacturer or they may be written by the user. These are intricate programs. For a large system they take a long time to write and need skilled programmers. They are inevitably hardware-dependent and cannot be written in higher languages. Furthermore, they must be well-defined before detailed work can start on the Application Programs. It is, therefore, a big advantage to the user if these are provided for him. Often, however, it may be necessary to tailor them to a particular application. Little success has been achieved so far in the standardization of Supervisory Programs for complex real-time systems, although portions of them have been provided successfully as standard packages. The customer may also find a need to modify the Supervisory Programs. If his system is a success he is likely to expand the work on it. If it is not, he will want to change its way of operating. Either could mean a change in the Supervisory Programs. It is, therefore, advisable for some of the user's programming team to understand fully the way these programs were designed and coded.

INTERRUPTS   Real-time systems make extensive use of some sort of *interrupt* feature. For example, a new message arriving from a distant terminal operator may interrupt what the computer is doing so that it may be read into the core. The end of a "seek" on a random-access device causes an interrupt, so that the computer can initiate the reading of the record found; and when reading is complete there may be another interrupt, so that the computer knows that the record is available for use and, also, so that the random-access device may be given another instruction if work is waiting for it. Either a Supervisory Program or an Application Program may be interrupted. When an interrupt occurs it is serviced by a short "priority" routine which is normally part of the Supervisory System.

When the cause of the interrupt has been dealt with, control will usually be returned to the point at which the interrupt occurred. There can be reasons, which are discussed in a later chapter, why it may not return there in certain circumstances. In order that the computer may resume what it was doing before the interruption occurred, the priority routine must retain the exact conditions that existed at that time. If it changes any of these it must restore them and make sure that the interrupted program continues as though no interrupt had occurred.

MAIN SCHEDULER   Figure 20 illustrates this and shows the relationship between the programs on a typical real-time system. The heart of the system is the small routine labelled the *Main Scheduler*. When a chunk of Application Program or of Supervisory Program has finished its work it returns control to the Main Scheduler, and this decides what is to be done next. All portions of the system, with the exception of the interrupt processors, are entered from the Main Scheduler, and they all return control to the Main Scheduler as shown. This routine is the master of the system. It determines the sequence in which jobs are done, and allocates work to the other programs as required.

The Application Programs, which actually perform the processing on the real-time data, have no direct contact with the outside world. They receive data from the Supervisory Programs, process them and then return them to the Supervisory Programs. They may, however, be much the largest part of all the programming. Some of the systems, at the top end of the scale in Fig. 12, have 200,000 or so instructions in the Application Programs but not more than 20,000 in the Supervisory Programs.

The Main Scheduler transfers control to some of the Supervisory routines. These may, in fact, be written in the same way as Application Programs, i.e., obeying the same rules. They may be routines for handling errors, for generating file addresses, or for preparing a message to the computer. These three functions might, indeed, be regarded as the work of Application Programs. There is an area in which the distinction between the two becomes rather vague, and they would be differently defined for different systems.

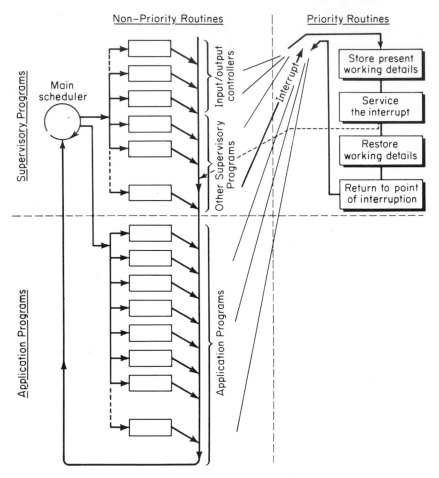

Fig. 20. The relationship between the Application Programs and Supervisory Programs.

COMMUNICATION LINES　　The control of a *communication network* may be an important function of the real-time programs.

The impulses on a communication line are translated by the hardware into bits. The bits are assembled either by hardware or program into characters or words. The characters or words are assembled by program into messages or transactions ready for processing. This may be happening on many lines at the same time. The lines must be constantly scanned. If the program is assembling bits, it must be sure that it never stops scanning long enough to lose a bit.

Conversely, outgoing messages must be broken down into words or characters, and these split into bits. The bits are transmitted down the line by the hardware in the form of pulses. Among the messages being sent down the line will be signals controlling the terminals. If a line has many terminals attached to it, they cannot all send their messages at once. Normally, they must wait until they are instructed by the computer to send. The instruction is one form of control message. Such messages have to be composed and sent at appropriate intervals.

The work of controlling the communication lines is normally a duty of the Supervisory Programs. The programs for doing this may be in the main computer or they may not. Often a separate line control unit or multiplexor has its own core storage and stored program. Alternatively, a small subsidiary computer may be attached to the main computer, and this has the duty of controlling the communications network and feeding complete checked out messages to the main machine.

In Reference System No. 1 in Fig. 13 the line control unit does not have a stored program. It may interrupt the computer when it has assembled a character or word, and the computer reads this. The computer has a routine to assemble the character or words into messages and to break down the output messages ready for transmission. The line control unit interrupts the computer when it needs another character or word to transmit.

In Reference System No. 5, however, the multiplexor has its own stored program. It assembles complete messages, performs an error check on them, queues them if necessary, and sends them ready for processing to the computer.

When more than one machine has a stored program the Supervisory System must coordinate their operation. The programs in a Line Control Computer may be regarded as a part of the Supervisory Programs of the System. In Reference System No. 6, there are four machines with a stored program. The Supervisory Programs for the system must coordinate all of these, arrange that when they interrupt each other the interrupts are processed correctly, and control the transfer of data from one system to another.

FILES   Real-time systems often have large random-access files attached to the computer for retrieving and updating information. Various programs are needed for organizing and locating data in these. They are described in Chapter 11. Locating an item in a large file is rather like looking up a number in a telephone directory, or finding an item in a room full of filing cabinets. In a commercial system this may take a much longer time than processing the item in question, and therefore a number of file operations are carried out at the same time. Where several such operations of varying length overlap, control becomes difficult. Interrupts signal the end of file operations, and the Supervisory Programs are made more complicated by this.

Items may be constantly added to the files or deleted from them. When items are deleted this leaves empty space which is wasteful, and when items are added they cannot be placed in the most convenient location immediately. A telephone list makes a good analogy. If names are struck off the list they leave unused lines. This does not matter on a sheet of paper, but on computer files it becomes expensive to have too much empty space. Similarly, when an item is added, it cannot be placed in alphabetical sequence but is added at the bottom of the list. For this reason, the list is reprinted periodically. A computer file with additions and deletions has to be reorganized periodically. It is rewritten with the items in the most convenient place.

SUPPORT PROGRAMS   The file reorganization programs are one example of the many Support Programs that may be needed. Like that part of an iceberg below the surface, the Support Programs have sometimes not been viewed in their true significance by teams planning and installing real-time systems. The man-years of effort they require may be considerable. It may be surprising to a new team to note that on most systems the Support Programs have taken considerably more programming manpower than the Supervisory Programs. In some systems the ratio has been as high as four to one.

A list of Support Programs for a typical real-time system will include such items as the following:

System loading and initializing programs

Restart programs

Diagnostics (see Chapter 12)

File reorganization programs

Fall-back programs (see Chapter 24)

Library tape and file maintenance programs

Data generation programs for program testing (see Chapter 29)

File loading routines

Supervisory Program Simulators for use in testing (see Chapter 27)

Application Program Simulators for use in testing (see Chapter 27)

Operator set and line control unit simulators (see Chapter 29)

Testing Supervisory Routine (see Chapter 29)

"Introspective" testing aids (see Chapter 28)

Core print programs

Debugging aids (see Chapter 27)

Testing output analysis programs and sorts (see Chapter 30)

7 UTILIZATION OF COMPUTER MEMORY

In order to understand a military campaign it is desirable to have maps showing the deployment of troops. This chapter attempts to give the reader maps of the computer memory and show how the programs and data are deployed in it. It leads up to the concept of *dynamic core allocation*.

TYPES OF MEMORY

Many real-time systems have two types of memory. The core storage or immediate-access working memory of the machine is often not large enough to hold all the data and programs, and thus a second-level backing store is used. This may range from a relatively small core store or drum to a gigantic set of random-access files holding, perhaps, billions of characters. There might possibly be more than one level of backing store. Some data might be referred to very frequently and therefore a rapid-access time is needed but not a massive storage. This would often be the case when programs are kept in the backing store. Other data might occupy a very large volume, and bulk storage is needed which cannot economically have a rapid-access time. Reference System No. 6, for example, has a few million characters of drum storage and many millions of disk storage. Such an arrangement is not uncommon. Table 1 gives an example of the types of memory that are likely to be found, indicating their capacities and access times. The cost per character or word of storage becomes progressively lower as one descends this table. Bulk storage with a relatively long-access time is much cheaper than more quickly accessible storage.

Normally, random-access is needed for real-time data. It is possible by appropriate system design to make use of magnetic tape, but this will

Table 1. TYPES OF COMPUTER MEMORY COMMONLY IN USE

	Probable access time	Capacity commonly found on real-time systems (in 1000 characters)
Small "scratch-pad" working memory:	10 nanosec* to 500 nanosec	1
Core storage, directly addressible:	1 μsec to 50 μsec	4 to 8,000
Core storage, addressible only as an input/output unit:	4 to 50 μsec per character	100 to 8,000
Drums:	5 to 30 μsec	400 to 20,000
Magnetic Disk Files:	30 to 600 μsec	5,000 to 600,000
Magnetic Tape Strip Files:	50 to 800 μsec	Up to 3,000,000
Magnetic Tapes:	Widely variable	Unlimited

$$*1 \text{ nanosec} = 10{-}^3 \text{ m sec}$$
$$= 10^{-6} \text{ μsec}$$
$$= 10^{-9} \text{ seconds}$$

almost invariably result in longer response times and/or higher system costs. Now that random-access devices are so readily available it is not recommended that tape should be used for data to be accessed in a real-time manner. It *may* be used for dumps, diagnostic procedures, emergency routines, for message logging and leaving audit trails. If too many messages arrive at once, they may be temporarily dumped on tape; when the burst subsides the tape is rewound, and they can be processed in the sequence in which they arrived.

LEVELS OF BACKING STORE   In a commercial application, using a large random-access memory, a major proportion of the records are often referred to only very infrequently. However, a small proportion may be referred to very frequently. Figure 21 illustrates this.

In an airline reservation system, for example, 80 per cent of the file may contain details of passengers who have booked flights. It is vital that these records are kept. They may be wanted at any time and must be readily accessible. However, the number of references made to them during their life will be very small. In many cases weeks will go by without a particular record being looked at. However, records saying whether seats are available on next week's flights will be referred to very frequently indeed.

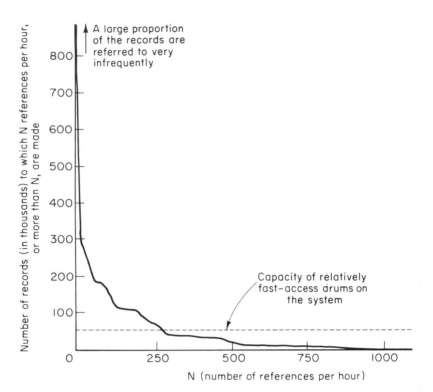

Fig. 21. An example of file usage: The frequency of reference to file records in a file of about six million records.

When records contain two extremes as sharply separated as this it is desirable to have two levels of backing store, one fast, but for reasons of economy not large, and one large but not fast. The choice of files will depend upon the shape of the distribution and upon the overall timing of the system such as in Fig. 21. In this particular case fast-access drums are available, each holding about 80,000 records; these will considerably help the timing of the system.

PROGRAM STORAGE In many real-time systems, programs as well as data will be kept on the backing store because there are too many programs to be held in the core. It is generally desirable to keep programs in a file area where they are quickly accessible. If a system has drums and disks, the programs would normally be on the drums. The programs may be divided into blocks. When the computer determines a need for one or more blocks not in core, it will enter the file and read them into core.

IBM drum files installed at American Airlines SABRE center. These give quick access to 1.2 million characters each. Other disk files on the same system give slower access to more than half a billion characters of information. The drums in the picture store frequently-used data such as programs and American Airlines' seat inventory and availability records.

One of the earliest machines using random-access storage and enquiry terminals—the IBM 305 RAMAC. This was announced in 1957 and had 5 million characters of random-access storage.

The blocks of programs may also be classified according to frequency of use. Table 2 illustrates this. Some of the programs will be kept permanently in the core. The remainder may be either in the core or in the backing store. In a large system such as that referred to in Table 2, perhaps 100 blocks of this program could be permanently in core. Another 100 blocks of core might be available for program read-in from the backing store. If a block of nonpermanent programs is required, and it is not already in core, it will have to be read in. With the figures of Table 2, this would mean that on average approximately eight blocks of program are being read every second.

The situation might be very different in a small system, such as Reference Systems 1 and 2, because here it would be a rare occurrence to call a program in from files. Everything stops until the program call-in is completed. Programs kept on files will be exception routines such as programs to handle errors, programs to process infrequently occurring message-types, or programs to handle exceptional conditions such as an overdraft on a banking application.

Table 2. FREQUENCY OF PROGRAM USE ON A LARGE COMMERCIAL SYSTEM, e.g., REFERENCE SYSTEM NO. 6*

Average number of times used in one hour	Number of blocks of program with this usage	
Less than 1	507	
1 to 2	192	
2 to 4	286	
4 to 8	210	
8 to 16	180	In backing
16 to 32	103	store, and
32 to 64	67	sometimes
64 to 128	59	in core
128 to 256	43	
256 to 512	48	
512 to 1024	32	
1024 to 2048	60	
2048 to 4096	33	Permanently
4096 to 8192	5	in core

* The Programs are divided into relatively small blocks of about 100 instructions each.

If the response time can be long and the decisions to be made are complex, the programs for making these decisions might be read into core and executed a slice at a time. This would avoid the high cost of a large core to hold all the programs.

On many applications processing time is not short but core is, because the cost must be kept low. A complex program is therefore continually overlayed. This is often the case, for example, on production control applications where the computer uses a complex program for re-scheduling the work in a job shop.

FIVE USES The core of a real-time system must then provide:
OF CORE 1. *Space for programs permanently in core.* These will include the main part of the Supervisory Programs and the frequently used Application Programs. Some parts of the Supervisory Programs may be used very rarely, for example, error routines, emergency routines and routines for switching to an alternate computer: these need not be in core permanently. On the other hand, certain Application Programs may be used on almost every transaction, for example, routines for determining the file address of a required record. Such routines must never be overwritten.

2. *Space for programs temporarily in core,* or overlay areas for programs read in from the file. On a system in which programs are read in only infrequently, other programs which are otherwise regarded as permanent may be overwritten and later returned. Where Programs are constantly being read in, as in Reference System No. 6, the system will be doing something else while they are arriving. It may not be able to use them as soon as they arrive, and thus queues of programs may form, waiting for the Supervisory Programs to authorize the processing of the particular message that needs them.

3. *Space for data that are temporarily in core.* This will include the transactions to be processed and data retrieved from the files to be used in their processing. In the simplest systems only one transaction will be in core at one time, and hence it is clear what data areas must be provided. In others an input and output area must be provided for each communication line. In many systems queues of transactions waiting to be processed may build up. Where multi-programming is used, half-processed transactions will be left waiting for records or programs to be retrieved, and thus queues of half-processed transactions will exist. Similarly, records read in from the files may not be used immediately, and these occupy core space. The data storage area becomes complex. It needs careful organization as will be discussed below.

4. *Space for data that are permanently in core.* This includes constants and tables such as file-addressing tables or terminal address and "polling" tables.

5. *Working space and space where temporary working data can be kept.* If multi-programming is used, one working area may not be sufficient, as working data left there for future use by one transaction may be overwritten by other transactions. It may, therefore, be necessary to have a working area for each transaction in the system or, at least, an area where working data can be preserved.

CORE LAYOUT OF A SMALL SYSTEM   Examples of typical core layouts are shown in Figs. 22 and 23. Figure 22, illustrating a small non-multi-programmed system such as Reference System No. 1 in Fig. 13, is relatively straightforward. The Supervisory and Application Programs are in one fixed core position, though the Application Programs may be overwritten by exception Programs read in from the backing store.

A buffer the size of one message is provided for each terminal, in core. When this buffer is full, the terminal can send no more until it has received

Fig. 22. Core map for a small system, e.g., Reference System No. 1 (Fig. 13), used on a savings bank application. The areas in the figure are drawn roughly to scale so that they are proportional to the core areas they represent.

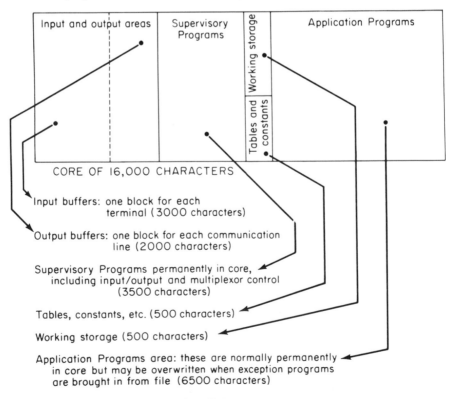

the reply to the message. When a terminal is sending, the line control part of the Supervisory Program is collecting the characters and building up the message in the buffer area. When this is complete the message waits its turn there for processing. It is processed as an individual transaction as though there were no other transaction in core. Its processing may be interrupted occasionally while the Supervisory Program carries on line control functions of sending characters to, or receiving characters from, the Communication Line Control Unit. But there will be no overlapping of the processing of separate transactions. When processing is complete, the answer-back message is stored in a buffer associated with the output line. This will be transmitted in parallel with other output messages while the next transaction is being worked on.

CORE LAYOUT
OF A LARGE
SYSTEM
On a larger system two factors make this straightforward approach impractical. First, in a system with a large number of terminals it would be uneconomical to use a buffer for each terminal. Second, the serial processing of messages, one after another, would not be fast enough. Where many time-consuming references are made to random-access files, it would be very wasteful on a big computer to execute these serially. They must be executed in parallel and must overlap with as much of the processing as possible.

This means that in large systems, such as Reference Systems 5 and 6 in Figs. 17 and 18, multi-programming will be used. Transactions will be processed in parallel. When a transaction is being processed and the need arises to refer to the files to obtain some data, to update a record, or to read in a new block of program, this request will be passed on to the Supervisory Program which will handle it. It will take some time to satisfy the request, and hence work will proceed on another transaction. If this were not so, the central processing unit would be idle until the request was satisfied. The processing, therefore, jumps to and fro from one item to another in a manner designed to optimize the use of the equipment.

The number and type of messages in the system that are being processed in this way varies from one moment to another, and difficult messages will take up different amounts of core space. There will be a queue of half-processed items waiting for a record to be read from files and then waiting for work to be resumed on them. Core space will be needed for data read from the files, but it cannot be predicted how long these data will occupy the core before they are used and finished with. New messages arriving will cause interrupts and have to be read into core. In many systems the messages are sent by independent human operators, and there is nothing to prevent a large number of them sending their messages by chance within the same few seconds.

FIXED AND DYNAMIC CORE ALLOCATION The use of a large area of the core is thus unpredictable and constantly varying. There are two ways in which a core of this type may be allocated: fixed core allocation or *dynamic core allocation.*

With the former, specific areas are set apart for specific tasks. There are fixed areas into which new messages may be read, fixed areas into which records are read from file, fixed areas for programs and so on. If the capacity of any of these areas is exceeded, the work using that area stops until space becomes free again.

Dynamic core allocation does not impose this restriction because here any area of core may be used for any purpose. The queue of new messages is not confined to any area, like the chairs in a barber shop, but may spread through all the available space as though a barber's customers queued in the corridors at peak hours. Similarly, all the available space may be used for holding records read from the files, keeping half-processed messages, storing programs and so on. Core may be used for any function and is allocated by the Supervisory Program. Only when the whole of this area is full, or almost full, does work stop.

DYNAMICALLY ALLOCATED BLOCKS This is achieved by splitting the core up into blocks as shown in Fig. 23. The Supervisory Program knows how many of these blocks are uncommitted and allocates them to various functions as required. How it does this is described in more detail in later chapters. This situation is rather like having a large open office with desks or cubicles which are used by representatives for working or interviewing clients. It would cost too much to give each man his own desk or cubicle. However, only a small proportion of the representatives are in the office at one time. When one comes in he is allocated a desk or cubicle according to his needs. Dynamic desk and cubicle allocation results in an overall saving of desks and cubicles.

The blocks of core that are allocated in this manner are normally of fixed length. It is difficult to program the dynamic allocation of storage on a variable-length basis. There may, however, be more than one fixed length. A system may have small blocks and big blocks available or several sizes of blocks.

To obtain the storage he requires, a programmer writing the Application Programs may code a request for core into his program. He writes

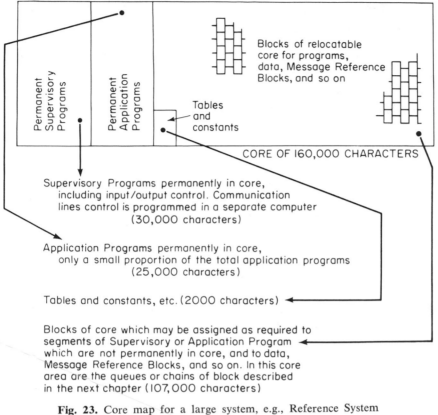

Blocks of relocatable core for programs, data, Message Reference Blocks, and so on

Tables and constants

CORE OF 160,000 CHARACTERS

Supervisory Programs permanently in core, including input/output control. Communication lines control is programmed in a separate computer (30,000 characters)

Application Programs permanently in core, only a small proportion of the total application programs (25,000 characters)

Tables and constants, etc. (2000 characters)

Blocks of core which may be assigned as required to segments of Supervisory or Application Program which are not permanently in core, and to data, Message Reference Blocks, and so on. In this core area are the queues or chains of block described in the next chapter (107,000 characters)

Fig. 23. Core map for a large system, e.g., Reference System No. 6 (Fig. 18), used for airline seat reservation. The areas in the figure are drawn roughly to scale so that they are proportional to the core areas they represent.

a macro-instruction which tells the Supervisory Program to allocate a block or several blocks to him. These are then his to use until he releases them with another macro-instruction. When the processing of a transaction is completed, all the core blocks used for this are released and may then be reallocated to any other function.

PROGRAM RELOCATION

One of the problems of dynamic core allocation is that when a block of core anywhere within an area of memory is used, the program must be written in such a way that it can operate on data that are anywhere in that area. To do this, it is normally necessary to make use of index, or indirect addressing, registers. Some systems without these features make use of high speed data moves to move the data to a fixed working area whenever they are operated upon, but this is slow and inefficient.

When programs are read into a core block which may be at any location,

77

they must be written so that they are "relocatable." In other words, a program must be capable of operating at one place in core at one time and in another place at another time. Here again hardware features can help greatly. The relocatability of programs is discussed in Chapter 20.

MESSAGE REFERENCE BLOCKS When using multi-programming it is desirable to have one area of memory associated with any given job for the entire in-computer life of the job. It must contain any information unique to that message and necessary for its processing. When work on a message is interrupted while it waits for a file record to be found, the working data associated with it must not be destroyed. Such data could be stored in fixed locations set aside as working storage areas, but again it is convenient to use one of the blocks of storage as described above. This gives rise to the concept of a *Message Reference Block*.

A Message Reference Block is an area which belongs uniquely to a message for the duration of its life in the system. When a new message arrives, a Message Reference Block is allocated to it. The message itself is stored in that block, and during its passage through the system any relevant indicators or data are collected in the block. When the message has been processed and leaves the system, the block is freed for other work. If the block allocated is not large enough, another block will be chained to it, like a truck with a trailer. This might be done, for example, if teletype messages of great length are to be processed.

The Message Reference Block may be compared to a pocket in a broker's filing cabinet. When a new client requires work, a pocket is taken from the available pockets and devoted entirely to this client. When this client is finished, the pocket is emptied and again available for other work.

The contents of the Message Reference Block differ from one system to another. In some systems the data related to a message are not all stored in one block but in different areas of core; but these areas are exactly equivalent to the Message Reference Block in other systems.

CONTENTS OF A MESSAGE REFERENCE BLOCK A Message Reference Block in a typical system may contain:

1. The original input message.
2. The address of the line and terminal from which it originated.

3. Working storage that can be preserved, if required, for the active life of the message.

4. A character giving the number of input/output requests to be completed for that entry. When this becomes zero, the entry may be placed in a queue ready for further processing.

5. In some Control Systems any input/output requests are defined by means of "Request Words" or control words, and these are stored in the Message Reference Block until the input/output is completed.

The detailed design of the Message Reference Block, or its equivalent, will vary with such factors as how many input/output requests are in process at one time, how many levels of a program in use at one time are to be recorded in the block, how much space the Application Programs require for storing data, and how long the messages are.

The core layout of a large system such as Reference System No. 6 is shown in Fig. 23. It contains permanent programs and subroutines, including Supervisory Programs and Application Programs. It contains permanent data such as constants and tables. The tables may be changed or overwritten, but their area remains constant. The remainder of the core is divided into blocks, and these are allocated dynamically to temporary programs and temporary data. They contain the queues of the system, including a Message Reference Block for every transaction. Their contents and functions are continually changing second-by-second to meet the ever changing needs of a real-time system.

8 QUEUES

Automobiles arrive at a gas station at times which are not precisely predictable. They arrive more or less at random. Because of this, the pump attendant will be idle one minute, and the next he will have a line of vehicles waiting.

The input to many real-time systems is similar: customers going into a Savings Bank, warehousemen sending transactions or airplanes reporting flight positions. Just as lines of vehicles build up at a pump, so lines of transactions accumulate in a computer. Transactions are kept waiting when they request data from the files. There accumulate queues of requests for a file unit, queues of half-completed items, queues of items on which processing has not yet started, and so on.

A small system such as Reference System No. 1 may be able to keep the queues outside the system. As described in the last chapter, it is likely to have a fixed buffer area for each terminal and strictly serial processing. There will be no variable-length lines of transactions waiting in core but instead a cyclic scanning of input areas. The queues, if any, are in the user's office, and in general it is easier to handle lines of customers waiting at the terminals than lines of transactions in the computer core.

Some systems do not have this kind of input. A computer for radar scanning or a process control system takes readings at set intervals as determined by a clock or similar device in the machine. To a certain extent the process can be timed and planned so that queues do not develop.

The larger systems with manual input, multi-programming and many terminals, such as Reference Systems 5 and 6, will have queuing problems. A major part of the work of the Supervisory Programs in such systems is the building of queues for input/output units and files, and queues of items requiring to be processed. Items are transferred to and from these queues according to considerations of timing and priority. This chapter discusses the nature of the queues and programming for them.

TYPES OF QUEUE
When new transactions arrive they cause an interrupt in the processing and are let into the core. If a separately programmed Line Control Unit is used, they are assembled in this, and a completed message is sent to the main computer. If this is not the case they will have to be assembled in the main computer. Either way, if many messages arrive in the same short space of time queues of waiting messages will build up. As the transactions arrive more or less at random the queues will occasionally grow long. Using queuing theory, it is possible to predict approximately the probabilities of various queue lengths.

The queues in a multi-programmed system are illustrated in Fig. 24.

As the processing on one item proceeds, a need will probably be found to obtain information from the backing store. It may be necessary to update a record, or to read in a table, or to obtain a new block of programs. This will involve a waiting time from 10 to 600 milliseconds if the request is serviced immediately. However, there may be other transactions already using the same input/output channel or waiting to use it. And so queues build up waiting for the channels. This constitutes too long a delay for a fast computer, and thus it will continue with other work, perhaps processing the next item in the input queue.

When the input/output request has been completed, work can start again on the processing of the transaction. It may then have to wait in another queue for the Supervisory Program to transfer control again to its Application Program.

In the course of processing the need may again arise for an input/output operation, and the transaction will find itself again in a Channel Waiting Queue. This may happen several times, perhaps many times, in the life of a transaction. Finally, its processing is complete. A reply message is composed, or possibly several messages to different terminals, and the instruction is given to send these. Again, there may be a queue because the channel to which the Line Control Unit is attached is busy.

In looking at Fig. 24 the reader can imagine a transaction going round the loop five or six times on the average, perhaps because it must make five or six references to files. The queues waiting for processing are often first-come-first-served. This might not be quite true of those waiting for input/output operations to be completed. One random-access "seek" may

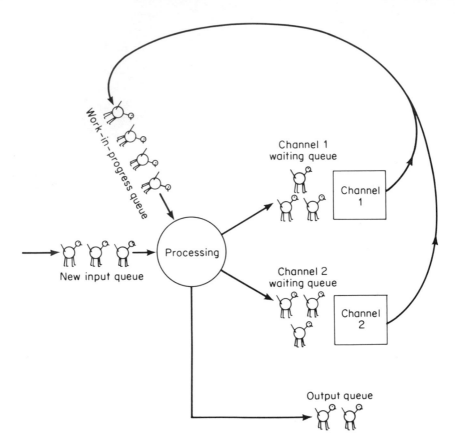

Fig. 24. The queues in a multiprogrammed system.

be completed long before another, and a transaction may have its request completed ahead of transactions that arrived earlier.

There are four common types of queue and these have been given the names:

(a) New Input Queue

(b) Channel Waiting Queue

(c) Work-in-Progress Queue

(d) Output Queue

These terms will be used consistently throughout the book. In technical literature the word "list" is sometimes used to mean the same as "queue" in this book.

There may be other types of queue, for example an overflow queue in which items are temporarily stored on a backing store, or tape because too many items have arrived at the computer at one time, or a non-real-time queue containing items of lower priority competing for processor time with the real-time transactions.

LINKAGE BETWEEN BLOCKS

In the core storage a queue consists of a sequence of blocks of data. These are not necessarily sequential but may be scattered throughout the core. If they are scattered they are connected by control words. This is illustrated in Fig. 25. These blocks may be anywhere in that area of core which is divided into blocks as described in the last chapter (Fig. 23).

The control words may be in the blocks themselves so that the blocks are chained together as illustrated in Fig. 25, or they may be in a separate index maintained by the Supervisory Program. If they are in the blocks the control word may be the first word in each block. It gives the location of the next block in the chain. For the last block in the list it will have a value such as 00000 to indicate that this is the end of the chain.

When a block is moved from one queue to another, for example, moved from the Channel Waiting Queue to the Work-in-Progress Queue because an input/output request has been completed, the block itself is not moved in the core; it merely has its control words changed so that it becomes a member of a different queue.

ALLOCATION OF BLOCKS

When queues of this type straggle at random across an area of core blocks, such as that in Fig. 23, it is necessary for the Supervisory Program to know which blocks are free so that it may quickly allocate a block for a new function. This may be achieved by a simple device. All the uncommitted blocks are chained together to form a type of queue of their own, referred to here as *Uncommitted Storage List*. When a block becomes free it is chained to this queue. When the Supervisory Program requires a block for a new function, it takes the first in this queue. The same mechanism that is used for programming the other queues may also be used for the Uncommitted Storage List.

The Supervisory Program may keep a count of the blocks in the Uncommitted Storage List. Whenever it takes a block from it or adds a block to it, it updates the count. If the count falls below a certain figure the Supervisory Program knows that the system is in danger of running out of core, and then it takes some form of emergency action. There may be different levels of emergency action for different degrees of shortage. These are discussed in a later chapter.

QUEUE DESIGN CONSIDERATIONS

In the design of a queuing system the following considerations may be relevant and should be carefully considered:

1. *Should there be a limit on the number of items in a queue?* If the

items are to be kept in core storage there will be a limit, though dynamic storage allocation allows several queues to occupy the same area, depending upon their requirements. This lessens the probability of one type of queue running out of available blocks. Blocks of core are taken from the Uncommitted Storage List and chained to the queue as necessary.

2. *Should the queue be all in the core of the main computer?* Probably the four main types of queue described above will be in the core of the main computer. A non-real-time queue and an overflow queue may be on disk, drum or tape.

It may be possible to put the real-time input and real-time output queues in a Line Control Computer rather than in the main computer. Some programmed Line Control Units are specifically designed to handle queues efficiently, and this capacity can be put to use.

3. *What should be the length of the items in the queue?* Can they be of a fixed length or is variable length essential?

A queue of variable length items may be difficult to control. On the other hand queue structure varies considerably from one application to another. It is usually possible to have fixed length queue blocks for messages, though long messages may have to occupy more than one block. In the pool of available blocks there may be blocks of different sizes. Two or more Uncommitted Storage Lists may be used, each with blocks of different sizes. Blocks of any size may then be chained onto one functional queue, though this may complicate programming the utilization of the block.

4. *What should be the priority structure of the queue?* Four types of queue mechanism are described below which distinguish between the priorities of items to be added or removed. They are illustrated in Figs. 25 to 28 in the form of scattered queues. Similar considerations apply to queues which are sequential in core or on tape or disk.

FOUR QUEUE MECHANISMS

1. *The Sequential Queue (Fig. 25)*

This is like a cafeteria queue. Items are added at the back and removed at the front. The priority is first-in-first-out (FIFO). The queue is defined by two words in the core which, at any instant, contain the location of the first and last items in the queue.

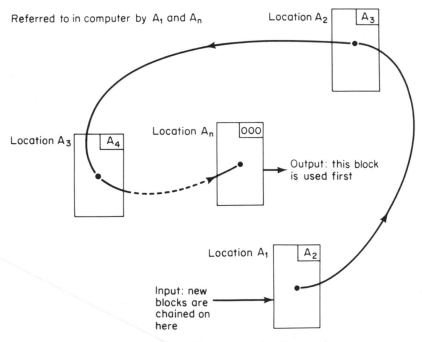

Referred to in computer by A_1 and A_n

Location A_2 | A_3

Location A_3 | A_4

Location A_n | 000

Output: this block is used first

Location A_1 | A_2

Input: new blocks are chained on here

Fig. 25. A sequential queue (cafeteria queue).

2. *The Push-Down Queue (Fig. 26)*

This is like a railway siding. Items are added at the front and must also be removed at the front. The priority is last-in-first-out (LIFO). The queue may be defined by the location of the first item and the number of items in the queue.

3. *The Any-Sequence Queue (Fig. 27)*

This is like a well-organized parking lot. Items are added at the front and may be removed from any place. There is no priority. In order to preserve the continuity, each item must carry the location of its predecessor and of its successor in the queue. The queue may then be defined by the location of the first item and the number of items in the queue. It is like a Push-down Queue but with back references.

There is one fundamental difference in the Any-Sequence Queue. When items are taken from it, or possibly when they are added to it, the queue is scanned. For example, a queue of messages may be scanned to find which of these messages requires an Application Program which is currently in core. A queue of random-access file requests may be scanned to

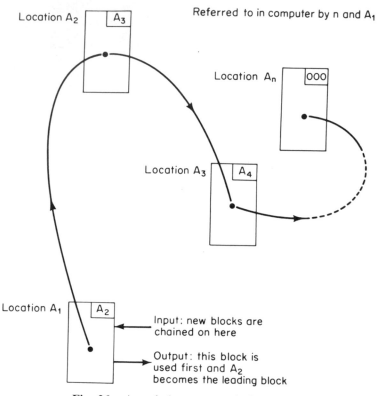

Fig. 26. A push-down queue (railway siding).

see if any other requests can use the current setting of the "seek" arm. As a record is read from tape the queue may be scanned for items which require that record.

4. *The Multi-Priority Queue (Fig. 28)*

It may be desirable to have in a queue items of different priorities. Priority 1 items will always be taken out before Priority 2, and so on; therefore, items are always taken out from the front of the queue. However, items of priority other than the lowest may be inserted in the middle of the queue, as shown in Fig. 28. This complicates the queue structure slightly.

It should be noted that all items in the first-in-first-out queue are sure to be processed eventually, whether in the most efficient manner or not. There is a finite probability, however, that items in the other types of queues may never be processed, or may have to wait an intolerable length of time. This must be guarded against in the design of the system. It may be better, for example, to have two Sequential Queues rather than one Multi-priority Queue with items of two different priorities. The Supervisory Programs could then make sure that the lower priority items are not delayed more than a certain time.

Some real-time systems use various of these mechanisms but others use only the Sequential FIFO Queue. The Uncommitted Storage List may be a Push-Down Queue which is the simplest to program. The Channel Waiting Queues may have items removed out of sequence if they are waiting for the completion of "seeks" of widely varying time. They may, therefore, be Any-Sequence Queues. The New Input Queue and Work-in-Progress Queue may be Sequential Queues unless priorities demand that items are removed out of sequence.

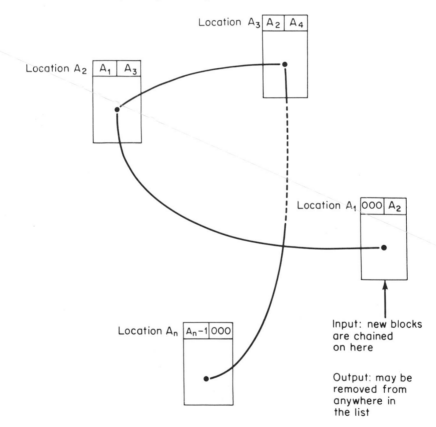

Fig. 27. An any-sequence queue.

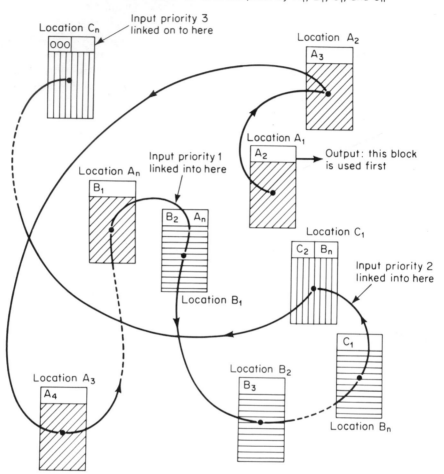

Referred to in computer by A_1, B_1, C_1, and C_n

Input priority 3 linked on to here

Location C_n

Location A_2

Location A_1

Output: this block is used first

Input priority 1 linked into here

Location A_n

Location C_1

Input priority 2 linked into here

Location B_1

Location A_3

Location B_2

Location B_n

Fig. 28. A multi-priority queue with three priorities.

EVALUATING SIZES OF QUEUES When programmers or systems analysts are planning the queueing structure of a system they must have some means of calculating how large the queues are likely to become. This will have an effect on basic decisions such as how much core the computer requires, or, given a fixed memory size, how the queues will be programmed.

Knowing the number of messages that a system is designed to handle at its peak periods, it should be possible to estimate what queue sizes will be involved. To do this accurately may require an elaborate technique such as *simulation* in which a model of the proposed system is built in the form of a program which may be experimented with to predict the queue sizes under various conditions. A special simulation language may be used for building the model. This has frequently been used in existing systems, but it is an elaborate, time-consuming and expensive technique. It requires a systems analyst skilled in the use of simulation and may not give any better results than simpler methods. Often the accuracy of the input data and knowledge of the Application Programs is insufficient to warrant the use of simulation.

An alternative to simulation in many cases will be calculation and the use of basic queuing theory. To a first approximation, queuing theory may be used to give the number of items waiting for file requests to be completed, the size of the New Input Queue and the Work-in-Progress Queue, and hence the number of Message Reference Blocks and the response time.

Queuing theory must however be used with caution. Formulae that assume exponential inter-arrival times may be invalid with some types of Supervisory Program because these routines flatten out any peaks. They may be deliberately designed, in fact, to minimize the queues in core.

9 THE UTILIZATION OF TIME

In a conventional computer application the utilization of time can be mapped out in detail when the programs are designed. In a real-time system this is not so because events happen at times which are not exactly known beforehand. The following times are unpredictable:

1. The times at which external events occur. For example, the time when a contact is closed on a machine tool, or a human operator depresses an enter key on a terminal.

2. Times of clock interrupts. A clock may be set to make the computer perform some action at a given time and may interrupt it at a point which might be anywhere in a program.

3. The times of completion of input/ouput actions, especially of references to random-access files.

Because of this unpredictability the computer cannot follow a repetitive cycle of events but must allocate the time on its various units according to requirements. As with the allocation of core, this may be done in a very simple manner in a small system like Reference System No. 1.; but, in a large system such as Reference System No. 5, it becomes economical to have a high degree of multi-programming, and the allocation of time becomes complex.

COMPUTER UTILIZATION   When the input varies with time the utilization of the computer will be less than 100 per cent. Figure 29 illustrates this. The dotted line represents the capacity of the computer from the point of view of timing. At moments of peak load the capacity will be exceeded, and there will be a delay in processing the transactions. The system might have been designed with a higher computer capacity, in which case the delay would be less. On the other hand, the dotted line might be lower, giving more efficient computer utilization but greater delays and thus greater queues. Greater queues might mean that more core space is occupied, and this would offset the advantage of higher computer time utilization.

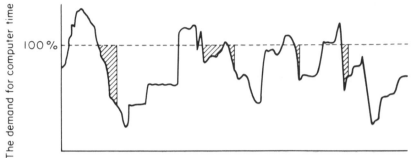

Fig. 29. The variation in demand for computer time. When the demand temporarily exceeds the capacity of the machine, there is a delay in processing transactions, as indicated by the shaded portions.

Figure 29 is oversimplified as the utilization of time for the files, channels and other components must be considered, as well as the effect of core utilization. In practice the sizes of available machines will be taken into account to determine the utilization of these facilities.

TIMING ON A SMALL SYSTEM   In a small system, such as Reference System No. 1, the processing may be strictly sequential with the exception of the servicing of the communications control hardware. No transactions are processed in parallel, but the processing is continuously and automatically interrupted to carry out the assembly of new messages.

Timing a system of this type is relatively straightforward. It is shown in Fig. 30. In a random-access system the lengths of the file references are likely to be great compared with the processing times, as illustrated. As these occur sequentially, not in parallel, the total time taken is largely determined by the sum of the file reference times.

Where small computers have been used for commercial real-time work, they are often far from fully loaded from the timing point of view. Frequently core storage represents a more serious bottleneck in the system design than timing. This is perhaps less likely to happen in a larger system. Where a large number of transactions have to be processed per minute, efficient use of time becomes more important.

TIMING WITH   Inspection of Fig. 30 shows that if the file actions
MULTI-PROGRAMMING could overlap, that is if two or more seeks, reads or
                        writes could go on at the same time, a larger through-
put of transactions could be handled. With present day hardware, if a faster computer is used the file reference times may not be shorter, and thus the need for overlapping file references is even greater.

If file references overlap, this means that transactions are processed in parallel, i.e., there is *multi-programming*. Several messages, which may or may not require different programs, are handled concurrently. It is generally true that multi-programming of this type is more valuable in a computing system when the ratio of input/output time or file access time

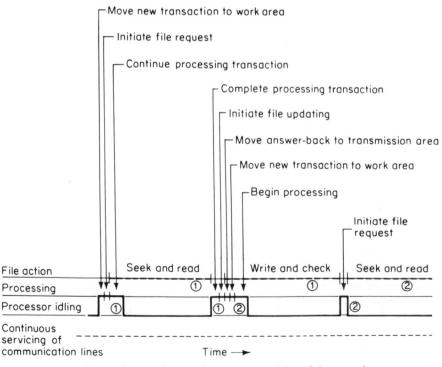

Fig. 30. A timing diagram for a system with serial processing, e.g., Reference System No. 1.

becomes high. A high degree of multi-programming is found in Reference System No. 6, much less in Reference System No. 5, and none with a small system.

Multi-programming is illustrated in Figs. 31 and 32. Suppose, for the sake of simplicity, that all transactions entering a system require identical processing; this is illustrated in Fig. 31. After the transaction has been read into the computer from the Line Control Unit, Program A works on it first, making a request for information to be read on File Channel A. When these data have been read, Program B works on the transaction, making a second file request on File Channel B. When this is completed, Program C can prepare the output, and this is sent to the Line Control Unit for transmitting. When no messages are in the system the computer idles in a scanning loop.

Figure 32 shows six messages of this type arriving and parallel processing taking place. The second message arrives while the request on File Channel B is being completed for the first message; therefore Program A starts work on the second message and initiates the File Channel A request for it before Program C starts on the first message.

Before the reply to the second message is finally transmitted another four have arrived. By this time queues are beginning to build up, both for the File Channels and for the central processing unit. Processing does not drop back to the idling loop as it did earlier.

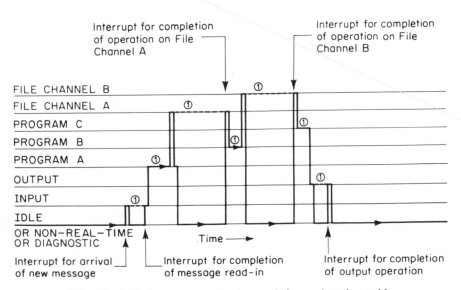

Fig. 31. A timing diagram to be used in conjunction with Fig. 32. Fig. 32 shows transactions of this type being processed in parallel.

SUPERVISORY PROGRAM FOR MULTI-PROGRAMMING
An elaborate Supervisory Program is needed for controlling the jumps from one type of program to another. In an actual system the programs are likely to be more complex than in these illustrations, with more than two file actions to each message. Different messages may have different numbers of file actions and use different programs. File references may, in fact, be needed to call in the appropriate programs. In a large system it will be possible to overlap more than two file actions, and possibly as many as twelve. If this were sketched in a diagram, such as Fig. 32, it would become very complex indeed. The use of parallel programming bears some resemblance to an engineering job shop. Just as the jobs to be handled in a job shop are split up into tasks that may be performed concurrently on the available facilities, so programs may be subdivided into such tasks. At any instant the tasks being executed simultaneously may belong to the same program or to different programs. In this way a much more balanced use of the facilities is achieved; however, as jobs of different types will be received at random, it is necessary to have a Supervisory Program which continuously schedules the work.

The scheduling consists of moving jobs into queues waiting for the processor and waiting for files and input/output units (Fig. 24). Those instructions which begin or terminate input/output operations are in priority routines for which the main routines are interrupted. All input/output operations overlap with processing, and when one of these ends an interrupt occurs, and a priority routine will start another operation on that input/output unit if possible.

TIMING ON A HYBRID SYSTEM
A hybrid system in which only a portion of the work is real-time may use its time in a different manner. In a system such as that in Fig. 15, the main computer may be doing other work while the small satellite computer collects messages and prepares them for processing in the main machines. The satellite computer interrupts the main computer when it has enough messages ready for this to be worthwhile, or possibly at preset intervals. The main computer stops the work it is doing at a convenient point, reads in the messages from the satellite machine, reads in the necessary programs, and processes them. It sends its replies to the satellite machine, and while the big machine continues its other work the small machine edits them if necessary and transmits them, at the same time accepting new messages. This is illustrated in Fig. 33. The satellite machine may keep its queue of messages on an auxiliary file or drum if necessary.

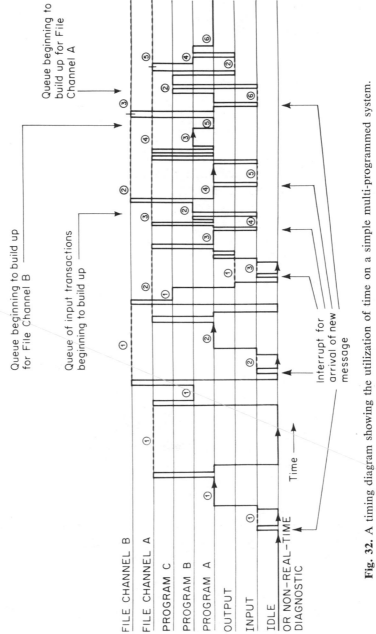

Fig. 32. A timing diagram showing the utilization of time on a simple multi-programmed system.

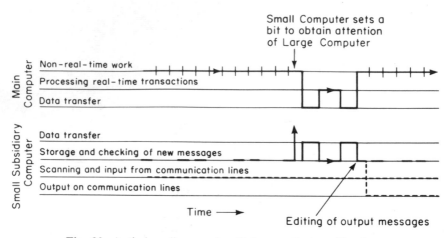

Fig. 33. A timing diagram for Reference System No. 3 on which a small proportion of the work is real-time.

Where the response time can be long, say of the order of minutes, there can be other variations of processing messages at a time different from that at which they are read in. For example, in a small commercial system with a low throughput, a computer may read in and store messages for a few minutes, then seal off the communication lines and load itself with the appropriate programs for processing them. When processing is complete it opens up the lines again, transmits the replies, and reads in more messages. The advantage of doing this is that a smaller computer can be used than if line control and processing take place at the same time.

One of the commonest types of hybrid systems is that in which conventional data-processing takes place in a computer which also handles infrequent real-time transactions or inquiries. These systems must have a Supervisory Program which allows the main work to be interrupted as required. The main work may possibly proceed to a check point before the real-time transaction is processed. It may then be rolled out of core, or the programs temporarily over-written by the real-time Application Programs. When the real-time transaction is dealt with, the non-real-time programs will be restored and their work continued.

10 RANDOM-ACCESS FILE TECHNIQUES

Most real-time systems, especially those for commercial applications, need a large backing store of information. This may contain fixed and unchanging files, or files or records which are constantly being updated by the Application Programs, or files to which new records are frequently being added or in which old records are deleted. The programs must be able to have access to any record fairly quickly, without having to scan through a magnetic tape, for example. In other words, there must be random-access to the records.

Some real-time systems will have both random- and serial-access files. Serial-access files, such as magnetic tape, might be used, for example, for logging messages or storing data with respect to a set of events that occurs in a strict sequence, such as the starting up of power station generators.

THE MECHANISMS
A random-access file is normally kept today on drums, disks, or card or tape strip file. To read a record on the file it may be necessary for the computer to physically move a reading mechanism or the recording media. This may take from 10 to 600 milliseconds and may require a separate program instruction referred to in this book as a *seek*. Some files require for a "seek" movements of a read arm on a disk file. Others do not because there is a read head on every recording track, for example, on every track on a drum. When the "seek" has been completed an instruction is given to read the record in question. There may, however, be some delay in the execution of this instruction because the record is on a rotating disk or drum or tape strip carrier and is not yet positioned over the reading head.

A disk random-access file in use with England's I.C.T. 1900
Series.

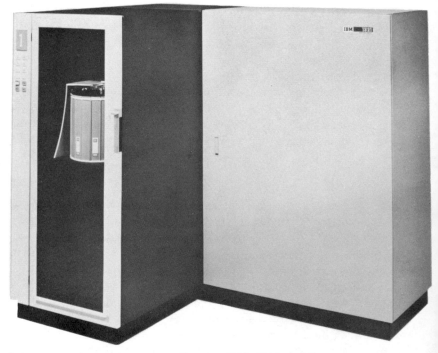

A large capacity random-access file, the IBM 2321, holding
400 million 8-bit characters or 800 packed numeric digits. The
data is recorded on magnetic strips which are stored in interchangeable bins.

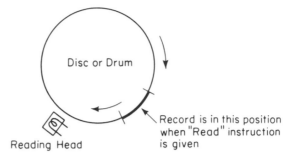

Fig. 34. Reading a record from disk or drum.

As illustrated in Fig. 34, the read instruction may be given at any point in time relative to the mechanical rotation of the disk or drum. The record is likely to be some way away from the reading head and will have to travel that distance before reading starts. This may vary from 0 to 10 milliseconds on a small drum or from 0 to about 40 milliseconds on a large disk. Because of the delay in obtaining a record, the programs will be planned, if possible, so that other processing takes place while the record is being retrieved.

The sequence of events in retrieving a record will be as follows:

1. The program must first generate or obtain the machine address of the record in question. This function may itself require reference to the files as described below.

2. A "seek" is executed, if necessary, to move the mechanisms into position.

3. A "read" instruction is given, but there is a random delay before the record is read, due to disk or drum rotation.

4. The record is finally passing over the read head and is transmitted to core storage.

THE PROBLEMS OF RANDOM-ACCESS   There are three main problems concerned with the programming for random-access files. First, there is the problem of timing. The file references must overlap so that the delays in referring to records are absorbed as efficiently as possible. This was discussed in the last chapter (Figs. 30, 31 and 32).

Second, a means of locating the required record must be devised. One way to find a record is to scan the files or part of a file, inspecting various records until the required one is found. To scan a large file sequentially is a very time-consuming operation. It may be shortened by first sorting all the records into a sequence of their key fields and then executing a *binary search;* but this also takes too long to be practical on most real-time applications, especially where large files are involved. Many systems, however, scan one track to find a record which is likely to be on that track. The computer has to wait for the disk or drum rotation, and it will take no additional time to scan this track if this can be done automatically. An addressing technique will locate the track in question. However, to find the address of the track can be a complex problem which will be discussed below.

Third, the data on the file must be organized as efficiently as possible. They must be organized so that the quantity of information packed into a backing store of given physical size is large. The "file packing density" will not normally be 100 per cent because addressing techniques do not permit this. It may be 90 per cent or 70 per cent or lower, and this will depend on how the file is organized. The file must also be planned so that records can be retrieved fairly quickly. With some methods of file organization two or more "seeks" will be required to locate one record. With others a record may be found directly. Data should be placed in such a position that those records which are referred to most frequently require short seeks. In some commercial systems, for example, a very small proportion of the records are referred to in 90 per cent of the seeks. The records should be packed together in a quickly accessible area. Last, the file must be organized in such a way that additions and deletions may be made without prolonging the seek times unduly, and without making the file packing efficiency too low. If there are a large number of additions and deletions this becomes a problem.

FILE ORGANIZATION   In planning the files a decision must be made as to what records are to be stored where, and how much space is needed for them.

By adding up the numbers of records needed for an application and taking into account their size, the volume required for their storage may be found. There are, however, four factors which may change the overall space demand for files.

1. *Future Growth*

The volume of records may increase during the years the system will be in use. Also, additional types of records may be added. This, and its effect on addressing procedures, should be considered at the time the files are initially planned.

The Card Random Access Memory developed for use with the N.C.R. 315 computer. Information is stored on magnetic cards housed in readily interchangeable cartridges. Picture shows three CRAM units, up to 16 of which can be simultaneously on-line, providing a file store of nearly 90 million alphanumeric characters.

A cartridge being removed from the CRAM files above.

2. Record Compaction

The space required for records may be reduced by compressing the records, using special formatting or coding. The data will be reformatted or coded and decoded by a programmed routine. Record compaction will reduce the file size and reduce channel utilization at the expense of processing time and core storage. The balance of critical factors in the system will determine whether or not various types of compaction are worthwhile.

Compaction techniques are likely to be valuable in any system, whether large or small. In some systems they result in substantial savings and should be considered when making the original design estimates. The following are typical record compaction techniques:

A multiple-choice index may be used in which bits or combinations of bits are coded for possible alternatives.

High order zeros may be compressed into one character.

Code may be substituted for certain names, places, identity characteristics, dates, etc., and decoded, if necessary, by a table look-up or possibly a mathematical conversion.

Variable-length fields may be compressed together in variable-length records.

On machines using seven-bit alphanumeric character coding, two numeric digits may be coded into one seven-bit character using binary-coded centesimal coding.

A field may be replaced by code on a probabilistic basis. For example, of over 600 common English names in Webster's New Collegiate Dictionary, the ten most popular comprise about 30 per cent of the first names in a typical name file. These may be replaced by a code character and less common names can be written in full.

Knowledge of such techniques is useful when designing a system. They should be used with care, however, and ease of maintenance must be considered along with the computer time and core requirements.

3. Additions and Deletions

In some file applications the records loaded initially are a fairly stable set, such as bank customer records or manufacturing product specifications. New records may be added to the file and old records deleted at a rate of less than 0.1 per cent per day. In other types of applications, however, records such as Airline Passenger Name Records may have an addition and deletion rate as high as 25 per cent per day. This means that periodically the file must be reorganized as the additions have not filled the space left by the deletions. On a sequentially-organized file it may be necessary to batch additions and deletions and sort them into the file when the system is not on-line 24 hours a day.

To assess the additional space required for additions and deletions it is necessary to decide how these will be organized. It must be decided what type of addressing scheme will be used and how often the file will be reorganized. As is indicated in the discussion of addressing below, the number of additions and deletions is likely to effect the scheme used.

4. *Addressing Techniques*

The basic problem of file addressing is this: records in the logical files are identified by a number, or key, which is determined by the application. This may be, for example, an account number in a bank, a part number in a factory, a flight number and date in an airline reservation system, or a passenger name. It is this number or key which will reach the computer in the input transaction, and from this the machine address of the record must be determined so that the computer can locate it quickly from the mass of records it has stored.

Much of the remainder of this chapter is concerned with the problem of file addressing and the effect it has on the organization of the files. Five fundamental methods of addressing are discussed below. Most systems will use one or a combination of these methods:

(a) *Direct addressing.* The easiest, and often the most economical, way to solve the addressing problem is to have in the input transaction the machine address of the record in question. For example, in some banking applications the account numbers have been changed so that the account number or part of the number is the file address of that account.

The account records for this customer withdrawing cash from his bank are kept on the random-access files at the rear right side of the picture. The bank teller in the picture, and other tellers at distant branches, have immediate access to these records. As a transaction is made, the records will be updated.

For many applications this is not possible. For example, the part numbers in a factory or warehouse could not normally be changed as they have a significance to the firm in question.

In some cases the method can be used, even though it is inconvenient to change the reference numbers in question. For example, in an application for updating savings passbooks the file address of the account record may be written on the passbook, and this is keyed in by the clerk operating the terminal.

Where direct addressing can be used it can give a high file packing ratio and usually a brief file reference time.

(b) *Algorithm*. It may be possible to organize a logical file so that the addresses within that file may be calculated from the reference information, such as account number or flight number and date.

This is not possible in the majority of applications, but where it can be done it is a simple and fast method of addressing the files. It may not, however, be efficient in its use of file space. An airline, for example, may have perhaps 150 flight numbers. The algorithm uses these and the date to calculate the file address. However, not every flight flies on every day; hence some of the addresses generated will not contain a record. There will be gaps in the file layout.

This must be taken into account when estimating the file requirements. It differs completely from one application to another and requires individual assessment.

(c) *Scanning*. In most systems there will be no logical relationship between the reference number (part number, account number, etc.) and the address where that item is kept in the files.

One method of locating the item would be to scan the files. It is obviously not practical to scan the whole of a large randomly-ordered file. However, if all the items in the file are sorted into the sequence of their reference numbers it becomes more practical to locate a given item. The problem becomes rather like finding a person's telephone number in a telephone directory. An analysis of the reference number will direct the search to approximately the right area of the files. From then on a *binary search* might take place to locate the item exactly. A binary search goes to the midpoint of the area to be searched and compares the reference number of the item sought with that on the file. It thus successively halves the area of search. When the area of search is sufficiently small it may be scanned sequentially to locate the item. This is illustrated in Fig. 35.

In general, scanning or searching the files in this way is a lengthy process. It is normally too time-consuming to be used on its own in a real-time system, but is often used to pinpoint an item within a small area when some other technique has found that area. If scanning a disk or drum track can be made to overlap with the disk or drum rotation time, this would be a worthwhile method.

(d) *Table look-up*. A table is often used as an index to a random-access file. It lists the reference numbers of items along with the addresses where they are stored. When this is done the computer has to search through the table rather than search through the file. A considerable amount of time may be saved, but space is needed to store the table.

The table may, or may not, be in sequential order, just as the file may or may not be in sequential order. In general, if one uses this method it pays to sort both the table and the file with a view to shortening the table look-up time and the file access time. Items that are frequently referred to are placed at the start of the table and are in file locations that can be reached quickly.

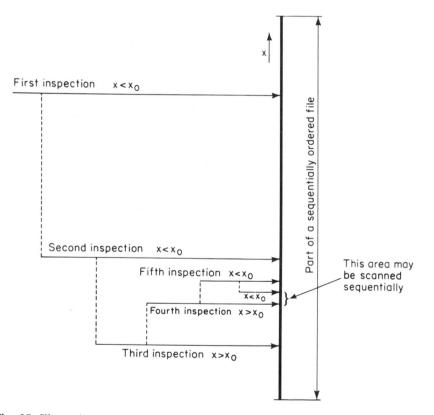

Fig. 35. Illustration of a binary search: a search for an item with reference number X_0. Six inspections of the file each halve the area to be searched, narrowing it down to the small area shown, which can be scanned sequentially.

The difficulty with using a sequential file is that additions cannot normally be made in sequence, and deletions leave gaps. This may not matter if the number of additions and deletions is small, but if there are many of them the file will frequently need reorganizing, that is resorting, if it is to operate efficiently.

Some space will have to be left for additions to the file, and this may be divided into "overflow areas" at points throughout the file. New records will reside in these areas until the next reorganization of the file. They will then be merged with the other records, in sequence, and the obsolete records will be removed.

There would not normally be one table for all the records in the files but rather primary and secondary tables, or a whole hierarchy of tables. The primary table would give the location of the secondary table, and this would give the location of the item in the files (Fig. 36).

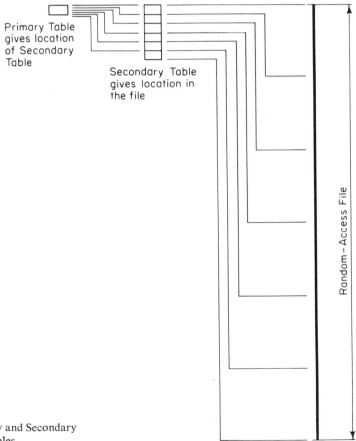

Fig. 36. Primary and Secondary File Address Tables.

Suppose that the files contained half a million records. It would be quite impractical to scan a table of half a million reference numbers and addresses. Instead, a brief inspection of the reference number might indicate that it is in one of, say, five areas of the file. A primary table might indicate which of 100 secondary tables is to be used. The secondary table would be read into the core, if it is not there already, and this would have about 100 items indicating the address of the item in the file.

This means that two short table look-up operations and two file references are needed to locate an item. It may be possible to store the secondary table in the same area of the file as the record so that only one "seek" would be required. On a disk file where different cylinders have to be "sought," a table for each cylinder might be stored on that cylinder. The first action, when a reading arm is positioned on a cylinder, might be to read the table for that cylinder into the core.

There is often scope for some ingenuity in making the scanning of the table coincide with the disk rotation so that the time involved can be minimized.

(e) *Randomizing.* This is one of the most common methods of addressing. It locates the majority of items but never all items with one file reference. Hence it is quicker than file scanning or table look-up. However, it does not give a high file density. Seventy to eighty per cent packing is a reasonable figure to aim at. With higher packing than this the number of records that need more than one file reference increases rapidly.

The first step in this type of addressing is to convert the item's reference number into a random (approximate) number that lies within the range of the file addresses where the record is to be located. There are many methods of generating this random number, and these must be evaluated for each specific application by means of the utility programs that are available for this. Several methods are described below.

It is desirable that the transform selected has two properties:

(i) It must have an almost equal probability of generating any address in the desired range.

(ii) In some cases two reference numbers will generate the same machine address. The quantity of such "synonyms" must be as low as possible.

With this method of addressing there is a probability that the correct record will not be found the first time, and a new reference will have to be made to an overflow location. The overflow record may be among the other records in the main file, or it may be in a specially planned overflow area (Fig. 37).

In making file estimates the methods of handling overflows must be decided, and characters for locating overflow records must be included in the estimates of track packing.

POCKETS   This technique is considerably improved if the randomizing routine produces the address of a group of records rather than one record. Records may be located together in "pockets", just as the documents stored in a set of filing cabinets are

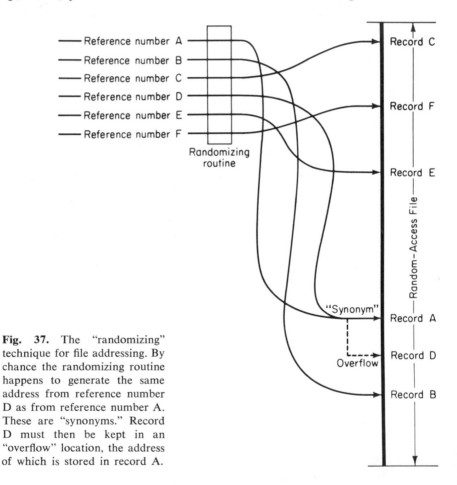

Fig. 37. The "randomizing" technique for file addressing. By chance the randomizing routine happens to generate the same address from reference number D as from reference number A. These are "synonyms." Record D must then be kept in an "overflow" location, the address of which is stored in record A.

placed in pockets, with each pocket containing a number of documents. If filing cabinets stored each piece of paper by itself it would be more difficult to find a particular item than when they are grouped together in "pockets" of a suitable size. The same is true of random-access files.

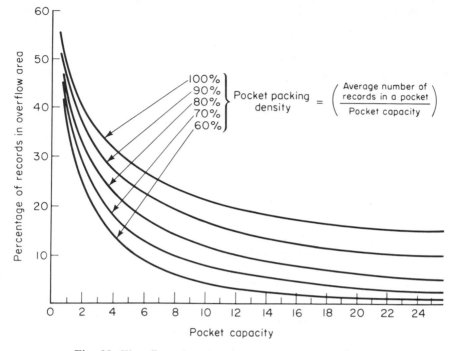

Fig. 38. The effect of pocket size on number of overflows.

OVERFLOW POCKETS   The randomizing routine will locate the required pocket, and this pocket will then be scanned for the record in question. The record is recognized because the reference number is stored in it, perhaps as the first field.

If the record is not in the pocket, an overflow pocket must be sought. The address of the overflow pocket will be stored in the original pocket. If the record is not in the overflow pocket, a second overflow must be sought. This is "chained" to the first. In rare cases more than two overflow pockets will have to be inspected before the record is found.

The location of an overflow pocket may or may not require a further "seek." A disk file arranged in cylinders would probably be organized so that the overflow pockets are on the same cylinder. In this case the reading mechanism need not be repositioned. A read would be necessary but not a "seek."

A pocket may be a natural division of the file, such as a track of a disk or drum. Scanning the pocket or track might then be done automatically.

When a new record is to be given a place in the files its reference number will be fed to the randomizing transform. This will give a pocket address. If there is room in the pocket the record will be stored there. If there is not, it is stored in an overflow pocket; if the item takes the last place in a pocket, an overflow pocket must be allocated for the next item. The address of the overflow pocket will be contained in the original pocket.

The greater the number of items in each pocket, the less is the chance of an overflow. However, a large number of items in a pocket means that the time taken to scan the pocket is long. A compromise between these factors must be reached, and this to some extent will be dictated by equipment features such as track size.

Figure 38 illustrates the relationship between pocket size and the number of overflows. It will be seen that with ten items in a pocket there is far less overflow than with one, or even five, per pocket. However, with 20 or 50 items in a pocket there is little to be gained by further increasing the pocket capacity.

OVERFLOWS AND FILE PACKING DENSITY The number of overflow pockets will also be a function of the file packing density. If the packing density is high, so that most pockets are full or almost full, a new record being placed in the files will often not find an empty slot with the first file reference. It must then be placed in an overflow location, and subsequent references to it will have to look first in the "home" location and then in the overflow.

A balance must be struck in the system design between saving file space and saving time. This is illustrated in Fig. 39.

TECHNIQUES FOR RANDOMIZING There are many methods for generating the requisite randomized number.

Generally, the original reference number or key is longer than the address into which it must be converted. Such keys by themselves are normally unusable as addresses. They may be numeric or alphanumeric. In general, the more randomly distributed they are the better.

If the key is not numeric it must first be converted into the format best suited to the computer in question. An alphanumeric key might, for example, be turned into a binary number. On a fixed-word-length machine the number might be compressed to the length of the words by adding some of the bits together.

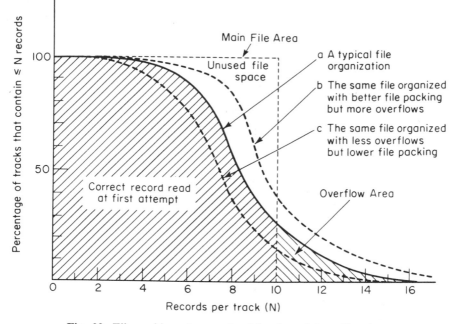

Fig. 39. File packing when randomizing is used for addressing.

The key must then be converted into a randomized number and this number must be processed so that it falls within the range of addresses in question. It will not be possible to find a randomizing method which cause no "overflows," i.e., too many keys transforming to the same address. An attempt should be made, however, to find a method which produces as few overflows as possible.

Typical of randomizing methods that may be tried are the following:

(a) *Division.* If the range of addresses is N, that is N address locations are available with consecutive numbering, the reference number or key may be divided by N and the remainder used as the randomized number. If P is the lowest of the addresses, this is added to the remainder.

(b) *Division by prime number.* With most sets of keys the above method gives a better distribution if the division is by a *prime number.* A prime number slightly less than the number of available addresses might be used. Prime numbers do not always give the best results, but usually the distribution within the range is such that there are fewer overflows. Different possibilities should be investigated for each application.

(c) *Truncating.* The quickest form of the above technique is to divide by 100, 1,000, 10,000 and so on. This is effectively truncating the reference number and retaining the requisite numbers of low order digits. If the set of reference numbers is irregular this method will give many overflows.

(d) *Folding.* Truncating throws away some of the information in the key set. Any information thrown away tends to destroy the uniqueness of the key set, and so to worsen the distribution. A better method would be *folding,* in which parts of the reference number are added to each other to give the required number of digits.

(e) *Radix conversion.* The radix of a number may be converted, for example to radix-11. The excess high order digits may then be truncated. This technique might be employed on a computer without automatic division. It is superior to truncating alone. The radix conversion can be performed by a series of additions and shifts.

(f) *Squaring.* The number may be squared and the center digits of the square used. This can produce an excessive number of zeros.

There are many methods that may be used to transform the reference number. For any one application it is usually necessary to experiment to see which gives the best results with the set of reference numbers that exist for that application. Generally, the most fruitful technique for investigation is the division by various prime and other numbers.

One error that must be avoided is accidental duplication of any reference numbers. If two different records have the same key due to a procedural or other error, a transaction may overwrite the wrong record.

11 PROGRAMMING FOR COMMUNICATION LINES

With any input/output unit such as tape or disk the main programs in the computer receive, or prepare for output, a complete record or message. A short routine writes or reads the record and checks that this has been done correctly. This is what is required also with the communication lines, but here the input/output routine may be more complicated.

The digital information is transmitted on the communication lines a "bit" at a time. The messages to be transmitted must therefore be broken into 'bits' and these sent at the speed of the line. Similarly, on receiving a message, 'bits' are assembled one at a time into characters, and the characters are assembled into messages. Both the characters and messages must be error-checked and the errors corrected if possible. Suitable control signals must be generated for operating the distant terminals at the correct times.

Depending upon the nature of the hardware in use, this may be done in the following ways:

(a) Entirely by programming.

(b) Entirely by electronic circuitry.

(c) Half-and-half, for example, with the electronics assembling 'bits' into characters and the programs assembling characters into messages.

The communication lines may go straight into the main computer. When programs are needed to service the lines the main programs will be interrupted for this purpose. There may be many such interrupts per second.

Alternatively, the communication lines may terminate in a device which feeds characters to the main computer and accepts data characters and

113

control characters from it. The main programs will then be interrupted to assemble characters into messages or feed characters to the line control equipment.

Or, a third alternative, the communication lines may terminate in a separate device, often a subsidiary computer specially designed for the purpose, which feeds complete, checked-out, edited messages to the computer, and receives complete messages for transmission.

The choice among these approaches is to some extent determined by the number of communication lines that must be handled. If the system has only one communication line this may go straight into the computer, or into a device with a buffer storage which automatically assembles or disassembles a complete message. If, however, there are fifty or a hundred communication lines, these are best terminated in a separate *Line Control Computer,* or *Multiplexor* as in Reference Systems 5 and 6. For the sake of flexibility the multiplexor may be a stored-program computer capable of handling messages of any length and of controlling different numbers of lines. It would have an instruction set different from conventional computers and designed for the handling of communication lines. It may have the facility to log messages on its own random-access file or tape unit. It may send English-language messages to the terminal operators as part of its control procedures. Because it is a programmable unit its procedures may be modified as circumstances demand.

OPERATIONS THAT MUST BE PERFORMED   Whichever of these approaches are used, the interface between the communication lines and the main programs of the computer is likely to have the following functions:

1. *To initiate and control the reception* of data from the lines. The lines may be of different speeds. Many lines may be transmitting or receiving at once. The terminals may have to be scanned or polled to see when they are ready to transmit.

2. *To assemble the bits* into characters and characters into messages.

3. *To convert the coding* of the characters. The coding for the communication lines may be different from that used by the computer. The lines may, for example, use Baudot code, whereas the computer uses binary coded decimal.

4. *To check for errors,* both in the characters by means of a parity check, and in the messages by means of longitudinal redundancy checks, such as analyzing polynominal checking characters.

This display board gives the status of circuits and stations within the U.S. Defense Communication System. It assists military commanders in identifying trouble anywhere in the 19-million mile network of communications channels. Traffic loads may be indicated on a selected portion of the system.

5. *To edit the messages* if necessary. For example, an operator may make mistakes in typing on the keyboard, use backspace, or erase characters. The message must be edited into its correct format before it is ready for processing. Control characters must be recognized and removed.

6. *To recognize End-of-Record or End-of-Transmission characters,* and carry out the housekeeping, preparing for another transmission if necessary. If an error was detected the same message should be sent again.

7. *To deliver messages to the main programs,* one at a time, edited and converted. For this purpose it may have to maintain a queue of messages waiting for the main programs.

8. *To accept messages from the main programs* when they are ready for transmission to the terminals.

9. *To prepare these messages for output.* It will be necessary to convert them from computer code to communication line code. Control characters may have to be added.

10. *To initiate the transmission* of these messages. Messages may have to be queued before they can be transmitted if there are more than one message for one line, as is often the case when a line serves several operator sets.

11. *To monitor the sending process,* repeating characters or messages if the terminal detects an error in transmission.

12. *To signal End-of-Transmission* to the terminal and carry out the necessary housekeeping functions and line control functions.

The IBM 1050 data communication system can send or receive business information in a number of different ways. The operator is shown transmitting information by placing punched cards in the 1050's card reader. Data also can be sent via the typewriter keyboard. To the left, behind the operator, are other components of the system. On the top shelf is an auxiliary printer, which prints incoming information. Below it are a paper tape punch and a paper tape reader. Information can be transmitted directly over communication lines to a computer for immediate processing, or to another 1050 at a distant point.

In addition to this, a stored-program 'multiplexor' may be required to *log messages* on to a file or to *add a sequential number* to the messages for control purposes. It may be programmed to take some type of *fallback action* if the main computer breaks down, or, in a duplexed system, to take part in an *organized switchover* in the event of a failure as described in Chapter 23.

SYSTEM WITH ONE COMMUNICATION LINE   Where an on-line system has only one communication line the control of this will be relatively simple. Probably one core storage buffer will be allocated to the line. This will be filled with characters from the line when the computer is receiving, and will be filled by the computer when transmitting. If the line is "full-duplex", that is, capable of transmitting in both directions at once, two such buffers will probably be used.

As indicated above, assembly of bits into a complete message and *vice versa* may be done by programming or by electronic circuitry. With only one line in use it is more likely to be done entirely by hardware. An input/output device may have its own core buffer of, for example, two hundred characters. This would be filled automatically from the lines, with automatic parity checks and longitudinal checks being done. If errors are detected, automatic retransmission would occur. Similarily, transmission from the buffer would occur automatically to the terminal or terminals indicated in an address which may be in the first characters of the message as it is assembled by the computer. Hardware logic may also do the code conversion between the computer code and the line code, and *vice versa,* and may delete characters which are not part of the data message before passing this to the computer.

The programs in the main computer then merely have to read and write the contents of the buffer as in any normal input/output operation, for example, reading and writing paper tape. They may need to edit the input messages and possibly queue them. They will add terminal addresses and control characters to the output messages.

SYSTEM WITH SEVERAL COMMUNICATION LINES   Where a number of communication lines are on-line, the problem becomes much more complicated. There is a probability that any or all of the lines may be in action at one time, transmitting or receiving. The lines must therefore be scanned regularly. If characters arrive on the lines at the rate of 120 bits per second, for example, this means one bit every 8⅓ milliseconds. The machine will normally sample each bit several times to nullify the effort of very short noise pulses, and hence a scan may have to occur about every 1 or 2 milliseconds.

The line control hardware may assemble the bits into characters, and the programs assemble the characters into messages. Suppose that 8-bit

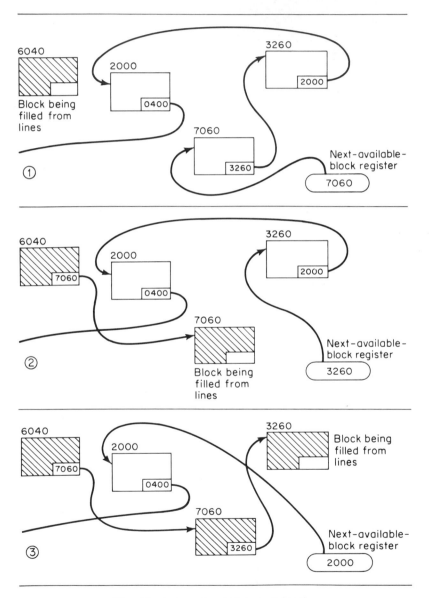

Fig. 40. Automatic chaining of blocks.

characters are used and that the communication control device has a buffer of two characters for each line. One hundred and twenty bits per second then give a character every 66⅔ milliseconds, and the character buffers will have to be scanned with this interval. Every 66⅔ milliseconds, approximately, the other programs must be interrupted while a scan takes place, and characters are transferred to or from the appropriate input/output area in the computer storage. A fair sized segment of a program can be executed between these interrupts.

DYNAMIC BUFFER ALLOCATION   Where many communication lines enter the system it is economic to allocate input/output storage in as flexible a manner as possible. Suppose that the system has 100 lines, each of which can handle messages of up to 300 characters. It is unlikely that all the lines would be in use at any one moment, and the average message length may be much less than 300 characters—say, 50 characters. It would then be uneconomical to allocate 100×300 characters of storage for input/output. This is especially so where a terminal's transmission rate is that at which an operator types in data, and the operator may be slow and tie up the core allocated to the terminal. Rather, the storage should be assigned dynamically, in blocks, as it is required, in a similar manner to the *dynamic core allocation* described in Chapter 7.

CHAINING   Initially, each input communication line has a block of core assigned to it by the program. The data being received from the line are stored in this, character by character. When the block is full another block is *chained* to it, and the storing of the message continues in this. Blocks are linked to the chain until the entire message is received. The last few characters in the blocks will contain the address of the next block in the chain. This is illustrated in Fig. 40.

AUTOMATIC BLOCK CHAINING   Some *programmed transmission control* computers have logic circuitry that is designed to handle the allocation and chaining of blocks of core automatically. When a block is filled the characters go automatically to the next block. This may be assigned by means of a "Next Available Block Register." When one block from a chain of available blocks is assigned, the address of the next block is automatically stored in this register (Fig. 40). A similar process occurs when a message is being sent to a host computer, or when an output message is being transmitted.

Suppose that one such machine has 30 characters to each block that is automatically assigned. If a long message, say 300 characters, arrives, it will continue to take blocks—10 blocks—until it is all in core. When the machine's program is initially loaded it will go through all the blocks in the core that are used for data and will chain them together. The address of the first block in the chain will be placed in the Next Available Block Register. One block near to the end of the chain may have a code placed in it which is automatically recognized. This code alerts the program that the supply of buffer storage is running low. The program will then take corrective action such as slowing down input or speeding up output to gain more storage space.

If this dynamic storage approach were not used, it is likely that a large amount of core would be tied up for long periods of time waiting to be filled, processed or emptied. This would be the case especially for long messages, or for messages which come from a manual unbuffered keyboard.

LINE CONTROL

The *control* of the communication lines and terminals is also likely to be done partly by programming, partly by hardware. The major part of this control consists of telling each terminal when to start transmitting.

In a system in which the input from terminals is not randomly timed, the terminals may be scanned on a strictly timed cycle. For example, ten channels of input data might be sampled 50 times per second. This leads to a basic cycle time of 20 milliseconds. The Supervisory Programs must make sure that every 20 milliseconds all six channels will be read. This would probably be done by using a real-time clock interrupt which would have high priority.

CONTENTION AND POLLING

Input which is random and at the whim of a human operator needs a different approach. The operator will probably press a key requesting attention from the distant computer. The computer, when it is ready, will signal the operator to go ahead or will initiate the reading of some medium such as a card or paper tape. There are two methods in common usage for organizing this: "contention" and "polling."

In a "contention network" the terminal will make a request to transmit. If the channel in question is free, transmission will go ahead. If it is not free the terminal will have to wait. A queue of "contention requests" will be built up, and this will be scanned either in a prearranged sequence or in the sequence in which the requests were made.

In a "polling network" the communication control device will send signals to the terminals saying "Terminal A. Have you anything to send?" If not: "Terminal B. Have you anything to send?" And so on. Terminal A may have control equipment which automatically sends the signal on to Terminal B, or the computer may originate both signals. Polling, rather than contention, is likely to be used on a network with a large number of terminals, especially one with many terminals on a line, because it allows tighter control over the network. It ensures that no terminal is kept waiting for a long time, as could conceivably happen with a contention network.

The polling signals will usually be sent under program control. The program will have a "polling list" in core for each channel which tells it the sequence in which the terminals are to be polled. If one terminal has a higher priority than the others its address may appear more than once in the polling list. The polling list may be modified under program control.

**LINE
STATUS**
A communication line may be in any of various types of status. Three of these are *receive status, transmit status,* and *control status.* As the lines are scanned, their status will be examined and this will inform the program or hardware whether to take receive, transmit or control actions. If the line is in control status, then polling signals will be sent to or replies received from these.

The communication lines are thus scanned by the transmission control equipment on a preset schedule, and simultaneous message assembly and distribution operations occur on all channels. The status of the existing conditions is examined on each channel as it is scanned, and appropriate action is taken.

**MESSAGE
PROCESSING**
The messages may be processed character by character; this processing will include functions such as deleting control characters, looking for end-of-message characters, code conversion if this is not done automatically, and so on. Such processing will start before the whole message is received in order to shorten the time during which the message is occupying the core. It will proceed from area to area in a predetermined sequence, scanning and processing those characters that have arrived since it last processed that area. In this manner it will check output areas as well as input areas.

The IBM 7740, a stored program machine which controls data transfers in a communication network. It can stand alone as a small computer and have random-access files attached to it, or it can act as an input/output device for a larger computer.

When a complete message is received it may be transmitted to a main computer, or logged on files or tape. Longitudinal check characters will be examined, and if errors are found, appropriate action will be taken. The transmission control computer may be programmed to carry out other functions, such as taking check totals or adding serial numbers to messages.

MULTI-PROGRAMMING   *Multi-programming* is necessary in such a computer because the timing is dictated by the times at which characters arrive on the lines. The programmer must estimate how much processing can be allowed for servicing one communication line without unduly delaying service to the others. The programming must be stopped at certain logical points, even if it could be continued, in order to provide service to the next line on the schedule.

The programs will thus be an intricate array of short routines, with the processor's attention darting from one line to another, doing what it can in the time available to it as it scans. The work of assembling a message and preparing it for the main computer will be done a section at a time.

When exceptional conditions occur, such as noise errors on a line, or a terminal failing and the polling list needing to be modified, this must have high priority, but as far as possible without interfering with the work on other lines.

LOGIC
REQUIREMENTS

It will be seen that the logic requirements of a programmed transmission control computer are different from those of computers in general. For this reason many real-time systems utilize a machine for controlling the communication lines which is separate from that doing the main processing. The transmission control computer may have facilities for automatically allocating chained blocks of core. It may have several levels of priority programs so that the programs for one function can interrupt those for another function with the minimum inconvenience. The interaction between the programmed and non-programmed functions will be made as easy as possible. Line or equipment errors will be detected automatically, but without stopping the machine. The nature of these errors would be transmitted to the programs by means of registers or control words, and programs with the highest possible priority would take the required evasive action. As far as possible, the machine should be able to isolate faulty components and notify its operator while continuing other operations.

A manufacturing employee reports on her specific production job via one of 127 remote terminals. Flashed in a fraction of a second to a central computer center will be: name and number of employee, job work order number, aircraft ship serial number, shop department number, cost center to be charged, type of work, and exact time for beginning or ending of operation. Conceived by Lockheed and designed and produced by the Radio Corporation of America, this data acquisition system speeds up and simplifies the flow of production information to management.

DIVISION OF
FUNCTIONS

If two computers are used in this way the functions to be programmed may be divided into the following categories:

(a) Functions assigned to the main computer because of its superior data-processing ability, or because of its access to files.

(b) Functions assigned to the transmission control computer because of its unique logic.

(c) Functions that may be programmed in either.

(d) Fall-back functions that occur in the transmission control computer only when the main computer has failed.

The functions which may be done in either machine should be placed so as to increase the system's efficiency and throughput, and to give it maximum flexibility for growth and change.

Flexibility is, indeed, a key factor in designing the communication network control. On almost all real-time systems it is likely that the transmission requirements will be modified frequently. New terminals and lines will be added as the system expands. Terminals will be closed down temporarily. Priorities will change. Traffic volumes will change. Message lengths will change. New types of terminals may be added.

It is for this reason that the control of the communication lines on a complex system should be a programmed function rather than a function handled entirely by hardware.

12 DIAGNOSTICS

Diagnostic programs are a tool used to test computers, isolate component malfunctions and improve overall computer system operation.

In conventional systems the engineer uses such programs to diagnose the causes of errors that have occurred, and, in some cases, to detect faulty circuitry before it gives trouble. The systems analysts, or programmers have little or no knowledge of the diagnostics as these are the province of the engineer. However, in complex systems, especially in real-time systems, the systems analyst must become more familiar with diagnostic techniques as these affect the ability of the system to meet its requirements. The purpose of this chapter is not to discuss the type of diagnostics that are familiar on conventional systems, but those additional programs that may be needed when a system is used for real-time work.

In a real-time system it is generally desirable that the machine should not stop when an error occurs if there is some way of circumventing the trouble. This is often the case, and methods of error circumvention can be built into the system. These can range from a simple repetition of the action if the error does not repeat itself, to switchover to a second set of equipment if the error is catastrophic.

The errors may or may not be permanent errors. A permanent or *solid* error, once it has occurred, is always present whenever the faulty part of the circuitry is tested.

Some errors, however, are *intermittent* since they occur only occasionally. These are difficult to reproduce, and diagnostics may not detect or pinpoint them because they may not occur at the right time. These types of errors generally occur under unfavorable environmental tolerance conditions, for example voltage, clock frequency, or temperature variations beyond safe limits. Certain combinations of data, frequency rates of special instructions or sequences of certain conditions may cause them to occur. They may be caused by components which are aging or wearing out.

A third type of error is that which occurs only once and cannot be made to repeat itself. These are called *transient* errors. When they occur the operation must be re-performed. Diagnostics are not used to trace them. They may be caused by noise, or cross-talk, or a brief abnormal condition in a supply line.

Reliability is usually a prime consideration in a real-time system. The reason for its being real-time is usually the same reason as for not wanting it to go "off the air" because of failures. Its "Mean Time to Failure" and "Mean Time to Repair," when a failure occurs, are important criteria. The maximum time taken to repair a failure may also be of importance in some systems. Skillful use of diagnostics and preventative maintenance can help to improve these time figures.

ON-LINE DIAGNOSTICS   In some systems diagnostic routines will be run while the system is operating in real-time. On others this will not be necessary, as there is plenty of time to check out the system when it is off-line. Diagnostics may, however, be run when the system is on-line without any waste of time. The volume of transactions it processes is not constant. The system will normally be built to handle peaks of traffic. During off-peak hours or minutes diagnostic routines may be run. They would be given a low priority so that they would not interfere with any of the data processing.

Not all of the necessary diagnostic work *can* be run on-line. By their nature some of the important diagnostics must have full control of the system so that no real-time work can take place concurrently.

In a simple system there may be no need or desire to complicate matters by running diagnostics for checking the computer and its peripheral units while the system is on-line. It may, however, be necessary to have a program for checking the communication lines and terminal equipment, on-line.

An engineer in a distant city may repair a terminal or a piece of transmission equipment. He wishes to test that it is now correctly connected to the computer. Rather than stop the computer so that this test can be made, the engineer may send a message from the terminal which the computer interprets as needing a real-time response. It loads into its core a diagnostic routine which exercises all the functions of the terminal and its communication link. The engineer also sends messages that use all these functions and checks that everything is working correctly. To the Supervisory Programs in the computer this may look like a normal real-time transaction.

TYPES OF DIAGNOSTICS   A conventional computer uses *Unit Diagnostics* to detect and isolate faults in the various units. Separate unit diagnostics will check such items as the arithmetic circuitry, transfer instructions, each input and output unit, and so on. These will be used off-line when the computer is entirely in the hands of the engineer.

With a real-time system off-line unit diagnostics will be used in the same way, but some on-line diagnostics will supplement these. A system with a communication network on-line will periodically check out parts of the network, possibly every morning as the system opens up.

When errors occur in the system, the computer, on detecting these, will use "quick look" diagnostic routines to determine the cause of the error and then decide what action it should take. In a system which needs a very high degree of reliability the diagnostic routines will locate the source of the trouble that has occurred, and an *Automatic Recovery Program* will bring into play duplexed circuitry or a standby computer, or a switch may occur to a fall-back mode of limited operation as described in Chapter 24.

SYSTEM DIAGNOSTICS   In a complex system unit diagnostics, however well written, are not sufficient to test all the combinations of circumstances that may occur. A test is necessary which exercises the whole system in a random manner, involving all the elements of the system in a constantly changing pattern. *System diagnostics* must utilize the whole system in a manner similar to its operational running. Programs resembling the operational programs will be used rather than systematic programs that run logical test patterns.

The system check-out program may, for example, run problems on the system and check their solution rather than intermediate results. It attempts to establish worst-case conditions, and it maximizes the utilization of all available machine elements. It is random in its operations, use of units and in the data it manipulates. It is, in fact, rather like the real-time system working under peak conditions. The randomness is a key factor in a program of this type. If the program runs long enough, every

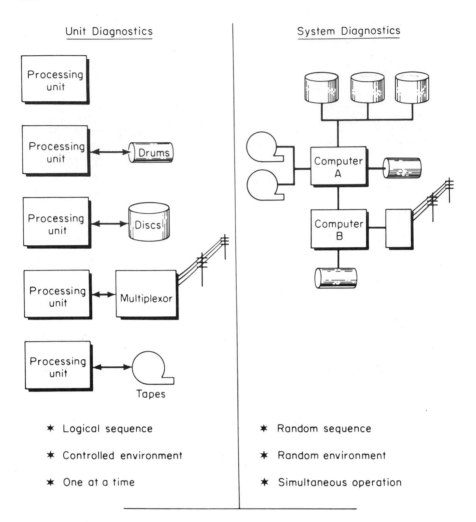

Unit Diagnostics

System Diagnostics

* Logical sequence

* Controlled environment

* One at a time

* Random sequence

* Random environment

* Simultaneous operation

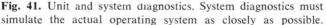

Fig. 41. Unit and system diagnostics. System diagnostics must simulate the actual operating system as closely as possible.

combination of interactions between central processing equipment and the input/output devices should be tested. Every combination of operations, data configurations and unfavorable machine conditions should be tested.

By its nature the system diagnostics routine does not isolate failures. However, experience has shown that there are certain malfunctions which this type of program detects and which unit diagnostics normally do not detect.

Diagnostics can, indeed, be divided into two categories: those which detect that errors are occurring and those which isolate the cause of errors. These two programs are contrary in nature and use different concepts. For this reason, error isolating programs usually have poor error detecting capabilities and *vice versa*. Error isolating programs are like a rifle shot aiming at a precise location, whereas error detecting programs aim broadly to hit anything there is to hit.

DIAGNOSTICS WORKING WITH THE SUPERVISORY PROGRAMS The concept of the system diagnostics can, with profit, be taken one step further. Instead of being written to operate by itself, it can utilize and operate with the Supervisory Programs. In this way it tests both the behavior of the hardware and the Supervisory Programs, and thus it is useful for system testing during the development of a system. To the user of the system it is the hardware working in conjunction with the Supervisory Programs that is of interest, and this forms an effective system diagnostics.

Diagnostics used in this way are written like the Application Programs. The programmers may make use of all the available macro-instructions. This means that they can operate easily while real-time work is going on, as the Supervisory Programs use the same methods for handling diagnostics as for processing transactions. It does, however, limit diagnostics slightly as they must accept the same restrictions as the Application Programs. All input and output operations must, for example, be carried out by the Supervisory Programs. This is tolerable if all the "prohibited" tests are performed in a scheduled maintenance mode when the computer is not on-line.

To operate with the Supervisory Programs the diagnostics may have to be *relocatable,* i.e., be capable of running from different positions in core. Minor problems arise when some of the programs are dependent upon knowing exactly where they are located in core. A relocated program does not normally know where it is operating. The program can calculate its own location if it is given the relocation factor. It may, however, be desirable not to relocate certain small parts of the diagnostics, for example, the routine that is entered when interrupts occur. This may have to be an addition to that part of core which is permanently allocated.

Diagnostics written to work with the Supervisory Programs cannot be written until the latter have been specified; they cannot be tested adequately until the Supervisory Programs are debugged. If the user of the system, rather than the manufacturer, writes the Supervisory Programs the question may arise as to who writes the diagnostics. Normally, a computer has its diagnostics provided as a "package" by its manufacturer. However, some of the diagnostics are specially written for one application only, and cannot be written until the programming of that application is well under way. If the manufacturer maintains a policy of providing all the diagnostics he needs a special team of diagnostic programmers to work in conjunction with the customer's programmers.

REASONS FOR ON-LINE DIAGNOSTICS   There are four main reasons for using diagnostics of this type which operate with the Supervisory Programs:

1. They can be used in checking out the communication network as indicated above. An engineer at a remote terminal can test its linkage to the computer.

2. They can save time. Certain system diagnostics can run while the system is still operating in real-time. This may be done periodically as a confidence check on the functioning of the system.

3. If the system has a fault in a non-vital component, and is still operating, perhaps in a fall-back mode, it is desirable to repair the error while the system is in operation. An error isolation diagnostic using the Supervisory Programs can be run on-line.

   If a fully duplexed system is used this may not be necessary. However, many real-time systems are not fully duplexed. Systems with a hierarchy of fall-back procedures such as Reference System No. 4 are generally a better economic proposition. These may need error isolation diagnostics running while real-time data processing continues.

4. When errors occur in an operational system, it will normally be desirable for the system to take some corrective action, if it can, rather than to stop. There are many different types of action that may be possible, as described in Chapters 22 to 25. These include switchover to a duplexed computer, fall-back to one of several types of degraded operation, or, if the error is a transient one, repetition of the processing that was under way when it occurred.

A computer system of the past would have stopped when an error was encountered. A real-time system will not stop, but an *interrupt* occurs. The system must then decide what type of action it is going to take. It must find out what has gone wrong and must see whether any of its own components are faulty before it decides whether switchover or a mode of fall-back is necessary. For this on-line diagnostics are needed. This is probably the most important use for diagnostics which work with the Supervisory Programs.

ERROR DETECTION
DURING OPERATIONAL
RUNNING

When an error occurs and an interrupt transfers control from the working program to a diagnostic, several possibilities for continued operation exist:

1. In the case of a transient or intermittent error it is possible that the instruction which led to the error can be re-executed and the program operation can be resumed. Only with certain instructions in the system is this possible without creating a logic fault.

2. It may not be possible to restart at the instruction where the failure occurred, but the program may be restarted at a certain restart address. As a program is loaded into core its restart point must be recorded in case this emergency action is needed.

3. If the failure destroyed part of the contents of core or otherwise caused damage to the environment of the program so that it cannot be rerun, it may be necessary to reload the program or other programs. A restart procedure may automatically do this.

4. The damage to the contents of the core may be such that the computer cannot reload its own programs. In this case a standby computer may take over, or an operator may reload the programs.

5. The fault may be "solid," in which case a repetition of the program during which it occurred will not suffice. It may be possible for the system to keep working without the faulty component, perhaps in a fall-back mode. The diagnostics must decide this and, if necessary, initiate the fall-back.

6. The fault may be "solid" and in a vital component, so that the computer in question is inoperable. In this case, switchover may occur to a standby machine, or the system goes "off the air" for repairs.

This process is illustrated in Fig. 42. The process of determining the requisite action is complicated by the fact that the program running when the error occurs may be an Application Program or a Supervisory Program. It may be a priority program following an interrupt, or even a diagnostic routine itself.

A small diagnostic Supervisory Program will be needed for selecting and transferring control to the appropriate diagnostic routine.

AUTOMATIC
RECOVERY
PROGRAMS

Using this concept of correcting errors in real-time can lead to a system in which the hardware and programs are jointly designed to recover from most fault conditions. Additional circuitry has been used on some systems, so that the recovery programs and the corresponding

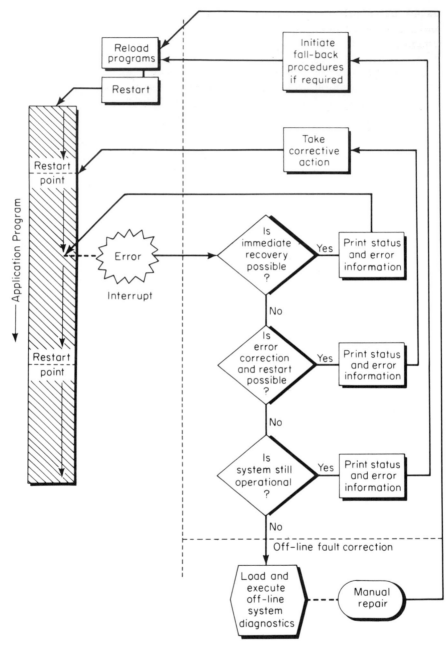

Fig. 42. Error treatment during operational running.

circuitry must be planned in an integrated fashion at the design stage.

In providing automatic recovery, the following features in the equipment are desirable:

1. An efficient error detection system to indicate an error immediately it becomes apparent. This is necessary on *all* real-time systems.

2. An automatic interrupt system which immediately gives control to the automatic recovery program when an error occurs. This is also needed on *all* real-time systems.

3. An instruction set capable of testing error status, examining error data, and resetting and releasing equipment.

4. Means to save and restore the program conditions that existed when the error occurred and return, if desirable, to the point of interrupt. This is necessary for restarting the program. It is also necessary for reconstructing the circumstances in which the error occurred, so that its cause may be sought.

5. When automatic error detection circuitry is used, it is desirable to have an automatic means of checking this. Otherwise it may fail and errors may go undetected. Many machines do not have this.

6. An output printer for logging errors may be used which is independent of the output units for the operational programs.

7. A non-destructive memory is valuable for the error detection and automatic recovery programs.

8. Certain hardware facilities may be duplicated. For example, vital data may be duplicated on separate files. Drum tracks may have duplicate read/write heads.

The desirability of additional hardware for automatic recovery will depend upon the size of the system, and the degree of reliability demanded of it. In a single computer system, automatic recovery facilities may add 20 per cent or 30 per cent to the cost of the system and enable it to recover immediately from, perhaps, 80 per cent of its error conditions.

13 THE RELATIONSHIP BETWEEN THE PROGRAMS

On a real-time computer a very large number of programs may have to fit together to make one operating system. These are likely to be written by different programmers or even different programming teams. Sometimes the Supervisory Programs are written by a team working for the computer manufacturer, and the Application Programs are written by the customer. In cases where an American manufacturer has sold systems in Europe, different programs have been written by teams working on different sides of the Atlantic.

Where programs must fit together in this way it is essential that the relationship between the programs is clearly defined at the outset. Programmers must be able to write the programs largely independently of each other, and therefore the interface between programs must be specified in detail.

For example, the Application Programs use and continually refer to the Supervisory Programs. The latter must therefore be defined in detail, and the means of linking with them specified, before the work starts on the Application Programs. The definitions and linkages may be modified later, and if there is any change, the Application Programmers must know about it. Similar problems occur when one Application Program uses another or when they use a common subroutine. In a large system some of the programs are likely to be *relocatable* so that the linkage may not be straightforward.

It would be more correct to refer to a set of Supervisory Programs than to a single program. The nucleus of this system may be a central scanning loop referred to in Fig. 43 as the Main Scheduler to which control is always returned when an Application Program or another Supervisory Program finishes its work. This central routine determines what work is to be done next and transfers control to the appropriate program (see Fig. 43). The central scanning loop may be regarded as the main program, and all Application Programs and other Supervisory Programs are subroutines to this. Some of these programs may themselves have subroutines. Application Programs will have subroutines which may be classed as other Application Programs or as Supervisory Programs, such as input/output routines.

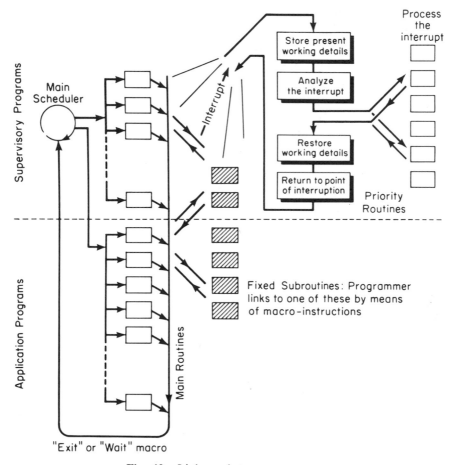

Fig. 43. Linkages between programs.

MACRO-INSTRUCTIONS The link which the Application Programmer uses to transfer control from his routine either to the Main Scheduler or to a subroutine is normally a *macro-instruction*. This is one line of code which, when the program is compiled, generates a number of instructions; it either gives the required link or it forms the complete subroutine. A set of accurately defined macro-instructions must be available for the Application Programmer to write into his coding. Some of the macro-instructions, with the library routines necessary for compiling them, will be part of the Supervisory Program Package. Others will be written by the Application Programmers.

This is similar to the use of macro-instructions in conventional programming which combine a language with, for example, an Input/Output Control System. In a conventional system, however, the programmer may have a choice as to whether he uses such routines or whether he writes his own. In a real-time system he normally has no choice because all input/output must be a function of the Supervisory Programs. The programmer is not concerned with timing this in detail. He merely says what he requires to be done, and the Supervisory Programs execute it at the correct time.

Much of the Supervisory Package thus consists of macro-instruction routines for inclusion in the computer's processor tape. Some computers may have standard routines for real-time work, written independently of specific applications. The user would then adjust the specifications of his Supervisory Routines, when they are compiled, in the same way that input/output control systems are compiled in conventional applications.

LEVELS OF PROGRAM   The levels of program are illustrated in Fig. 44. There may be several levels of subroutines. Some of these may be fixed in core; others may have to be brought in from files when required, and may be relocatable. Multiple subroutines are discussed in a later chapter.

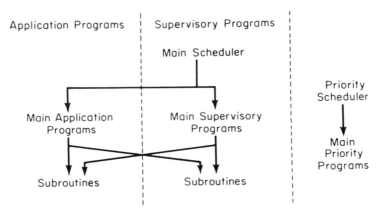

Fig. 44. Levels of program.

The dividing line between what are called Supervisory Programs and Application Programs is a diffuse one. There are some programs that might be in either category. For example, the first program that works on a message, once it has been read into the system, may be an Initializer Routine which checks for errors in transmission and analyzes an action code on the message to determine what program shall work on it. The Initializer Routine then transfers control to the Main Scheduler, indicating what Application Program is required for the message.

RULES FOR RELATIONSHIPS BETWEEN PROGRAMS When programs are being used together in an integrated fashion as in the systems described here and are sharing a common memory, certain conditions need to be established. These are:

1. *Independence of Preparation*

The scheme should permit programs to be written and compiled quite independently. This is particularly important if the programs are not related to one another. In a multi-programmed system, the programmer cannot judge which programs will be co-executed with which.

2. *No Reduction in Logical Power*

When any program is in control of the processor, there should be little or no reduction in the effective logical power available to it. In practice, there is always some reduction in the facilities available. For example, it may not be able to use all the index registers. Such restrictions are discussed later.

3. *No Interference*

No program should be allowed to introduce error or undue delay into another program. Hardware devices are in use to prevent such interference. These include "Memory Protection" to prevent a branch to a non-permissible area of core or the overwriting of one program by another, and a "Watchdog Timer" to prevent a program staying in a closed loop.

4. *Automatic Supervision*

Instructions to the operator for handling tapes, forms, etc., should originate from the Supervisory System. Hardware malfunctions and possibly program or operator errors should be reported in a standard manner.

5. *Flexible Allocation of Space and Time*

Allocation of space in core and disk, assignment of input/output units, and the control of time sharing should be based on the needs of the programs being executed.

The Application Programmer refers to the various subroutines of the Supervisory System by means of macro-instructions, which are provided as part of the Supervisory Package. The programmer writes these into his source program; when the program is compiled, machine-language instructions are generated which cause the appropriate action to occur, for example, the placing of a file request in the appropriate queue.

Macro-instructions will be used for functions such as obtaining the requisite core areas for a program and releasing these when they are finished with, executing all input/output operations, setting up Message Reference Blocks, giving linkages with subroutines, and so on.

There is one type of macro-instruction that is especially important and will be referred to again throughout the book. This is the macro-instruction which returns control to the central scanning loop when a segment of an Application Program has completed its work. This might be referred to as an *EXIT Macro*. It may signal the end of the message processing or it may not; it may be merely a temporary delay in which no more processing can be done until a file record has been retrieved. Two macro-instructions might in fact be used for these two cases, and in the description that follows these are called EXIT and WAIT respectively. These and other typical examples of Supervisory Package macro-instructions are described below:

1. WAIT

When an Application Program gives a file request and cannot do any more processing until this is complete, it must not hold up the processor. In this and similar situations, the programmer writes a WAIT macro-instruction. The program location and conditions, which must be preserved for restoring later, are stored in a suitable place such as the Message Reference Block, and control is transferred to the central scanning loop. When an input/output or file request is made, the input/output control routine may increment a counter located, for example, in the Message Reference Block. As each such operation is completed this counter is decremented. When the counter equals zero the Message Reference Block is chained to an appropriate queue ready for work again, and eventually the Main Scheduler will return control to the Application Program (as described later in the book.)

2. EXIT

This is the last instruction in an Application Program signifying that processing is complete. When this has been given, as soon as all input/ output operations are complete, the Supervisory Programs will release any working storage blocks held by this entry, including the Message Reference Block itself. Thus, the life of the message in the computer is ended. When the instruction is given, the count of input/output operations mentioned above may be checked. If it is not zero an indication may be stored in the Message Reference Block that the next routine to be executed is the EXIT routine. Control will then return to other processing.

3. GET CORE

This macro is used when a storage block is required for the processing of a message. If the core is divided into blocks which are dynamically allocated as described in Chapter 7, a core block is removed from the Uncommitted Storage List and is assigned to the message in question.

The count of the number of uncommitted blocks is decremented, and if this count falls below a certain level the system may be in danger of running out of core. The program then transfers control to a routine which will take corrective action. This corrective action may possibly be the completion of a partially processed message, or the removal to a disk of some of the Application Programs that are normally in the core.

All interrupts should be inhibited during the process of removing and allocating a block if it is possible for a program, operating in a priority mode, to remove the same block and assign it elsewhere.

4. RELEASE CORE

This is the converse of GET CORE. It is, of course, important that core blocks should be released as soon as possible. There may therefore be macro-instructions which request both an output operation and a release of the associated core block, e.g., a WRITE FILE would be given as a WRITE FILE and RELEASE CORE.

5. INPUT/OUTPUT MACRO-INSTRUCTIONS

A Supervisory Package may provide many input/output macro-instructions. Some typical ones are:
WRITE DISK (meaning Seek disk record and Write. The Seek may be given separately from the Write).

WRITE BOTH DISKS (in a system on which records are duplicated on different files for safety, this would write both of them).

READ DISK.

READ DISK AND WAIT (a READ DISK combined with a WAIT).

WRITE DISK and RELEASE CORE (a WRITE DISK combined with a RELEASE CORE macro-instruction).

READ TAPE, WRITE TAPE, REWIND TAPE, PUT or GET (with block or unblocking), and so on.

PRINT, TYPE, PUNCH A CARD, DISPLAY, and so on.

MESSAGE OUT (this might be used to transmit a message to the multiplexor).

OUTPUT TELETYPE (this is used separately from MESSAGE OUT where teletype messages are of a different length and nature).

All such input/output macro-instructions are likely to result in a request to an Input/Output Scheduler which is part of the Supervisory Programs. This routine will execute the instructions as soon as possible. Many may not be executed immediately because the Input/Output Channel or Unit is in use.

6. CREATE MESSAGE REFERENCE BLOCK

A Message Reference Block, designed to contain all the details needed in the processing of a message and to save these throughout the in-system life of the message, is created in the required format. It may be desirable to split a transaction, producing duplicate Message Reference Blocks, so that more than one output message may be sent.

7. MACRO-INSTRUCTIONS FOR TIME-INITIATED ACTIONS

These cause a designated program to be called in and used at a specified time. To use time-initiated macros a special Time-Initiated Supervisor Routine will be needed.

8. LINKAGE MACRO-INSTRUCTIONS

There may be a variety of macro-instructions for making logical linkages between programs and subroutines and for saving data from one program for use by another. A set of macro-instructions for subroutine linkage is described in Chapter 21.

9. LOGGING DATA AND DEBUGGING

Macro-instructions which may strictly be thought of as part of the Support Programs can be of great value in program testing, tracing system faults and in monitoring the performance of a system. These are described in later sections of the book.

RESTRICTIONS ON APPLICATION PROGRAMS The Application Programmer is both helped and hindered by the Supervisory Programs. They help him by providing a set of macro-instructions such as those mentioned above. These, in a way, make programming easier than in a conventional system. He does not have to think in the same way, for example, about input/output timing. This is handled for him by the Supervisory System. There are, however, certain restrictions placed on the Application Programmer. These are necessary when several programs share the same facilities. The restrictions vary considerably from one system to another. They need to be stated in detail by the designers of the Supervisory Package.

Typical of such restrictions are the following:

1. No core storage may be referred to by an Application Program outside of its own assigned area or blocks; the constants, tables or common subroutine area it may use are also specified.

2. Input/output instructions and interrupt-type instructions may never be executed by Application Programs. These may only use the provided macro-instructions.

3. In a machine with index registers or latches, only a certain number of these may be used by the Application Programs. The others are exclusively for use by the Supervisory Programs.

4. Registers used by an Application Program are normally not saved when control is switched to another program via a WAIT or EXIT macro-instruction. In other macro-instructions (which do not switch to another Application Program), the registers may be saved.

5. Certain switches and indicators may not be saved when a macro-instruction is given. These should be specified. None will be saved when a WAIT or EXIT macro-instruction is given.

6. An Application Program may be limited in the time for which it can exclusively occupy the central processor. An automatic time-down device may prevent, for example, a longer interval than 500 milli-seconds between successive WAIT or EXIT macro-instructions.

7. The length of an output message may be restricted to the size of a buffer area. Messages in excess of this length must be split up and sent as more than one message.

With a set of facilities and restrictions such as these above, the Application Programmer is not merely programming the computer he is used to, but rather a combination of computer and Supervisory System. The programmer needs two manuals of operation, one for the machine and one for its Supervisor. In programming a multi-programmed system there is perhaps less scope for a gifted programmer than with a conventional system. The programmer must obey the rules very carefully lest errors will occur when his programs are interfaced with the work of the other programmers. In these systems, especially in the more complex ones like Reference Systems 5 and 6, teamwork between the programmers is the overriding necessity. The "prima donna" must be restrained or he might upset the apple cart.

A CODING
EXAMPLE

In conclusion, to illustrate the relationship between programs, a simplified piece of coding of a typical Application Program is given in Fig. 45. The Supervisory Program macro-instructions are shown. The purpose of this program is as follows:

When a message is received two records must be found in order to process it. The file addressing is such that when record from file 2 is found, this may turn out not to be the correct record. In this case an overflow address must be calculated and an overflow record read.

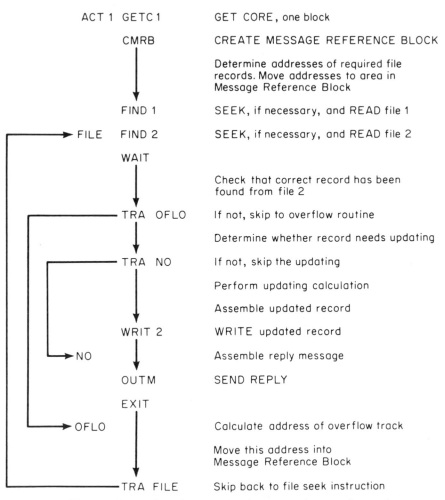

Fig. 45. Illustration of coding showing common macro-instructions.

The processing will determine whether or not file 2 needs updating. If it does, the updated record is assembled and written. A reply to the message is assembled and sent.

To do this processing the program must first obtain some core and set up a Message Reference Block. This is done with two macro-instructions as shown. It must then determine the addresses of the required file records, SEEK them and READ them. This is done with FIND macro-instructions, and these must be followed by a WAIT, so that the system can carry on with other processing while they are being found.

Control is eventually returned to the program after the records have been read. The program checks that they are the right records and, if so, it carries on with the processing. In the file 2 record is incorrect the overflow location is found.

When the reply message has been sent an EXIT is given. After the file actions are completed and checked, the EXIT releases the core that this processing used, and this core may then be used by other messages. Thus the life of the message in the computer is ended.

AN INTRODUCTION TO
SUPERVISORY PROGRAMS

14 THE FUNCTIONS OF SUPERVISORY PROGRAMS

The Supervisory Programs used for real-time systems vary greatly from one type of application to another. The smallest system with a low number of inquiries may have a very rudimentary control routine. At the other end of the spectrum a system such as Reference System No. 6 with a very large number of Application Programs, a high throughput and low response time will require a complex and intricate set of Supervisory Programs that will take many man-years to write. Such a set of programs is described in Chapter 16.

The Supervisory Programs are designed to coordinate, service, and augment the machine components of the system. The Supervisory Programs handle input and output and the queuing of messages and data. They schedule the work in the system. They may assess priorities between Application Programs and carry out housekeeping functions for them. They process interrupts and deal with error and emergency conditions. They are designed to coordinate the functions of the system under varying loads.

A computer used for a conventional data processing application normally follows a repetitive cycle of events which may be planned and timed in detail by the programmer. Input and output operations are usually of a known length and time and may be balanced with each other and with the processing that is to be done.

In an on-line system this is unlikely to be true. Messages arrive at random times and are probably varied in their length and nature. The sequence of operations is unpredictable. However, the data are still to be handled in minimum time and computer facilities are to be used fully. Events will occur in real-time that cannot be built into any predicted timing

147

pattern. Failure of a machine component will necessitate immediate emergency procedures and these may be automatic.

In addition, in a large real-time system the volume and variability of messages received may be such that several transactions must be in the computer at once if reasonable efficiency of operation and the required response time is to be maintained. These transactions may require different programs.

For reasons such as these a Control or Supervisory Program is used to continuously schedule the work, allocate core storage and assess priorities, as this cannot be done in advance in a rigid manner by the programmer.

Application Programs are written for a specific application, whereas Supervisory Programs can be used for a variety of different applications. In this respect the Supervisory Programs are almost like part of the hardware. In large systems, however, the requirements differ so much from one application to another, as will be described later, that many of the Supervisory Programs also have to be rewritten for each application. Software now being planned for computers by manufacturers is, however, introducing more and more standardization here.

THE RANGE OF SUPERVISORY PROGRAM REQUIREMENTS   Not all real-time systems require very elaborate Supervisory Programs. The following examples show the range of techniques and functions that are found in these programs:

1. A very elementary application would be one in which enquiries are received while other work is being done; the enquiries request the contents of a record to be transmitted in reply. The processor would interrupt its conventional data-processing applications at convenient points in the cycle and test whether an enquiry has been made. If it has, a small routine in core answers the enquiry and then returns control to the main routine.

2. The enquiry or command which is received on the communications line may require a program to be moved into core in order to handle it. The sequence of operations here might be as follows:

   (a) The processing unit interrupts its normal work at convenient points to test whether a message has been received or whether an operator is ready to send a message.

   (b) If so, the message is transmitted to the core and the processing unit analyzes a code to find what program is required.

   (c) The appropriate program will be moved into the core from a file in such a manner that it does not destroy working data or indicators in use in the main program.

(d) The message is then processed, file references are made and the reply is sent, if necessary.

(e) If there are no more messages, the original program is again moved into the core from the file, and the computer continues with its normal work.

With this method of operation only one enquiry can be processed by the system at a time. A new enquiry will be held up until the processing of the previous one is completed.

This method of operation is likely to be common in small commercial computer applications, and perhaps in larger ones in which the volume of messages is low in proportion to the non-real-time work.

Such a technique requires a rudimentary Supervisory Routine, which will mainly handle the communication lines.

3. The Supervisory Program becomes more complicated when:

(a) The volume of messages is higher.

(b) A fast response time is required.

(c) A high reliability is required and the computer must take action in the event of a component failure or other error.

(d) The messages vary in type and can require many different functions to be performed, so that the Supervisory Program must select and read in the appropriate Application Programs.

(e) Complex input/output devices are used. Then, for example, elaborate communication line control is needed.

4. There is a considerable increase in complication when more than one transaction is to be processed *at the same time*. In other words the operations is *multi-thread* rather than *single-thread*.

There are two reasons for making an on-line system multi-thread. The first is that the time interval between events is less than the response time. Suppose that messages arrive at the system during the peak period at the rate of four messages per second. Although the Application Programs do not occupy the central processing unit for more than 100 milliseconds, eight or so random-access file references are required which take almost one second in total. In this case four or more "threads" must be processed in parallel. When input/output operations are slow compared with processing in this way, it is generally true that multi-programming improves the efficiency of the system. Some of the large systems that have been installed require ten or twenty threads to be processed in parallel, and this is likely to increase in future systems.

The second reason for multi-thread processing is that certain messages have a high degree of urgency, so that the processing of the other, lower priority, messages is interrupted for them. This is the case, for example, in the computer systems monitoring the manned space flights from Cape Kennedy. The Supervisory Programs used for Project Mercury allowed multi-thread programming with a central priority routine which gave preference to urgent messages.

It is generally true that multi-thread operation causes considerable difficulties in implementing a working system. Much of this book is concerned with the problems of multi-thread programming and the system testing difficulties it causes. An alternative to multi-thread operation is multi-processing, i.e., the use of more than one computer working in parallel. Some real-time systems use this approach, and there is much to be said for it. However, it can become impractical when large files have to be updated, as it is uneconomic to have several copies of these; also, logical difficulties arise when more than one processor is able to update the same file records. Furthermore, to run one large computer is usually cheaper than many small computers, and this makes a multi-thread approach economic.

5. In Reference Systems 5 and 6, duplexed computers are used to give added reliability. Where reliability becomes critical, the duties of the Supervisory Programs increase. They must perform checks to help detect faults, and if there are faults, they must assist in switching computers or operating in a limited fall-back mode.

In a large system there may be many interrupts from various input/output units and other machine components.

To summarize, a list is given below of the functions that are likely to be performed by the Supervisory Programs in a complex, multi-programmed system. Simpler systems will not require all these functions:

1. *Input/output control.* Scheduling the operations on input/output units and channels, checking for correct functioning, and so on.

2. *Communication line control.* Reading bits or characters from the line control equipment and assembling them into messages; polling and controlling the terminals; feeding messages bit-by-bit or character-by-character to the communication equipment; error checking, and so on.

3. *Message set-up services.* Giving an edited, checked-out message to the main programs and setting up a Message Reference Block in the required format.

4. *Handling displays,* for example, light panel displays, or cathode ray tube displays which need repetitive scanning.

5. *Communicating with the operator.* Notifying the operator, possibly on the machine console, of error or exceptional conditions, requirements for tape changing, and so on. Permitting the operator to give instructions to the system.

6. *Scheduling the message processing.* Deciding which message to work on next on a basis of priorities, response time requirements and other factors.

7. *Scheduling the machine functions.* Deciding which machine function is to be done when these conflict.

8. *Queue control.* Building up queues of items or of requests for input/ output operations; working off the queues in the best sequence.

9. *Core storage allocation.* Assigning core to various functions as required.

10. *Allocation of other equipment.* As well as assigning core, it may be necessary to assign other components of the system to various functions as required.

11. *Communication between separate computers.* Transmitting data to, or receiving data from, another computer in a multi-computer system.

12. *Control of an off-line computer,* where this has a standby function, as well as doing off-line processing; it will take over when a failure occurs in the on-line machine.

13. *Linkage between programs and subroutines,* when these may be fixed in core or relocatable.

14. *Handling interrupts.* Analyzing the cause of the interrupt; transferring control to the appropriate priority routine; storing registers, switches or data from the interrupted program to make sure that a logically correct return can be made.

15. *Selecting and calling in the required programs.* Deciding whether these are already in core or whether they must be read in; deciding which used programs can be overwritten when core is needed.

16. *Retaining working data, registers, and so on,* when control switches from one program to another without an interrupt.

17. *Controlling time-initiated actions.* Initiating a given action at a predetermined clock time, or after a given elapsed period.

18. *File security.* Ensuring, as far as possible, that file records are not overwritten incorrectly by testing programs or by errors in operational programs.

19. *Fault indication and reliability checks.* Taking appropriate action when errors of all the various types are detected.

20. *Diagnostics.* Operating on-line diagnostics to increase confidence in the system or to assist the equipment engineers.

21. *Switchover.* Organizing switchover to a standby computer when a failure occurs.

22. *Fall-back.* Organizing a degraded mode of operation when a component of the system fails, for example a file or a communication buffer; switching to the twin in a duplexed file system; organizing recovery from fallback, for example, returning a file to the system and updating records that would otherwise have been updated during its down period.

23. *Handling overloads.* Taking emergency action in a system which can be jammed by an overload.

24. *System testing aids.* Temporary routines to aid in real-time program debugging and the testing of the operational system.

25. *Performance monitoring.* Temporary routines to gather statistics on system performance.

These functions will be discussed in more detail in the remainder of the book.

15 SUPERVISORY PROGRAMS FOR A PROCESS-CONTROL APPLICATION

This chapter describes a typical set of Supervisory Programs for a system like Reference System No. 2. This might be used in applications such as paper mill or blast furnace control, optimization of the operation of a chemical plant, logging technical data in jet engine tests, and so on.

The Application Programs may be fairly complex. Some of them may be too large to be all in the core at one instant. However, the number of interrupts and disk references may be lower than in a commercial system such as Reference Systems 4, 5, or 6. The number of times the program in use will be changed will also be lower. A random-access backing file is used. A reference to this may be fairly slow so that it is desirable to carry out some processing while the "seek" is being made. However, unlike Reference Systems 4 and 5, only one file action can take place at one time. Interrupts will occur, caused by external events needing quick attention, as well as for internal hardware reasons, but there will be only one level of interrupt. In other words, when one interrupt is being serviced, this interrupt program may not itself be interrupted by a second event.

In this illustration there are two states when a program is not interruptable: first, when the program is already servicing an interrupt, and second, when an Application Program has inhibited interrupts because the programmer has determined that the current program is more important than the immediate recognition of interrupts. When the computer is in this non-interruptable mode it records all interrupt conditions by setting indicators which will be tested later. This makes the Supervisory Programs much simpler than in a system in which control can dart back and forth from one interrupt condition to another, such as will be discussed later.

The system has strictly *single-thread* processing. With the exception of

Operator instructions from the IBM 1710 control system are relayed to the remote typewriter at right located in the control center of Northwestern States' completely automated rotary cement kiln. Readings from 58 instruments situated along, around, and inside both the kiln and cooler are relayed to the computer, where they are analyzed and balanced. The computer generates kiln operator instructions necessary to maintain optimum production.

occasional interrupt programs one piece of work is completed before another begins.

A process-control system with these characteristics is likely to need a Supervisory Program that will carry out the following functions:

1. *It will schedule the work.* When one activity is completed it will determine what is to be done next and will transfer control to the appropriate program. The decision will be based on the current demands on the system, what processing is partially completed, what interrupts have not yet been serviced, what overlapped input/output actions are taking place, such as printing or "seeks," and so on.

2. *It will handle all interrupts.* When an interrupt occurs the Supervisory Program must identify its nature and, at a suitable time, transfer control to the appropriate priority routine to handle it. If a further interrupt occurs while the first is being processed, an indicator must be set for subsequent recognition and service. After servicing one or more interrupts the Supervisory Program must return control to the Application Program at the point at which it was interrupted.

3. *It will handle all file actions.* When instructed to read from, or write on, the files, it will carry out all the actions necessary to do this, such as "seeking," possibly scanning a track, and error checking. It will probably allow further Application Program work to continue while a "seek" goes on.

4. *It will handle the loading of Application Programs and subroutines.* When a new Application Program is needed it will be requested by a program in core at that time. The Supervisory Program will check whether it is in core; if it is not, it will read it in and transfer control to it. It will sometimes be necessary to dump a program presently in core and replace it by another. Working data or indicators from the first program must be preserved by dumping them on the file. This will be done by the Supervisory Programs.

5. *It will handle the input reading and check it for errors.* In a process-control application the input is likely to be from analogue-digital converters and the reading of contact settings. These may be scanned periodically or read at random. Error checks on the readings from the analogue-digital converters are likely to check that the value is within specified limits, and/or that the change since the last reading is not too great.

6. *It will handle the output.* This may involve adjusting controller set points to the nearest trim automatically. It may require contacts opening or closing, perhaps with a check that they have in fact operated. The computer may send serial output such as typewriter messages or digital

displays. It may compose cathode ray tube displays or operate a chart plotting machine.

7. *It will handle error conditions.* When an error is detected it analyzes it to determine its cause and records its occurrence. Depending upon the operating conditions, it will decide which of the following corrective procedures to follow:

(a) Restart, using a program specified by the writer of the Application Program in current use.

(b) Branch to an exception program specified by the writer of the Application Program in current use.

(c) Record the error but not halt.

(d) Halt and notify the operator.

The Supervisory Programs are likely to have different sections for carrying out these seven functions. The sections may be quite separate programs, separately compiled and replaceable.

PROGRAMS NOT IN CORE Not all of the Supervisory Programs need be in core all of the time. It would be a waste of valuable core space to keep them there. The majority will be on the backing file and will be read into core only when required. It will, however, be necessary to have a nucleus of Supervisory Programs permanently in core. These may represent as much as a quarter of the whole.

Among those parts permanently in core will be the routines for deciding what work to do next, for handling file actions and the routine for calling in programs from the file. Using these two, any other Supervisory Programs may quickly be read into core when they are required. The routine for identifying interrupts will also be there. This will handle all entries and exits from interrupt routines. The interrupt routines may or may not themselves be in the core. Similarly, the routine for analyzing error conditions will be permanently in core, though the exception routines for dealing with errors will be required only very infrequently and thus can be kept in the files. The exception routines for dealing with certain file errors may be kept in core because, if there is a file fault, it may not be possible to read them in.

Whether or not the other Supervisory Programs are kept in core will probably depend upon their frequency of use. For example, if an input scanning routine is constantly in use it will be kept permanently in core. If, however, the system takes readings for a time, and, afterwards, processes these and prepares the output before it takes further readings, then the input program can be kept on the files and brought in when required.

The Supervisory Programs must maintain in core a storage area for various programming switches and other pertinent data that they refer to. The status of all the various activities must be recorded. In particular, there are various tables which tell the Supervisory Programs the status and the addresses of programs in core and on disk.

CORE
LOADS
Those Supervisory Programs and their tables, which must be permanently in core, are referred to below as the *Resident Executive*.

The system may be thought of as operating with one "core load" at a time. An Application Program with the subroutines it requires for carrying out one particular function would constitute one core load, along with the Resident Executive. The programs to carry out one function may occupy only a fraction of the available core, in which case there will be other programs there at the same time, such as programs for handling interrupts. They may, however, require a larger space than the available core. In this case, part of the programs for the one function must be on the file. Macro-instructions, to call them in as required, will be written into the Application Program in question, and executed by the Resident Executive.

INTERRUPTS
One Application Program constituting a core load may run for a period of time until its work is done. During this time, however, there may be interrupts. The work of the Application Program will stop temporarily while the interrupt is dealt with, and then continue. Dealing with the interrupt may require a new program to be brought in, and the half-completed Application Program, with its working storage to be dumped on the file until the interrupt program has been executed.

A simple process-control application may be able to cycle sequentially through its Application Programs. Each "core load" would then contain the address of the core load that must follow. The cycle of events may be, for example: to scan various readings in the plant under control, construct a plant log, perform calculations to evaluate how the operation should be optimized under these conditions, send back control information to set valves or inform an operator, and then repeat this cycle. The cycle goes on continuously except during start-up or shut-down or some change in operating. The Application Programs will, however, be interrupted occasionally, due both to internal and external conditions.

Figure 46 illustrates a relatively simple use of such a system. Many

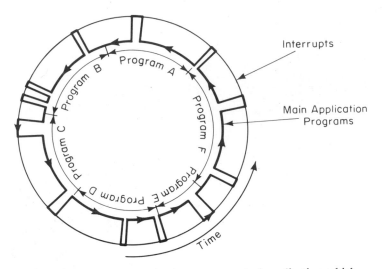

Fig. 46. Timing of a simple process-control application which cycles sequentially through six "main-line" application programs, but occasionally has to service internal or external interrupts. Many systems will not be able to operate in this simple cyclic manner as the programs are needed in an unpredictable sequence.

systems will change the sequence in which Application Programs are called into core and used, depending upon events in the process under control.

The external interrupts come from the plant or the environment that are being controlled. They may be caused by the closing of an electrical contact, a rise in temperature above a set limit, and so on. They may come from a plant operator who is sending information or instructions to the computer, or making an enquiry. The internal interrupts come from the computer itself and may be caused by an error condition being detected, an input/output operation being completed, a clock interrupt, a computer operator setting a switch, and so on.

INTERRUPT CONTROL ROUTINE   The interrupt subroutines to handle these conditions are in some cases part of the Supervisory Programs, but in general they are part of the Application Programs. In either case entry to and exit from them must be via a Supervisory routine which is permanently in core for this purpose. This is referred to below as the *Interrupt Control Routine*.

It must first identify each interrupt and determine which subroutine is needed for its processing. It must determine whether a desired interrupt subroutine is in core storage, and, if not, call it into core when needed, dumping the current "core load" if necessary. When the interrupt routine is completed and no more interrupts remain to be serviced, it must return control to the main line Application Program at the point where it broke off.

An interrupt may occur at a time when it is inconvenient to process it. In this case the Interrupt Control Routine will record the interrupt for servicing at a later time. When this happens or when several interrupts occur close together, the Interrupt Control Routine may have to select between a number of interrupts contending for service. It will do this on a priority basis, the priority rules being determined by the nature of the application. Error interrupts will always be checked for before other types to ensure that the computer and its units are functioning correctly.

STATUS MAPS It is necessary for the Supervisory Programs to maintain a running record of the status of the various programs which are being interchanged between the core storage and the file and to be able to locate them when required. The scheduling of the required programs and the "housekeeping" this requires is performed with the aid of tables or maps. A Supervisory routine will refer to these maps to determine how particular situations must be handled.

A typical map of this type is shown in Fig. 47. This example is taken from the "Executive II" package provided for the IBM 1710 Control System. The main body of this map is kept on the file; when a "core load" is brought into core storage the appropriate strip of the map is loaded with it. When this is completed, another core load with its strip of the map is brought in. The strip tells the Supervisory Program the next sequential core load and what exception or restart procedures must be used if an error occurs. It gives the file address of the area where the program is stored on the files and the number of sectors it occupies. It gives its address when it is in core, which is also its starting address. This information enables the Supervisory Program to dump it on the file if necessary and to read it from the file into core storage.

Certain of the required Application Programs will have more subroutines than can be held in core storage at one time. Some provision must be made for instructing the Supervisory Program which of the subroutines should be loaded into core at the beginning of the core load, and which should be brought in from the file when needed. A *Subroutine Status Table* does this and maintains a log of subroutines in core storage. It is used in conjunction with a map giving the addresses of subroutines, to enable the Supervisory Program to locate and transfer control to appropriate subroutines.

Another function of the map in Fig. 47 is to indicate the sequence

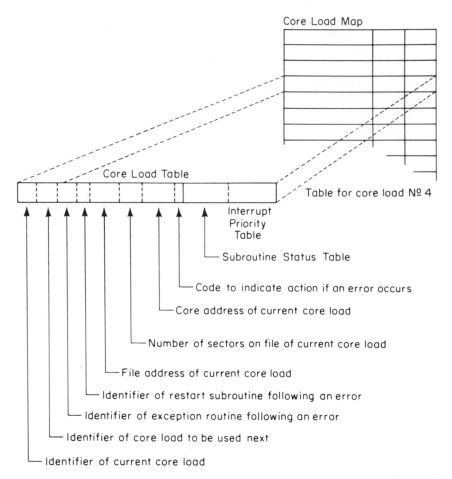

Fig. 47. Map giving supervisory program details of address and status of programs it schedules (taken from IBM 1710 Executive II).

in which the various interrupt conditions shall be dealt with. The *Interrupt Priority Table* lists the sequence in which interrupt indicators should be tested.

RANDOM-ACCESS FILE ROUTINES One section of the Supervisory Programs handles all actions involving the random-access files. It will read or write, with appropriate error checks, scan the files or position the "seek" arm. The Application Program requesting a file read or write may hang up until that action is completed, or it may continue processing while a relatively lengthy "seek" or disk rotation is taking place.

As with other requests to the Supervisory Programs, the Application Programmer will write a macro-instruction or equivalent into his coding to provide the appropriate linkage. The file read and write routines provide an alternative method of obtaining a subroutine from the file. Rather than using the Supervisory Program which normally does this, an Application Program may be permitted to read its own subroutines directly on those occasions when this is more efficient.

INPUT AND   Much of the remainder of the Supervisory Programs
OUTPUT   in this type of system are concerned with input to, and output from, the system.

The input is likely to be a serial scanning of instruments or contacts, or a random reading of one or several input devices. It may be necessary to read a message from a device like a typewriter or from manually set dials. An operator or a device may trigger an interrupt which causes an interrupt routine to make the reading, but here the input routine required is the same. Different versions of input routines may be included, depending upon what error checks are required. The input routine may check that readings, for example from an analogue-digital converter, do not lie outside certain set limits, or that the change since the last time a reading was made is not too great. The input routine may then be provided with a table in which an entry for each point will say what checks must be made and what the limits of permissible variations are.

The output routines may be required to send a digital or alphabetical message to a plant operator, to close or open relays, or to select and adjust the various set-point positioners within the user's process. They may be required to present displays on panels or cathode ray screens or to operate graphical plotters. A variety of output routines are possible for these different functions.

A common requirement is to adjust valves or set-point positioners in a plant. The routine that does this may allow the user to specify different rates of adjustment so that set-point movements can be synchronized. To ensure accuracy the computer may read a feedback signal from the point. It will take a period of time—long in terms of computer instructions —to make the adjustment, and this may be geared to a cycle of fixed duration. The computer must be interrupted at the appropriate points on this cycle to take the required action. The cycle may be divided into a set-up time and an action time. In the former, a table is constructed giving details of the required output. An entry for each set-point will give the output address, the setting or the change required, the rate of change required—for example, whether a movement is required in every cycle or in every n^{th} cycle, whether feedback is available, and so on. In the action time of the cycle the instructions in the table will be followed.

ERRORS   A last function of the Supervisory Programs is to take over control if an error is detected. The machine will normally be built so that error conditions trigger an interrupt. The Supervisory Programs may themselves test the correct functioning of components by operating diagnostics periodically. When an error is detected the Supervisory routine will log it, print out a console message, analyze the error with respect to operating conditions and decide what action to take. The types of action possible on error conditions are discussed in Chapter 22.

In a computer with two-address instructions and a fairly comprehensive set of operation codes, a set of Supervisory Programs such as these might require between one and two thousand instructions.

16

SUPERVISORY PROGRAMS FOR A COMPLEX COMMERCIAL APPLICATION

This chapter describes a typical set of Supervisory Programs for a system such as Reference System No. 6. This might be used in applications such as airline seat reservations, railroad truck control, a large enquiry system and so on.

Unlike the system discussed in the last chapter, the individual Application Programs may be fairly simple; they could be, for example, routines for updating files, scanning records for information, and doing commercial data-processing. There may however be a large number of different Application Programs or exception routines to be used in different circumstances. The total number of lines of Application Program coding is likely to be higher than in a process-control system. The system will be continuously selecting segments of programs from the files and reading them into the core ready for use.

There will be a large amount of varied commercial data in the files. Many accesses to this will be made per second. As a high proportion of the file accesses take from 100 to 600 milliseconds, several of them will be taking place at the same time. Since accesses connected with different transactions and different programs will be occurring simultaneously, processing will be multi-thread, with control darting to and fro between one Application Program and another. At any time there will be many partially completed pieces of work in core. The Supervisory Programs control all this.

The Supervisory Programs are further complicated by the fact that all, or almost all, of the input is random. In a large system there may be many hundreds of people using operator sets and keying transactions into devices

163

such as typewriter-like keyboards which are connected to the computer. Transactions arrive at times when the computer is engaged in another activity, and frequently they require programs for their processing which are not currently in core. A system such as this might have to accept messages arriving at the maximum rate of from 3 per second to perhaps as many as 20 per second.

In addition, the system may also be required to handle some non-real-time transactions, such as magnetic tape processing. It can only do this when there is a lull in the real-time traffic which leaves sufficient time and core storage for non-real-time work.

There will be many more interrupts than in the system described in the last chapter. They occur for the same reasons: external events needing quick attention, end of input/output actions, end of "seeks" or file references, and error conditions. A system of this type may need speedy attention to interrupts, and therefore multiple levels of interrupt may be allowed. A subroutine which is handling an interrupt condition may itself be capable of being interrupted in some systems. There will always be certain points in the program, however, at which interrupts must not be allowed because they might cause a logic error. During the execution of these few critical instructions interrupts will be inhibited.

The control of communication lines from distant operator sets is much more complex than the cyclical scanning of instruments in a process-control application. There the function is programmed in a line control computer separate from the main computer. Communication control programs are discussed in Chapter 11. They will assemble complete messages and then cause the main machine to be interrupted. A Supervisory Program in the main machine will read the message into the core and initiate its processing. Similarly, messages being sent by the system will be passed to the line control computer whose programs transmit the message character-by-character, bit-by-bit. The line control programs will check for errors in transmission and, if these are detected, will arrange for retransmission. If errors or other circumstances occur which are beyond its control, it will inform the main computer and this will take appropriate action.

A high degree of reliability is likely to be required from a system such as this. It has two main computers, so that if one fails the other can take over. If one line control computer fails, the other can be switched into action. Data on the files are written in duplicate, so that if one file develops a fault the duplicate copy can be used. When a part of the system goes wrong and the rest of the hardware limps on without it, the system may not be able to carry out all its functions. It may continue in a "fallback" mode and execute only the vital part of its work. Switchover and fall-back present many problems for the Supervisory Programs which have to initiate the change of mode and assign the appropriate units. These are discussed in Chapters 24 and 25.

The functions of the Supervisory Programs are likely to include all those listed at the end of Chapter 14.

Because the Application Programs are executed in relatively short segments, with control darting from one to another, and because new messages are arriving continually and file references are being executed all the time, a larger proportion of the Supervisory Programs will be permanently in core than with the system described in the last chapter. Only exception routines will be kept on the files, such as those for handling switchover, fall-back, errors and other infrequent events. These will be called in when required in the same manner as the Application Programs.

CORE ALLOCATION   As described in Chapter 7, there will be certain fixed areas in core, but the majority of core will be split up in blocks or areas and will be dynamically allocated. The use to which a block is put will vary second-by-second. The fixed areas in core will be used for that part of the Supervisory Programs which are permanently in core—the *Resident Executive*—for those Application Programs which are used sufficiently frequently, and for permanent data or tables. The rest of core will be allocated, a block at a time, to any function that may need it, by the Supervisory Programs. It may be used for either programs or data. Figure 23 in Chapter 7 illustrates this use of the core.

The blocks of core may be all of the same size, or there may be two or three or so different sizes. As mentioned in previous chapters, all the blocks not actually in use are chained together to form "Uncommitted Storage Lists." There may be one of these, or one for each size of block. When an Application Program requests some core by use of a macro-instruction, this links to a Supervisory Program subroutine which allocates a block from the end of the chain of available blocks. When the Application Program finishes with this or vacates the core by means of an EXIT macro-instruction, the block will be re-chained to the appropriate "Uncommitted Storage List" so that it may later be used for another function. The Supervisory routine will keep a count of the number of available blocks, just as a storekeeper records the number of items he has in stock. When the number falls below a certain limit, this will indicate that the system is in danger of running out of core, and emergency action will be taken by the Supervisory Programs. There may be several levels of emergency action depending upon the degree of the shortage. The possible action is discussed in Chapter 23.

MESSAGE
REFERENCE
BLOCKS
Each message entering the system is given a block, a storage referred to in this book as a *Message Reference Block* as described in Chapter 7. This will remain unique to that message until the message leaves the system, like a pocket in a broker's filing cabinet, and will contain the message itself and data and indicators that must be kept for the processing of that message. When a message is accepted into the system and has been checked for validity, the first job of the Supervisory Programs will be to set up a Message Reference Block for it in the required format.

QUEUES
The Message Reference Blocks waiting for processing to begin will form a queue, the blocks being chained together as described in Chapter 8. Similarly Message Reference Blocks containing partially completed work, and again requiring the attention of the Central Processing Unit, will form another queue. There will also be queues of items waiting to use the file channels and the output channels. These are illustrated pictorially in Fig. 22 in Chapter 8.

Much of the work of the Supervisory Programs will consist of manipulating these queues. Items will be added to and taken from the queues by a Supervisory routine when required. The queues of Message Reference Blocks may straggle across any area in core as determined by which available blocks are allocated from the Uncommitted Storage List. On some systems of this type the queues of requests for file actions may be listed in a fixed areas of core.

MAIN
SCHEDULING
ROUTINE
In a multi-programmed application such as this, control will continually switch from one segment of Application Program to another. When one segment completes its work it will transfer control to the Main Scheduling Routine which forms the nucleus of the system. This will examine all the incompleted work and decide what is to be done next. It will transfer control to the next segment of program to be used. This is illustrated in Fig. 43 in Chapter 13.

In order to decide which segment of program is to be used next, some form of scheduling algorithm or set of rules must be used. This will be a function of parameters such as the priorities of various tasks, the response times that are required, the available equipment, and so on. The size of the Main Scheduling Routine will depend upon the complexity of the set of rules used. It will differ very considerably from one system to another because their requirements differ.

In a system such as the one in this illustration, in which there is a high degree of multi-programming with short individual Application Programs, it is desirable that the Main Scheduling Routine be as simple as possible because it is entered many times per second. In some otherwise very complex systems this central scanning routine has been so simple that it consists of only a few instructions. Figure 48 is an illustration of this. Here no

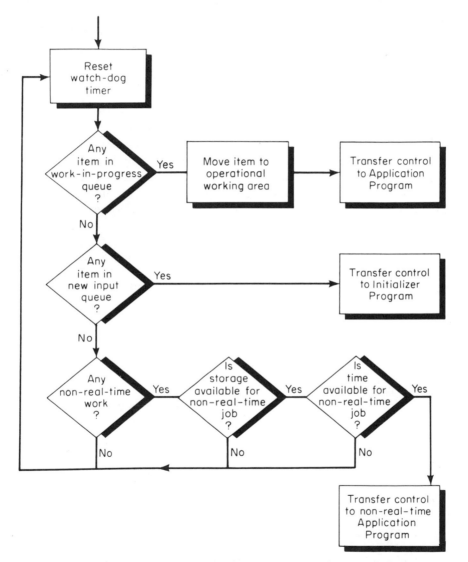

Fig. 48. A simple example of the Central Scanning Loop of a Supervisory Program (see also Chap. 18).

differentiation is made between the priorities of different real-time trans-actions. The Main Scheduling Routine merely services the queues sequen-tially. Input/Output scheduling is done by a different routine when input/output interrupts occur.

In describing the flow of work through the system, it would be possible to think of all queues as belonging to one of two categories. The first in-cludes those entries waiting for an input/output or file request to be serv-iced. The second includes those entries ready for further processing (Fig. 24). In this illustration the former are checked in Input/Output Schedul-ing Routines and the latter are checked by the Central Scanning Loop of Fig. 48.

This routine scans the Work-in-Progress Queue and the New Input Queue. It takes items from these queues and transfers control to the Appli-cation Program needed to process them. If there is no real-time item ready for further processing it will see whether there is non-real-time work such as tape processing to carry on with. This will only be done if there is a shortage of real-time work. Tests will be made as to the core storage and time that are currently available and unless these exceed given amounts no non-real-time work will be attempted. The available core may be checked by inspecting the count of blocks in the "Uncommitted Storage List." The available time may be checked by inspecting a count of the number of transactions currently in the system.

If there are no items ready for processing and no non-real-time work, the computer cycles in a closed loop waiting for an interrupt to occur. As soon as an input/output or file operation is completed, or a new mes-sage enters the system, the item will be placed in one of the queues being scanned by the Main Scheduling Routine, and this will transfer control to the next routine required to process the item. As soon as this program is finished or is held up waiting for an input/output or file action, it will re-turn control by means of a WAIT or EXIT macro-instruction to the Main Scheduling Routine. By this time, other interrupts may have resulted in further items being placed in the queues.

WATCHDOG
TIMER
The Main Scheduling Routine is the one routine in the system which is entered regularly several times a second. In a system of this type none of the Applica-tion Programs occupy the central processing unit for more than a fraction of a second at a time. When they relinquish it they return control to the Main Scheduling Routine. Thus, if this is not entered every few hundred milliseconds, it indicates that something has gone wrong. Perhaps there has been a circuitry failure in the computer, or perhaps a logic fault in one of the Application Programs has stuck it in an endless closed loop. To

prevent such a failure which can hold up the entire system a hardware device may be used which causes a computer interrupt after a given period of time. This is sometimes known as a "Watchdog Timer." It is set by a program instruction for a given interval, say 500 milliseconds in this case. During the 500 milliseconds it will be reset again if all is going well. If it reaches the end of its time period without being reset this is an indication that something has gone wrong. It will then cause an interrupt to an error routine and perhaps sound a buzzer on the console. The watchdog timer will be reset every time the Main Scheduling Routine is entered.

INPUT/OUTPUT SCHEDULING   The Main Scheduling Routine schedules the use of the central processing unit. In a not entirely dissimilar manner another part of the Supervisory Programs schedules the work of the peripheral units, the files, tapes, printers, the data going to and from the line, the control computer and the input/output channels to which these are attached. These equipment-scheduling routines are permanently in core. When one operation on them is completed the scheduling routine decides what will be done next. In a system which, if loaded to capacity, would be input/output-bound, it is desirable to keep the input/output units continuously busy.

The input/output and file operations go on simultaneously with the processing and independently of it. When an input/output or file operation is completed the processing will be interrupted so that the next job can be started on the free unit as quickly as possible. When it has started the processing will resume where it left off and continue concurrently with the input/output or file action.

INTERRUPTS   It is the computer interrupt system which makes possible a full use of the input/output facilities. Both Application and Supervisory Programs can be interrupted to service an input/output unit. There are certain instructions which cannot be interrupted. When these are being executed, the interrupt feature will be inhibited and the interrupt stored until it is free to occur. Interrupts will occur when:

1. Any input/output operation is completed and that unit is free to start another operation.
2. A "seek" is completed on a random-access file.
3. An error or "unusual end" condition has occurred and requires to be serviced.

4. An interval timer reaches the end of its interval.

5. A new message is due to enter the system, e.g., when the line control computer demands attention.

When an interrupt occurs the computer leaves the program it is currently executing and goes into a priority routine which takes the required action, e.g., starts the next input/output operation. As soon as this routine is completed, control is returned to the program that was interrupted.

INPUT, OUTPUT AND FILE OPERATIONS   Assigning the input/output unit or file its next task is thus performed by a priority routine. The Input/Output and File Scheduling Routines though not the Main Scheduling Routine are priority programs.

Under normal circumstances there are three types of activity in a system: non-priority programs, priority routines for handling input/output and file actions, and the input/output and file actions which go on at the same time. This flow of data is illustrated in Fig. 49.

When an Application Program arrives at an input/output or file request, which has been generated from the programmer's macro-instruction, this operation will probably not be executed immediately because the channel or unit in question is busy. There may be other items ahead in the queue for the same channel or unit. The Application Program must therefore store a request for the operation in a place which the Input/Output Scheduler will inspect later at a suitable time. Only in this way can the input/output units be kept continuously busy.

A list, or queue, of requests for operations on each unit and channel will be formed. A scheduling routine for the unit and a scheduling routine for the channel will inspect these when a new operation is to be started on a unit and channel.

The Application Program making the request must furnish the following information:

1. A code giving the nature of the request, e.g., write file in duplicate, read tape, and so on.

2. The address of the input/output unit and channel. This may be in symbolic form if it is desirable for the Supervisory System to use some form of table look-up to determine the actual address. With tape, for example, the actual address will never be given if alternate reels are used.

3. The address, or an identification of the record in the unit. This also may possibly be an identification rather than the actual address, with the conversion being done by an addressing routine.

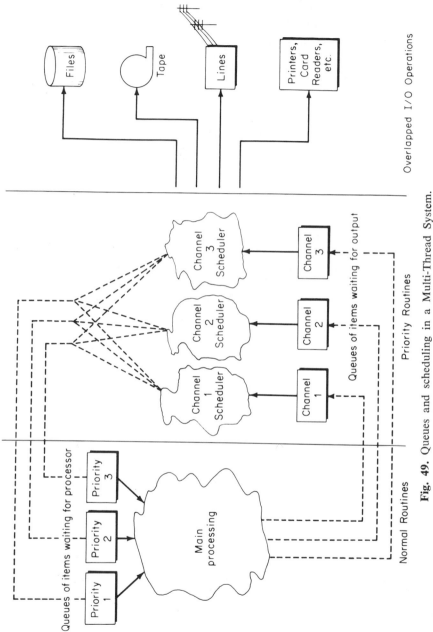

Fig. 49. Queues and scheduling in a Multi-Thread System.

4. An address to tell the input/output routine where in core the item is to be read to or read from.

This information will be stored in a control word, and a table of such control words will govern the input/output and file routines.

When all the requests associated with one Message Reference Block are satisfied, the item will either be ready for further processing or else it will be deleted from core, depending upon whether the last program segment used on it terminated with a "WAIT" or an "EXIT." If it was a "WAIT" the block will be chained to the Work-in-Progress queue.

Input/output and file requests are not necessarily executed in the sequence in which they were requested. Movements of the access mechanisms, for example, take varying periods of time, and thus the requests are completed at indeterminate times. The input/output routine must be ready to service the file requests with no regard to the order in which they were made. It must be able to determine which request control word relates to each completed action.

It is possible to shorten the access times on some applications by not executing file requests on a first-come-first-served basis. By scanning the existing requests, the sequence of file operations can be selected so that access time is minimized. This could increase the maximum throughput of the system at the expense of lengthening the response time.

THE FLOW OF WORK THROUGH THE SYSTEM

The flow of data in the system will be described with reference to Fig. 50, when a typical message is processed.

Consider a message which requires the following action:

1. It must be logged on tape.
2. A record must be sought from the random-access files. It is not, however, directly addressable, and to locate it a table look-up must determine the area of the files that must be "sought."
3. The required area is "sought" and a track index is read from it.
4. Another table look-up gives the contents of the track index, and this gives the required record address.
5. The required record is read into core.
6. A calculation is done on the contents of the record.
7. The record is updated and written back on the file.
8. A message is sent in reply.

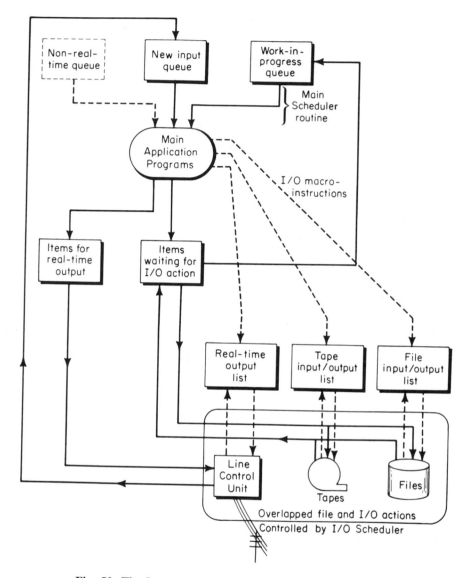

Fig. 50. The flow of data in a Multi-Thread Real-Time System.

The Supervisory Programs handle this message as follows:

1. An interrupt occurs, and a priority routine detects that a message requires to be read in. It acquires a block of core from the Uncommitted Storage List and initiates the read of the message into it. Control then returns to the interrupted program.

When new messages arrive on the communication lines and are read from the line control unit into a core block, the first program to examine the message and begin its processing will be an *Initializer Routine*. This is kept permanently in core. It may be regarded as an Application Program or as part of the Supervisory Programs. The functions of this routine may be as follows:

(a) It sets up a Message Reference Block in its specified format.

(b) It may perform a validity check or error check on the message. If the message is not correct it will transfer control to an exception routine for dealing with this.

(c) It selects the first required segment of Application Program to process the message. This is selected on a basis of the action code in the message.

(d) It transfers control to this program.

This Application Program will probably need to transfer control to other segments of program, which may or may not be in core storage at the time. The linkage to these will be done by a routine generated by a macro-instruction. This routine forms a part of the Supervisory System. If it needs to call the routine in question from the files it will generate a WAIT condition for this message.

2. The message will be read from the line control computer into the core of the main computer, and this operation will overlap with any processing that is taking place. When the read operation is completed an interrupt again occurs. The priority routine which is selected to service this interrupt chains the block of storage containing the new message into the New Input Queue. Control again returns to the program that was interrupted.

3. At some later time the Main Scheduler Routine works its way down to this message in the New Input Queue. It transfers control to the Initializer Routine which might be regarded as the first Application Program to work on the message.

4. The Initializer converts the message's storage block into the format of a Message Reference Block. It may check the message for validity and initiate corrective action if there is an error in it. It analyzes the message to decide what Application Program is needed to process it. It transfers control to this program by means of a linkage routine which is part of the Supervisory Programs. It may be necessary to read in the required Application Program from a backing file, in which case a file operation occurs as described below.

5. The first Application Program contains a macro-instruction to

write the message on the logging tape. A Request Word for this is set up and stored in the Message Reference Block. The request is placed in the Tape Output Queue. Messages logged on tape will probably be written in blocks of more than one message. The macro-instruction will automatically arrange for this to happen. If a complete block now exists, the macro-instruction will attempt to write the block to tape. If not, this will occur when some later message arrives and the partially completed block remains in a buffer area in core. If the tape unit or channel is busy the output operation cannot occur now, but a program will be interrupted sometime in the future, and it will occur then as a priority routine.

6. The Application Program executes a table look-up to find the area of the files that must be "sought." This table is stored permanently in core storage because it will be used by many messages.

7. The Application Program contains the macro-instruction to "seek" and read the track index. A Request Word for this is set up and stored in the Message Reference Block. If the access arm or channel is busy, or if there are earlier requests for that arm, the request is placed in the queue of requests for that channel and arm and will be dealt with later. If duplexed files are used, only one need be read. The seek and read will probably occur on a later priority routine on the first file that becomes available.

8. The Application Program can now do nothing until many milliseconds later when the file read is completed. It therefore contains a WAIT macro-instruction. This causes control to be returned to the Main Scheduler Routine, and this will in turn give control to another Application Program.

9. At some later time some different program will be interrupted because the above seek has been completed. The priority routine that occurs will select a block from the Uncommitted Storage List and commence a read into it.

10. Still later another routine will be interrupted because the read is completed. The priority routine will chain the new block into the Work-in-Progress Queue and initiate the next operation on access mechanisms.

11. The Main Scheduler Routine at some future time will detect this item in the Work-in-Progress Queue. It will select the required Application Program which will still be in core and transfer control to it.

12. The Application Program will execute a table look-up on the table contained in the track index that has been read in. This will tell it the address of the required track. It will then give a macro-instruction to

read that track, followed by a WAIT. The reading sequence described above will occur again. The access arm may or may not have been reserved during this period. In other words, a re-seek may or may not be required. In the large systems the access arm is often released because otherwise it could be tied up while a queue of other items are worked through. In small systems this may not be so.

13. When the Application Program is at last at work on the required record, it will update the record and then gives a Write File macro-instruction. This will instruct the File Scheduler Routine to write the updated record on both files, to check the written records and to release the core block in question. Again, it will be handled with a priority routine when the time is suitable.

14. A macro-instruction is then given to send out the replying message. A Request Word for this is set up and stored in the Message Reference Block. If the request cannot immediately be executed the request will be placed in the Real-Time Output Queue.

15. Finally, an EXIT macro is given. This will be executed as soon as the final message has been sent. It will erase the Message Reference Block from core. Control is transferred to the Main Scheduler Routine again for work on other messages.

This completes the life of this message in the system.

17 DIFFERENCES IN REQUIREMENTS FOR SUPERVISORY PROGRAMS

One of the most difficult problems that must be faced, when planning a real-time system for a new application, is estimating program requirements. If these are planned inadequately the result may be an unrealistic feasibility study and a system unable to meet its design requirements.

In a system with a high input rate or a complex priority structure, the computer requirements depend to a large extent on the system of Supervisory Programs, and the way these route data through the machine. Without a knowledge of this, and the scheduling mechanisms, and the way Application Programs are brought into core, no reliable estimates can be made as to the core requirements or the speed of the processing unit that is required. No real-time machine proposal for a complex system should be made or accepted without an understanding of the way the Supervisory Programs work, and how this affects the Application Programs, the core allocation, the queue sizes, and so on.

Unfortunately, this is not too easy as the mechanisms of the Supervisory Programs are likely to differ from one application to another.

It would be very useful to be able to employ standardized software for the Supervisory Programs. This is possible to some extent, especially on "single-thread" systems, but the more complex the system becomes, the more difficult or undesirable it is to use standardized "packages." As will be illustrated below, there are many differences between complex real-time systems. These systems have many specialities of their own or are unique in some way, so that it is difficult to use an off-the-shelf set of Supervisory Programs.

It is, however, of great advantage to use an existing and proved set of these. A system which uses debugged and error-free Supervisory

Programs is likely to have far fewer installation problems. The Application Programs will be made to work with the actual Supervisory Programs at an early stage. There will be no doubt whether program errors here are caused by the Application Programs or the Supervisory Programs. The types of program errors that are likely to occur will be understood early. If no Supervisory Programs were complete at that stage, as is often the case, they would have to be simulated in some way.

The design of the system around an existing set of Supervisory Programs would also be easier. There would be fewer uncertainties about the time and core requirements of the processing unit.

Another powerful reason for using standardized Supervisory Programs is the cost involved in writing them especially for one application. Applications in the top half of the spectrum in Fig. 12, Chapter 3, are likely to take twelve or more man-years for writing and testing specially designed Supervisory Programs. At least some of the programmers must be highly skilled. If the Support Programs needed to accompany these Supervisory Programs are included, the bill is likely to be more than $200,000.

Although it will often be impractical to use a complete set of Supervisory Programs in a standardized form, there are many partial solutions to this problem. Some of the Supervisory routines can and have been standardized successfully, especially for low throughput or non-multiprogrammed systems. Routines for specific applications on specific machines have been standardized, for example, a message-switching system.

This chapter indicates the different requirements for Supervisory Programs for different applications and then discusses methods of generalizing these programs. The next section of the book discusses in detail specific mechanisms of the Supervisory routines that differ according to the application requirements.

The different requirements for Supervisory Programs may be due to differences in the hardware, and perhaps to differences inherent in the application itself:

1. *Hardware Differences*

(a) *Different processing units.* The coding of a program will, of course, be quite different for different types of computer. However, because of differences in the logic of the computer the structure of the program also is likely to be different. For example, one machine may have a processing unit with alphanumeric characters, no index registers, but a high speed move instruction, whereas another is a binary machine with index registers and a program relocatability register. These two will need quite different techniques for positioning and executing the Application Program segments.

(b) *Specially engineered hardware.* Many real-time applications, especially the large and complex ones, have used computers with devices engineered specifically for that application. Special programming will be required for these devices.

(c) *Different input/output configurations.* Applications are likely to differ widely in the number and type of input/output units they use. They will have different types of files, different configurations of lines and operator sets, and different peripheral units such as tapes and printers. The routines handling input/output and files need to be written so that they can be recompiled to handle different configurations. In some real-time systems it will be difficult to do this without too great a sacrifice of efficiency.

(d) *Different core size.* Wide differences in core size and in sizes of core blocks will create different Supervisory requirements.

(e) *Different line control equipment.* Different systems will have different methods of attaching the communication lines. In some, a self-contained, separately programmed, special purpose line control computer will be used to deliver complete checked-out messages to the main computer. In others the communication lines will go directly into the main computer. Some will make use of analogue-digital converters for input from instruments or output to valves and so on. Others will have strictly digital input.

2. *Application Differences*

(a) *Throughput.* The number of messages per second handled by the system will vary drastically. If the number is large a higher degree of multi-programming will be required, and some Supervisory Systems restrict the number of messages that can be handled in parallel. If it is smaller it may be possible to simplify the system, which will make the testing phase easier.

(b) *Required response time.* A very wide range of requirements exists. If a longer response time is tolerable it is possible to use techniques in which processing need not be done entirely at random, and thus efficiency is improved.

(c) *Number of Application Programs.* In some systems all the Application Programs can be in core at any one time. In others some need to be kept on a backing file. Some systems have so many programs that only a very small proportion can be in core at one time. If many Application Programs are read in per second the read-in mechanism may be different from that of an application in which programs are read into core only on an exception basis.

(d) *Size and complexity of Application Programs.* In some systems the functions of the Application Programs are relatively simple, and short segments of Application Programs can be used. In other systems, the Application Programs may be very long and complex with much branching and looping. They may occupy the core for a long time and may be interrupted many times.

(e) *Message mix.* The majority of messages may be of the same type or of a small number of different types. On the other hand, some applications will have a much broader spread of message type. This may affect the mechanisms with which programs are scheduled and read in. It will affect the number of Application Programs that it is desirable to have permanently in core.

(f) *Priority considerations.* The priority structure is likely to differ widely from one application to another. In one system all messages have the same priority. In others there may be a wide range of different priorities between messages, with consequent complications in the mechanisms for scheduling.

(g) *Fallback procedures.* The techniques for fallback when certain input/output or other units cease to function are likely to differ considerably from one type of application to another. Some applications will log all messages on tape and use this for fallback. Others will duplicate information on files. Still others will duplicate only part of the information on files. Some may have one simple fallback procedure but in others a hierarchy of different procedures may be necessary. Some will use switching from a faulty computer to a standby, and this may be automatic or manual.

(h) *Multi-processing.* It may be an attractive prospect to have two computers sharing the load at peak hours, and only one of these handling it at non-peak hours. This technique may cut down the cost of the system. If one computer fails during the peak hour the system will fall back to a limited form of operation. This technique would require two sets of Supervisory Programs, one for use when both computers are working and the other for a single computer. It is possible to have hierarchies of different computers sharing the work.

There are many other differences in requirements besides those in this list. It will be seen from this that the job of providing standardized or generalized Supervisory Programs is very much more difficult than, for example, providing input/output control routines for conventional applications. And it is likely to remain a challenge to computer manufacturers' programming teams for some years to come.

Perhaps in the future a language may be developed by means of which Supervisory Programs can be specified, compiled, and perhaps simulated, for each individual application.

Meanwhile, the software provides parts of what is required. For a simple, single-thread application, with a standard method of handling communication lines, it may provide most of it. The standard file input/output and line control routines are linked together with a fairly short scanning loop and a program for selecting and reading in the required Application Programs.

Similarly, standard software is used for process control systems where instruments are scanned, calculations are done, and, finally, output is sent. Again, it may take a relatively small amount of programming to add simple queuing and scheduling routines to these.

But complex multi-programmed systems such as Reference Systems 5 and 6 have a more difficult task, and systems with special hardware will need much special programming.*

It is worthwhile to make these Supervisory Systems as *modular* as possible. One module may then be replaced by another. For example, a different program read-in mechanism may be plugged in, or different input/output routines, or a main scheduling routine with a different allocation of priorities, and so on.

This is one fairly simple approach towards increasing their generality. Another is to write programs which can be recompiled for different requirements, such as different input/output configurations, different core sizes, different block sizes, either of data or programs, and perhaps also for the selection of different types of Supervisory routines. Such programs have been written for use with a preassembly run which can modify the source program to cater to these different requirements in the compilation.

These techniques which are half-way stages to generalization may be used by a computer manufacturer in an attempt to provide some of the software for different real-time applications. It will often be worthwhile for a user also to write Supervisory Programs in this way because he is likely to have many requirements to modify his system, to add more input/ouput units or more core, and so on.

Any attempt at generalization, or even at modularization, may reduce the efficiency of the program by requiring more core or more time—these being more or less equivalent in a real-time system. This is the price that is paid for the reduction in manpower requirements. It is better to aim at simplicity and modularity rather than at the ultimate in efficiency. If

* Written before the announcement of programs such as IBM's 360 Operating System.

the system is simple and modular it will be possible to make modifications to it relatively easily when these are needed—as they always are.

When buying or planning a real-time system there is much to be said for choosing a computer or a configuration which has available a set of Supervisory Programs or some of these routines. In the past it was sometimes necessary to tailor an application to fit the available computers. It may now be worthwhile to tailor a real-time application to fit the available Supervisory Programs.

In either case, careful attention must be given to the problems of Supervisory Programs when the system is being planned. They affect the size of the computer needed, the manpower requirements and the installation schedule.

SECTION **IV**

THE MECHANISM OF CONTROL

18 THE TOP EXECUTIVE

In the real-time world it is not possible to plan ahead with exactitude. Except in the simplest scientific systems in which instruments are scanned cyclically, events occur in an unscheduled manner. The demands on the system will vary from moment to moment in an unpredictable fashion.

At the center of most real-time systems there is, therefore, a scheduling routine which looks periodically at the current demands on the system and decides what program shall operate next. Control returns to this central scheduling routine sufficiently frequently to ensure that the demands on the system are met.

The sets of rules that are used for scheduling the work differ considerably from one system to another, depending upon its needs. The scheduling routine scans the current status of messages or system functions and, according to its rules, transfers control to the required program. All the programs are in a sense subroutines of this top executive.

This chapter discusses the needs of the central scheduling routine and gives examples from different types of systems.

A scheduling routine is likely to be entered whenever an Application Program or segment of program ends its work, and the decision must be made what to do next. If the Application Program, for example a linear programming routine, takes a long time, interrupts may cause the scheduling routine to be entered. The interrupts could be caused by new transactions arriving, or they might be periodic interrupts caused by a clock.

A simple example of a central scheduling routine was given in Chapter 16 in Fig. 48. Here a routine which is entered very frequently scans the queues of items that may be waiting for processing. There is no priority differentiation between the messages, except that non-real-time messages

185

are only processed when there is enough time and core storage available to prevent the non-real-time work from interfering with the real-time work. If there are no items currently requiring the central processor and if the queues are empty, the scheduling routine cycles in a closed loop waiting for new additions.

In this example, items in the Work-in-Progress Queue requiring work are attended to before the items in the New Input Queue. The reason for this is that partially processed items normally tie up more core storage than new messages. It is desirable to release this storage as soon as possible; otherwise an emergency situation may arise when the system becomes short of available core blocks. Furthermore, if part of the system fails, for example one of the random-access files, or if the system becomes similarly degraded, it is preferable to complete half-processed messages rather than start on new ones.

A reason for examining new inputs first could exist, however. For example, some of the new messages might require a very quick response, and it would be desirable to preempt existing work. It may be necessary to preempt other running items in order to obtain equipment to execute this high priority work.

Priority considerations are likely to differ from one type of application to another. The sequence in which processing is done may differ on priority grounds in two ways. First, different messages may be of different importance and may have different priorities. In an airline reservations system, for example, all messages may have the same priority, but in a banking system it may be desirable to give customer enquiries from the bank counter priority over transaction processing in order to ensure a fast response time. In some systems there may be many different message priorities. Second, different functions of the system may have different priorities. For example, high speed output to data displays is likely to have priority over teletype output; vital calculations may have priority over data logging or other types of processing. A vital message or a vital function may have to jump the queues, either those waiting for the central processing unit or those waiting for an input/output unit or file.

Any difference in the priority of processing means a difference in the main scheduling routine. The simpler the priority structure, the simpler will be this routine. If, as in some airline applications, the Supervisory Programs recognize no difference in message priority and no difference in priorities of functions, then the central scanning loop will be a simple routine of ten or so instructions as above. If there are a number of different priorities between functions and messages, the scanning loop will need more elaborate logic, such as the testing of a priority table.

Although some large real-time systems give a fast response to all their messages, for example, most airline booking systems reply in three seconds or less, there are many applications in which only a portion of the messages require such fast reaction. This would be a reason for building a priority structure into the main scheduling routine.

On a small computer a program priority structure may be used when restricting the degree of multi-programming in the system. Suppose that a maximum of three messages may be processed in parallel. Messages may be assigned priorities 1, 2 and 3. Only messages of a higher priority may take control of the central processing unit when the program for the current message gives a WAIT macro-instruction.

Figure 51 illustrates such a scheduling routine. Here there are three priorities of program in the system, distinguished from one another by the degree to which they may interrupt each other:

(a) High Priorities Real-Time Programs (HRT). During a WAIT given by these programs, no other Application Programs may be entered.

(b) Low Priority Real-Time Programs (LRT). During a WAIT given by these programs, only a HRT program may be entered. The processing of the LRT program is thus suppressed until no High Priority messages are waiting for processing.

(c) Non-Real-Time Programs (NRT). During a WAIT given by these programs, HRT or LRT programs may be entered. The processing of the NRT program is thus suppressed until no real-time messages are in the system.

In a system with a high throughput the main scheduling routine is entered many times per second. It is therefore desirable that it should be tightly programmed to be as short as possible.

Certain infrequently occurring events or messages in the system may need more complex analysis than that above. It is sometimes desirable, therefore, to have an *exception* scheduling routine separate from the loop that is entered many times per second. This is illustrated in Fig. 52.

Some real-time systems execute their Application Programs in a *pre-set sequence* rather than selecting them at random. For example, read a group of plant instruments, perform calculations, print instruction to operator if required, read instruments again, and so on. Deviations from the preset cycle would occur only when exception conditions arise. In a system like this a latch may be set by any conditions needing exception scheduling. This would be tested between Application Programs and then, if necessary, a scheduling routine might be executed.

Most real-time systems will overlap their input/output operations with processing. In this case the scheduling of input/output and file operations is normally separate from the scheduling of Application Programs. The input/output scheduling routines may be entered when an interrupt signifies

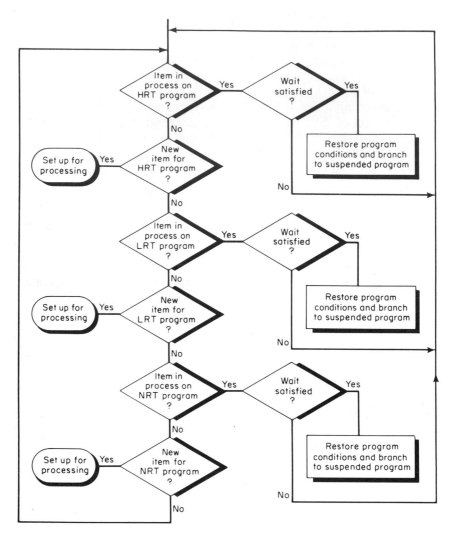

Fig. 51. A scheduling routine with three levels of priority.

that such an operation is complete, so that another one can be started on that channel and unit. On a slower or less sophisticated machine, however, there may not be such an interrupt. The main scheduling routine may then incorporate input/output scheduling also, testing first to see whether any input/output channel is not busy. This is illustrated in Fig. 53.

The decision as to what Application Program to execute next, or what message to process next, can, indeed, become involved with the availability

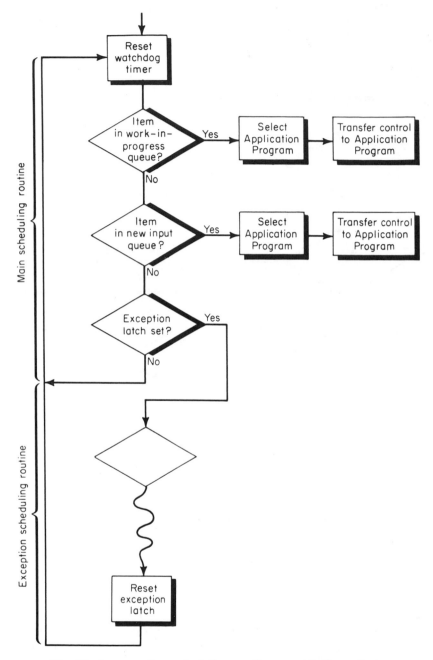

Fig. 52. An exception scheduling routine separate from the main scheduling routine. Messages or situations requiring exception action cause the exception latch to be set.

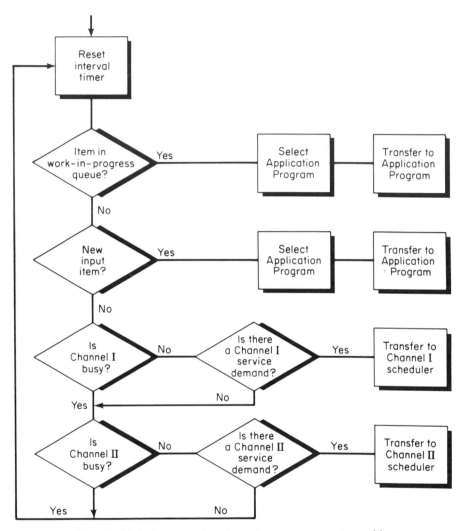

Fig. 53. Main loop test for channel status on a system with a low degree of multiprogramming.

of equipment. In systems using more than one computer and different memory units, channels and so on, the scheduling routine may have a dynamic record of how equipment is assigned, and it may check that the required equipment is available before allowing work to begin on a particular operation. This could become very complex, especially if multi-thread programming is in use.

Just as a Supervisory Program might check the availability of equipment, so also it might check the availability of other programs, and this could be a criterion in deciding which job is to be done next.

Consider a system with a large core storage in which all the Application Programs are in core, with the exception of those very infrequently used such as error routines. Of the messages entering the system some may be processed quickly, but others take a relatively long time. Some of the messages are urgent and need a quick response, and these must interrupt the processing of others. A program may thus be left partially completed for some time. Control will return to it when higher priority work has been done. But meanwhile it cannot be used by other messages, and for reasons of logic other associated programs or subroutines may have to be made unavailable to other messages.

Figure 54 illustrates the scheduling routine for such a system. This illustration is taken from the computer programs used for Project Mercury in which duplexed IBM 7090's were used to monitor the first manned space flights from Cape Kennedy.

In this system, there is a relatively small number of Application Programs (Ordinary Processors). A table, called the Priority Table, contains one word for each Application Program in the system. In that word one bit is used for various indicators—A, B, C, D, etc.—for that program. Indicator A is on when that Application Program is in the middle of being used and has been interrupted. Indicator B is on when a job is waiting to use that Application Program. Indicators C, D, etc., are suppression indicators. When a suppression bit is on for some reason or other, a transfer may not be made to that Application Program.

Immediately a routine is entered it switches on its A indicator and thus records the fact that it is active. If it is interrupted the A indicator remains on. When a routine is completed it switches its A indicator off.

Each routine has as many suppression indicators (C, D, etc.) as there are reasons for its being suppressed. Every condition which requires the suppression of a given routine is associated with a given suppression indicator of that routine. For example, a low priority routine may have some special relationship with a high priority routine which requires that the latter should not be entered for a period of time.

As is shown in Fig. 54, the scheduling routine scans through the Operational Programs in sequence 1, 2, 3 . . . up to n, the high priority programs being the first. On each program it looks first at the suppression indicators.

If any of these are on, it ignores that program. Next it looks at the A indicator to see whether a job is in the middle of being processed by that program. If this is the case, then control is returned to that program. Otherwise the scheduling routine tests whether there is a job waiting for that Application Program.

If there is no item for this Application Program, it looks at the next Application Program in the priority sequence, and so on, until it has checked all of them.

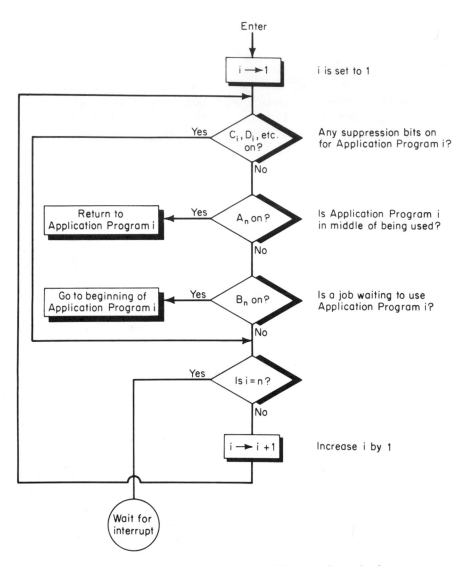

Fig. 54. The priority routine of Project Mercury. Items in the priority table are arranged so that those with high priority have a low value of i.

It will be seen that this procedure makes the main loop much longer and needs a computer with fast logic capacity. Such a scheme could only be used where there is a reasonably small number of Application Programs, though a variation of it could check all programs of one priority level with one instruction, rather than checking each program individually. A procedure of this type is of value only where priority considerations are of importance. The use of suppression indicators introduces a form of logical interaction between different Application Programs which could become complex—and perhaps unmanageably complex—where there are many such programs.

As will be seen, the main scheduling routine is likely to differ considerably from one application to another. Basically, a scheduling algorithm is needed for each application. This algorithm can be simple or it can become very complex. It is a function of factors such as:

1. The priority structure between different tasks.
2. The precedence rules. Can one task interrupt another? Can one message preempt another?
3. How is the available equipment allocated? Are the input/output schedulers separate from the main scheduler?
4. What response times or deadlines must be met?
5. Are real-time work and non-real-time work combined?

In general, when designing a real-time system, every attempt should be made to simplify the way work is scheduled. Too complex a mechanism for scheduling gives rise to many difficulties in the implementation of the systems, especially in program and system testing.

19 INTERRUPTS AND MULTI-PROGRAMMING

The conventional computer of the past was able to start at the beginning of a program and work its way through to the end. A variety of reasons grew up for complicating this approach, especially in commercial data processing work where the processing was simple but where many mechanical input and output units had to be operated. Multi-programming was used in systems in which the input/output times were out of balance with processing times, and interrupts were introduced to help keep the expensive and relatively slow input/output equipment continuously busy.

With an on-line system the handling of the input/output devices becomes a much more difficult task. The timing is likely to be even more out of balance. The numbers of units are greater. Input occurs at the whim of a distant operator rather than at the command of a programmed instruction. Timing is asynchronous and unpredictable. The need for interrupt mechanisms and multi-programming becomes much greater than on a conventional system.

The term *interrupt,* for which different computers have different words (trap, derailment, mode change, etc.), means that because of a hardware event of some type the program currently operating is temporarily stopped while a routine of higher priority is executed. When the priority routine is ended control will return to the point at which the original program was interrupted. In some circumstances the original program cannot necessarily be interrupted at *any* point because this might cause a logic error. Where desirable, instructions will be "tagged" or marked so that interrupts are inhibited. The interrupt will then have to wait until a non-tagged instruction is reached in the program.

REASONS FOR INTERRUPTS　　An interrupt is thus an automatic change in the program flow as a result of some condition arising in the data processing system. Typical of the conditions that may cause an interrupt are the following:

1. *A signal that an input/output operation may begin.* For example, a line control computer may signal that it is ready to transmit data to the central processing unit, or a file that has moved an access arm to a given location may signal that it is ready for a write operation to commence.

2. *A signal that an input/output or file operation is complete.* For example, when an input/output read or write is completed, the processing which was going on simultaneously with it is interrupted so that a priority routine can initiate a new read or write on than channel or unit without delay.

3. *A signal that an error or abnormal condition has been detected.* For example, a parity error in core, or an input/output error, will cause an interrupt to a priority routine for handling this condition rather than stopping the computer as it would have done on some older machines. A hardware feature such as memory protection will cause an interrupt if a program tries to refer to a core storage word beyond its specified area.

4. *A signal that indicates a special condition,* such as a watchdog timer reaching the end of its interval, or a real-time clock causing an interrupt at a given time.

Organization of the flow of data through a real-time system can be made more efficient with the help of these interrupts.

MODES OF OPERATION　　Many real-time computers have, as described above, two modes of operation, a normal mode and a priority mode which is used to process an interrupt. Some more sophisticated machines, especially certain machines designed specifically for handling communication networks, may have more than two modes of operation. This may mean simply that an interrupt routine can, itself, be interrupted. In other words, there are several depths of interrupt. Or it may mean that different modes exist for different functions. For example, one such computer has four modes, in order of decreasing priority:

> Service Mode
> Attention Mode
> Input/Output Mode
> Normal Mode

The function of Service Mode is to handle error conditions such as invalid words in core or communications line trouble. Attention Mode handles urgent conditions not associated with malfunctions, such as the need to update words which tell the time of day, or the situation that data storage for incoming messages is running low. Input/Output Mode handles all input/output to files or to another computer, and Normal Mode handles the normal processing.

A series of operation modes of this type, all with different priorities and each capable of interrupting those of lower priority, is especially useful in a computer that controls a communication network or has to scan input devices several times a second.

Multiple levels of interrupt are not necessarily required on a real-time computer which has a separate line control computer attached to it to handle the communication lines, though they may be valuable for error conditions. A hardware or programming error will probably cause an interrupt to an error routine, rather then causing the system to stop. If this error should occur when the system is already in a priority routine, then a second level of interrupt will be needed in order to handle it.

In a system with a high throughput and fast response time it is important that priority routines are programmed to operate speedily. The priority program must be fast enough to ensure that there will be no interference with the action that must be taken on other interrupts. In a machine with only one level of interrupt these will not be recognized immediately if they occur during a priority routine and, therefore, the possibility of losing data may arise. Consequently, individual routines must be fast enough so that the worst combination of simultaneous interrupts will not instantaneously overload the system. This possibility should be investigated if a program written for an existing system is being adapted to another system with a higher throughput or a different input/output configuration.

THE SEQUENCE OF EVENTS FOLLOWING AN INTERRUPT When an interrupt occurs a sequence of machine actions is necessary for dealing with it. Some of these will be programmed and some will be automatic, depending upon the sophistication of the hardware. The sequence of events in a system with only one level of interrupt will be as follows:

1. Further interrupts will be inhibited, or prevented from occurring, until this priority routine is over.

2. The location at which the previous program was interrupted will be stored, so that a return can be made to that point when the priority routine is over.

3. Certain indicator registers or latches must be preserved, as the contents or setting of these will be needed again by the interrupted program. Possibly the contents of accumulators, index registers and so on will be needed again. If these units are to be used by the priority routine it may be necessary to store their contents also.

4. The cause of the interrupt must be determined. The interrupting channel and device must be determined. This may be implicit in the location to which the interrupt branch occurred, or it may be necessary to test various indicators.

5. The required action must then be determined and control transferred to the program that will take this action if it is to be done immediately. There may be some cases in which action is not taken immediately but in which the request for the action is queued.

6. In most systems control is returned, after the priority routine, to the point where the previous program was interrupted. The indicators, registers and so on must first be restored.

Of these six actions, No. 5 will be programmed, No. 2 will usually be automatic, and the other four may be either programmed or automatic, depending upon the sophistication of the hardware. Computers without automatic interrupt features have often been used for real-time applications, but if the above functions are programmed they take a considerable amount of time. Fewer interrupts can be permitted to occur, and restrictions may be imposed on the interruptable programs.

A system may, for example, have priority routines which do not store all the pertinent registers and indicators because this would take too long. It only stores those in common use. If, then, any program uses these indicators which are not stored, it must inhibit interrupts until it has finished with them, unless the interrupt routines themselves are known not to interfere with them.

The numbers of interrupts used can be cut down at the expense of efficiency. For example, it is not necessarily desirable to have an interrupt at the end of each input/output operation. Instead, the main scheduling routine of the system could test to see which channels or units are free as in Fig. 53, Chapter 18.

RETURN
OF CONTROL
In most systems control will be returned after the priority routine is completed to the point at which the interrupt occurred. However, in some complex systems there are priority routines which do not return control to the point at which the interrupt occurred. For example, the IBM 7090 system for Project Mercury, the main scheduling routine of which was illustrated in

the last chapter, has a complex priority structure, and some messages must pass rapidly through the system. The interrupt may indicate the need for immediate use of a different routine. The priority program must recognize this and transfer control to the appropriate routine. This considerably complicates the structure of the Supervisory Programs. Similarly, in a system which handles error interrupts, the error may necessitate the use of a different program.

In commercial data processing systems little seems to be lost by having only one level of interrupt in a computer which does not handle the communication lines directly, and by making every priority routine return to the point at which the interrupt occurred. The simplification gained by this is worthwhile.

MULTI-PROGRAMMING The continuity of programs working on a message in a real-time computer will thus be broken occasionally by interrupts. In some systems, it will also be broken by the use of *multi-programming* of the concurrent processing of more than one message.

The term "multi-programming" has various shades of meaning in the computer world, and it is possibly clearer to use the term *multi-thread processing*. A "thread" refers to the passage of one message through the system and to the string of Application Programs that process it. In "single-thread processing" the work of Application Programs on one message is completed before the Application Programs begin on the next message. The messages are processed serially. With "multi-thread processing" they are handled in parallel. The Application Programs have not finished with one message, but break off while others work on the next message.

This is not automatic switching from one program to another of a higher priority, but programmed switching between programs of the same priority.

Multi-thread processing means that different programs, operating on different messages and with varying degrees of interdependence, are all in various stages of simultaneous execution, with control jumping back and forth among them in a manner determined by the sequence of external events. Different messages which may or may not require different programs are handled concurrently.

The individual programs are complete in themselves and cannot be considered as subordinate to one another, in the way that subroutines are subordinate to the main routine in conventional programming.

Multi-thread programming may take place in a system which can overlap certain functions. For example, if input/output overlaps with processing, then, while one transaction is waiting for an input operation to be completed, processing may begin on another transaction, possibly using a different program. This is illustrated in the timing diagram of Fig. 32 in Chapter 9.

DEGREE OF MULTI-THREAD PROGRAMMING The degree of multi-thread programming refers to the number of transactions that may be in process at one time, i.e., the number of "threads." If input/output is very slow compared to processing it will be economical to have many transactions in process at one time, provided that a sufficient number of input/output operations can be made to overlap. In most large real-time systems random-access files with a relatively long reference cycle are used, but a number of these can operate to overlap their "seeks" and reads. The majority of input/output operations refer to these at random; therefore, with a fast central processing unit which completes the Application Program segments quickly, it will be economical to have a fairly high number of "threads" running in parallel.

If input/output operations are not too slow compared with processing, or if the number of channels restricts the number of parallel input/output operations, the degree of multi-thread programming will be lower. Similarly, if the core storage size restricts the number of items that can be in core at one time, then the degree of multi-thread programming will be low.

Thus, a system such as Reference System No. 6, with large, fast computers and a number of random-access files, is likely to have many messages being processed at one time. Reference System No. 5, having smaller computers and fewer files may have only two or three "threads" running in parallel. Reference System No. 1., doing similar work, but on a small computer with a low throughput, completes one message before it starts processing the next.

The prime reason for multi-thread programming is, then, to increase the efficiency of a system that is out of balance from the timing point of view. If file reference times are long compared with processing times, then multi-thread programming will increase the throughput of the system.

It is generally true that parallel programming becomes more valuable in a computing system when the ratio of input/output speed or file access time to processing time becomes high.

There may be another reason for multi-programming where a complex priority structure exists. It may be desirable in some systems—for instance, in scientific or control systems as opposed to commercial data processing systems—that some messages should be handled quickly and should interrupt the processing of other messages. Long reiterative calculations will be suspended frequently to process control signals, scan instruments, or to continue the typing of messages to distant plant operators.

For any given system it is possible to calculate, or to evaluate by simulation methods, the optimum degree of multi-programming for a given throughput. In order to do this one must know approximately the input/output and file reference cycle times, the Application Program running times and the times for various Supervisory Program functions.

EFFECT ON SUPERVISORY PROGRAMS   The degree of multi-thread programming will have an effect on the structure of the Supervisory Programs. In a system with many parallel "threads" the main scheduling routine will be entered many times in the processing of one message. For a small system macro-instructions may be designed to enable a message to retain control of the central processing unit for a longer period of time, rather than to relinquish it constantly to other messages. For example, the system could be programmed so that when one Application Program reaches a WAIT condition only messages of higher priority than the one being processed can take advantage of this and break the "thread."

Again, if in a system with a low degree of multi-programming an Application Program gives an input/output instruction, the system might check to see whether this can take place immediately. If it can it does, and this Application Program retains control of the processing unit while it is happening, rather than allowing the "thread" to be broken. If it cannot take place immediately, or if it is a file action requiring a time-consuming "seek," then the input/output instruction would effectively execute a WAIT as defined earlier.

A system with a high degree of multi-programming will probably release the access arm on a file when it has found a required record. Another Application Program will then be free to move the access arm if it needs to. The access arm may, however, be needed again in its present location, perhaps to update the record it has just read, or to inspect another one in the same area. A small system would find it economic to retain the access arm if the Application Programmer so demanded, rather than allowing another "thread" to use it.

Many considerations of this type will be involved in determining the degree of multi-programming. In general, in the small, less sophisticated system with a lower throughput the messages will be handled in a more serial fashion. The main scheduling routine will be entered less frequently, and the occurrence of interrupts will be more restricted. Application

Programs may not be segmented so finely. Some of the larger systems currently in use which handle high traffic volumes use relatively small segments of Application Program. This is because a high degree of multi-thread programming is used.

It is worth noting that the decision to use multi-thread programming leads to many more difficulties in the implementation of the system than are normally anticipated when the decision is made. The Supervisory Programs become more complicated, and the use of multi-thread programming invariably produces many logic errors in the system that are very difficult to track down. If it is possible on a small system to use serial processing entirely this will simplify the installation, though a system which has to handle a high transaction rate and messages that need a number of long random-access file operations is often forced into multi-thread operation.

DESIRABLE COMPUTER FEATURES Where the characteristics of a real-time application require that multi-programming be used, or that there be a complex interrupt structure, a machine should be selected which is well-equipped to deal with these. It should have, if possible, an automatic interrupt and return mechanism with automatic storing of registers and latches. Interrupts to different locations, depending upon the cause of interrupt, are useful. Index registers are essential. A program relocation register is desirable if the same program is to be executed from different parts of core. On a computer which also handles a communication network, different modes or levels of interrupt are valuable. Where independently written programs are run concurrently, it is worthwhile to protect the system from logic errors in individual programs by using a watchdog timer and a memory protection device, which ensure that an individual program does not destroy data in areas of core it is not intended to enter.

20 THE MARSHALLING OF APPLICATION PROGRAMS

In most real-time applications there will be too many programs in the complete working system for all of them to be in the computer core storage at one time. It will be necessary to store the programs on backing drums or disk files, and if a program is needed which is not in core, it will be called in.

A large real-time application might have, say, 100,000 instructions in its programs and room for only 15,000 in core (with data, tables, etc.). If those kept on the files were all exception routines, infrequently executed, this would have little effect on the design of the system. However, this is often not the case. Programs that are in common use have to be kept on files because it would not be economic to have a core storage big enough for all of them. In some large systems with a high throughput the majority of messages need programs that are not necessarily in core. A system of the above dimensions might well have to make ten or twenty accesses per second to an external program store.

This chapter discusses the mechanisms for selecting and obtaining the necessary programs. This can be a critical factor in the design of a real-time system, especially one in which the queues for input/output channels are significant. It is not uncommon that underestimates are made of the sizes of Application Programs, or that more Application Programs are added when the system is working. This would probably not be of great significance in a conventional batch processing system. It may mean that a run is split into two, and the system works overtime. However, unless a real-time system is designed with such a possibility in mind, it may be prevented from doing the job it was designed for.

Consider a system designed so that 80 per cent of the programs in use are normally kept in core. The remaining 20 per cent are brought in from the files. Now suppose that the number of programs actually required were twice as large as this estimate. The core can still only hold the same number, i.e., 80 per cent of the original one hundred; this means that now 120 per cent must be brought in from the files. The number of file accesses for programs has gone up by a factor of six. This may make the file channel queues large, and it will take longer to have access to program segments and data. Messages will then spend a longer time in core, and the core shortage will be worse than is suggested by the above figures alone.

The position of any item on the files of a real-time system is determined to some extent by how frequently it is entered. Programs will usually be entered fairly frequently compared with most of the data on the files. They will therefore be kept on a part of the files to which quick access is possible. If the system has disks and drums, the programs will probably be on the drums as these have a quicker access time. To lessen the rotational delay time of the drums, a segment of program which is less than, say 500 words, may be written repetitively around the same track.

SELECTION OF PROGRAM SEGMENT   Selection of a program segment needs to be made in two situations:

(a) A new message arrives at the computer and a program must be selected to process it.

(b) An Application Program segment is in process and determines the need for another Application Program segment or a Supervisory Program segment.

Normally a new message is first given to an Initiator Program, fixed in core, which analyzes a code to determine what Application Program is required for processing the message.

Given a code to identify the required program segment, it may or may not be a function of the Supervisory Programs to obtain that program, read it into core and transfer control to it. The Application Program itself, may, generate the file address of the segment and read it into core as though it was reading data, using the Supervisory Programs only to execute the file actions. On the other hand, if the system has a large number of program read-in operations it will probably be more economical to have a Supervisory Program for organizing these.

METHODS OF PROGRAM READ-IN   There are certain fundamentally different methods by which the system may obtain the required programs:

1. *Fixed Programs*

All the programs required for one phase of operation are in core at the same time. This is sometimes the case in a technical control system. It is not the case in most commercial real-time applications because the programs are too numerous for all of them to fit in core.

2. *Serial Read-in*

Program groups are brought into core in a serial fashion and recycled. When program group A is temporarily finished with it, it is replaced by program group B. Program group B is followed by program group C, and so on until program group A is again in core (Fig. 55).

This scheme has the disadvantage of a long response time. The messages to be processed must wait until their particular program is in

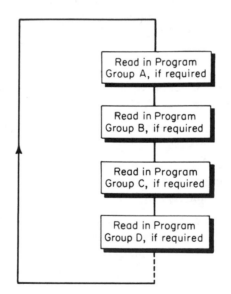

Fig. 55. Serial program read-in.

core. When a new program group is read into core the New Input Queue is scanned, and those messages requiring this group are processed. If a response time of ten or twenty seconds is adequate this may be the simplest method of program read-in.

This is likely to be of value in a system with not too many messages, and with Application Programs that run for a fair length of time. In a system requiring a large number of Application Programs, each of which are quickly executed, Random Read-in, described below, is more likely to be used. A combination of Serial Read-in and Random Read-in will sometimes be the most economic method.

3. *Random Read-in*

Programs are usually divided into segments, and these segments are brought into core at random as required.

When the processing of a message requires a program segment, a Supervisory Program may check to see whether it is in core. If it is not, it is read in from disk or drum. Checking to see whether it is in core requires an operation such as scanning a table and updating the table each time a program is read in. This may not be worthwhile, and in a system with a wide spread of Application Program usage segments may be read in without this check, in which case some segments may be in core twice at the same time.

Random read-in is useful where there are a large number of programs to be executed rapidly and for which a fast response time is required. These criteria apply to many commercial systems, especially systems for making enquiries and updating records.

Random read-in is generally more difficult to organize than the serial approach. The program has to be located on the files, and a decision has to be made where in core it is to be read to. Many randomly read-in segments are likely to be in core at one instant, and thus it becomes necessary to either move the programs around in core before executing them, or else to make them "relocatable" so that they can operate from any area in core. The former method is inefficient; the latter introduces problems. Methods of making programs "relocatable" are discussed later in this chapter.

4. *Combinations of the Above Methods*

All applications are likely to have some of the programs permanently in core. The remainder will be read randomly, serially, or with a combination of these methods.

Let us suppose that the approach shown in Fig. 55 is suitable, except that a small proportion of the messages require a wide range of infrequently used Application Programs—too numerous to be included in any of the program groups with which the core is cyclically loaded. There may be a periodic break in the sequence of planned core loads in which any items needing programs outside the serially-loaded program groups are using random (and relatively inefficient) program read-in (Fig. 56).

It may be found that one core load is enough to handle a large proportion of the messages. Consider an application in which a response time of 30 seconds is adequate and 90 per cent or so of the messages

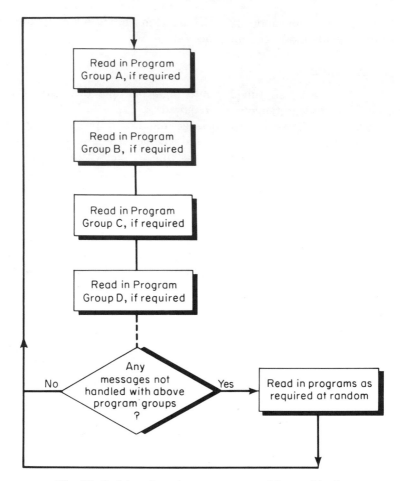

Fig. 56. Serial and random program read-in combined.

require a group of programs which could be entirely in core in fixed
locations. Here it would be possible to allow the system to operate for
perhaps 10 seconds with these programs only. All requests for other
programs would be placed in a queue. At the end of the 10 seconds,
this queue would be processed, and the programs required would be read
into core in segments at random. The sequence in which items in the
queue are processed would be determined by considerations of minimizing
program read-in operations. When the queue is emptied the main core
load of fixed programs would be restored, and work would continue on
this for another 10 seconds. It can be an advantage to have these main
programs in fixed locations rather than to have to relocate them.

ADVANTAGES AND
DISADVANTAGES OF
SMALL SEGMENTS
In general, reading the programs in at random in small segments saves core storage, but it is wasteful in processing time and file channel time. It may be necessitated by a fast response time, 3 seconds for example, which is demanded of some systems, and by a wide variation in the programs required for processing the messages. A more economic method may be found if:

(a) A longer response time can be tolerated.

(b) The majority of messages refer to a minority of programs which can be all in core at one time.

RANDOM
READ-IN
If a Supervisory routine is used to read in programs on a random basis, it may first inspect a table to determine whether the program is in core or not. On a multi-thread system the table may also state whether any of the items currently being processed have requested this program segment, and if so, how many. When the Supervisory routine brings in a program segment from the files it has to over-write a segment already in core. The above table will indicate which may be over-written.

When a program segment is needed three conditions may apply:

(a) *The program is in core.* If the program segment is in core, the count in the above table for that segment is increased by one, and the Supervisory Program may transfer control to this segment in turn.

(b) *The program is not in core.* If the program segment is not in core the Supervisory Program initiates a read of that program from the files, generating its file address from the program identification it is given.

(c) *The program has been requested already.* If the program is not in core but has been previously requested, the entry is placed on a special list to await the arrival of the program in core.

When programs are read from the files at random with a mechanism such as this, they will normally be divided up into blocks of fixed length. If the computer core is divided up into blocks as illustrated in Fig. 23 in Chapter 7, these may correspond to the size of a program block. It would be very difficult to organize the reading in of programs on a random basis if they were in segments of variable length. There may, however, be more than one block size. Block sizes may, for example, correspond to the record size on the drums or disks, and to the track size.

One of the problems with the random loading of variable-length program segments would be the tight packing of core. When a program is finished with, it would leave a gap which would be difficult to fill exactly. As many programs would be finished with at random points in time there would be many such gaps. This has been a problem in some systems that are using multi-programming. Suppose that several programs are to be read in at random times and are to occupy core for widely different lengths of time. Several programs must be in core at the same time, and they differ considerably in size. They leave core at random times and leave random-sized holes to fill.

It is necessary to reorganize the core at intervals, perhaps squeezing together the remaining programs. This necessitates setting up conventions for the preservation of registers or address values which are subject to change.

In some systems there is a need to use program segments of variable length. The requirement for this is likely to be stronger if the program segments themselves are complex. In a scientific system program routines may vary considerably in length, and the periods between input/output operations or the need for a WAIT may be long. It is probably not desirable to bring in such programs in fixed-length segments. If at all possible, serial rather than random loading should be used.

When programs are read into core from an external storage medium they may be always read to a fixed location in core. The programs are written for that location and executed in that location. This is possible in a simple "single-thread" system. For example, in Reference System No. 1 the program is read from the file, when it is wanted, to the location in core at which it will operate.

PROGRAM RELOCATION In the more complex multi-thread system the program may be read into a core block anywhere in the dynamically allocated area of core. It must then either be moved to a fixed area somewhere before it operates, which takes time, or else it must be *relocatable*.

Many multi-programming systems, real-time or otherwise, have to have relocatable programs, that is, programs which can operate from any part of core. Programs are written relative to core address zero and then relocated as and when required. The problem involved here is that when the program uses a branch (transfer) instruction or in any way refers to itself, it must know where it, itself, is located. Suppose that it is written relative to core address 00000 and operated relative to core address 05000 because that is where it happens to be sitting in core; then, before execution every instruction containing an address which refers to the program itself must be effectively modified by having 5000 added to it.

There are basically four methods by which the modification of the program may be performed.

1. *Software Relocation*

The program is processed when it enters core, so that its addresses are changed as required. This is a fairly lengthy operation which must be carried out every time the program is loaded into core. If it were to stay in core for a long period, as in some applications of multi-programming, this would be reasonably economic. However, in most real-time systems of this type, program segments are brought into core too frequently and are used for too brief a time for this to be a practical method.

2. *Hardware Relocation*

The machine has a piece of hardware logic which automatically adjusts any address referring to the program by adding the contents of a *relocation* register to that address. The appropriate value is loaded into the relocation register as the program is loaded into core.

3. *Index Registers*

The program can similarly be relocated by means of indexing. Any address which refers to the program has the contents of a specific index register added to it. Suitable index registers are a standard feature on most computers. This technique has the disadvantage (on machines without double indexing) that addresses which refer to the program cannot be indexed for purposes other than relocation. This may be a serious handicap as many machines use index registers for looping or branching, which they could not do at the same time as a relocation.

4. *Programmed Address Modification*

The relocation of programs on a machine without index or relocation registers could be done by programming the address modification. In other words, the program is written so that it is self-relocatable. Every time it refers to itself it adds a constant factor onto the address of that instruction. This makes the Application Programs tedious to program, and it is time-consuming and wasteful in core. On a machine with high speed move instructions it may even be faster to move the program segments to and from a fixed core area whenever it is executed, thus avoiding relocation.

Undoubtedly the best method of program relocation is (2) above, the use of special hardware logic. This was included in the list of machine features recommended for this type of application at the end of the previous chapter.

21 SUBROUTINES AND PROGRAM LOGIC

It will frequently be necessary for a program in a data-processing system to make use of a subroutine or to transfer control to another program. In systems such as those described in the previous chapters, programs are written in fixed-length segments so that they can be read into core from the files and can be relocated or manoeuvred in the core. Any of these segments may need to refer to other segments fairly frequently. These may be closed subroutines which return control to the previous program where it left off, or they may be open subroutines which do not return control to the previous program.

The subroutine may be:

(a) A routine of any length permanently in core in a fixed position.

(b) A relocatable program segment which is known to be in core at the time of the transfer, though its address in core may change.

(c) A program segment which is not known to be in core and which may have to be called in from the files.

In case (a) and possibly (b), the transfer to the subroutine may be made without reference to the Supervisory Programs' Scheduling Routine. This is desirable, especially in a system with a slow processing unit, as minimizing the number of references of this type to the Supervisory Programs will increase the efficiency.

Subroutines which are kept in core may be of variable length, as on a conventional computer application, and fixed in one position in the core, or they may be of a fixed length and relocatable. The advantage of the latter is an increased flexibility. The subroutine may be easily interchanged with other subroutines written in the same format. They may be Application Program segments, and it is desirable that the most frequently used ones be in core. Fixed-length format will enable the group in core to be changed if the frequency of use changes, or it will enable the number in core to be increased or decreased as circumstances demand.

If variable-length subroutines are used, these will probably be more efficient in their use of core. However, it will be difficult to relocate them, so that they will normally be in a fixed position. Routines of this type will include Supervisory routines and also the most frequently used Application Program routines.

Both these types of subroutines are common in existing systems of this type.

INDIRECT ADDRESSING

A transfer to a program segment which is relocatable cannot be made directly. Some form of *Indirect Addressing* must be used. Some computers have special hardware for indirect addressing, though it is quite easy to effect this by programming. If it is done by hardware it will need an instruction with logic such as: "transfer to the instruction the address of which is contained in location XXXXX,"; on other machines the address field XXXXX of any instruction may be tagged so that it means "the address which is contained in location XXXXX." The computer will then have a list of addresses of all the programs in core.

TRANSFER VECTOR

If it is done by programming, it will be necessary to use a device such as a *Transfer Table,* sometimes called a *Transfer Vector.* A simple example of this is given in Fig. 57. This will contain one or more instructions for each of the programs in core. Each of these instructions will be an unconditional branch to an entry point of the program. For a program with more than one entry point there will be one entry in the Transfer Table for each entry point. All references between relocatable programs will pass through the Transfer Table, as shown in Fig. 57. In this figure an instruction for an unconditional transfer to location XXXXX is represented by BXXXXX. Every program will end with such a transfer to an instruction in the table which links it to the next program.

When the location of a program in core is changed the address in the indirect addressing list or Transfer Table must be changed also. This technique permits the individual relocation or reassembling of any program without changing the others.

This type of mechanism is of value for program segments which are known to be in core at the time of transfer. The Transfer Table may refer also to some segments which are not always in core. As a segment is brought into core the appropriate address in the table is updated. If a group of programs is brought in, it may bring its own Transfer Table. If a transfer is attempted to a routine not always in core the table may cause a transfer to a routine for calling it in.

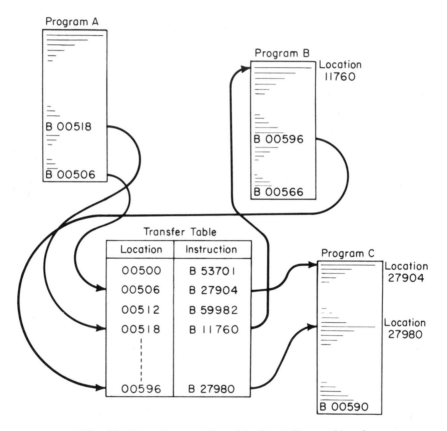

Fig. 57. Use of a transfer table for indirect addressing.

In general, however, a more elaborate mechanism is needed for programs normally kept on file, and a Supervisory routine must execute the transfer. This routine will be given a mnemonic table for the program it is to find. It may then execute a table look-up to determine whether or not it is in core at that moment. If not, it will convert the mnemonic to a file address and initiate a read-in of the program.

MACRO-INSTRUCTIONS FOR TRANSFERRING CONTROL   A real-time system will normally be provided with a set of macro-instructions for transferring control from one program to another and for linking with subroutines. A typical set of such macro-instructions is as follows:

First, there will be instructions such as WAIT and EXIT as described in previous chapters.

Second, there will be a set of ENTER macros for entering other programs. Let us define three of these:

1. ENTERA

This is for entering a subroutine permanently in core in a fixed location. It is a direct transfer without going through the Supervisory routines. A return address is stored in a location associated with the subroutine so that a return can be made to the original program if required.

2. ENTERB

This is for entering a subroutine which is known to be in core but which is relocatable. Such a subroutine may be permanently in core or may be known to be in core because a program connected with the message in question brought it in. A transfer to such a subroutine must be made via a *Transfer Table*.

3. ENTERC

This is for entering a subroutine which may or may not be in core. Normally, a Supervisory Routine will decide whether or not it is in core. If not, it will make a request to read it in and meanwhile treat this macro-instruction as a WAIT.

When a program in core transfers control to another routine in this manner, the first program may or may not be finished. If it is finished, it is important that it should not go on occupying valuable core space, unless it is one of those programs that reside permanently in core. The ENTER macro-instruction should indicate whether or not the program is to be retained for later use. If it is to be retained, a return address will be stored giving the instruction at which it is to be reentered when the return is made. If it is not to be retained, the block of core it occupies will be rechained to the Available Storage List.

Let us suppose that an "X" at the end of the macro-instruction mnemonic indicates that it will not be retained. This gives three more such instructions:

ENTERAX

ENTERBX

ENTERCX

If the subroutines that are entered are closed subroutines a return address will be stored in an area associated with them. A macro-instruction will enable them to return to the program from which they were entered. Let us call this macro-instruction RETURN.

This gives a possible set of nine macro-instructions for transferring control from one program to another (Table 3).

Table 3.

	Transfer is via main scheduling routine?
WAIT	YES
EXIT	YES
ENTERA	NO
ENTERB	YES or NO
ENTERC	YES
ENTERAX	NO
ENTERBX	YES or NO
ENTERCX	YES
RETURN	NO

These macro-instructions would be used by Supervisory routines as well as by Application Program routines.

Several levels of subroutine may be entered. That is, a program transfers control to subroutine X, X transfers control to Y, Y to Z, and so on, with control returning eventually Z to Y, Y to X and X to the original program. This is referred to as a *nest of subroutines*. There may be a limit to the number of subroutines that can be *nested*.

MULTI-THREAD OPERATION   One factor can make the relationship between the program segments much more complex. This is multi-programming, or a "multi-thread" operation, where more than one message is being processed in parallel. A system using relocatable programs in this way is likely to have also multi-thread processing. The reason for making the programs relocatable is that they can be read into different core blocks at different times. In a real-time multi-thread system any mixture of transactions may be contending for the computer's time. Messages wanting the same programs will, at times, be processed in parallel.

Suppose that message A is being processed by subroutine X, above, which transfers control to subroutine Y, and Y gives a WAIT. While the WAIT is taking place message B is being processed by subroutine W. W also transfers to Y. Y now needs a means of telling whether to return control to X or W. If there is no restriction on the degree of multi-thread programming, there is a finite probability that Y might be processing many messages in parallel.

One way of overcoming this is to store the return addresses in the Message Reference Block. There will then be a limit to the number of subroutines that may be in a "nest" for that message. A limit of four levels of subroutine may be enough for quite a complex system.

PROGRAM SELF-MODIFICATION   In conventional computer systems a common technique of programming is to allow a program to modify itself or to set a switch, so that a set of events occurring at one time effect the action of the program at a later time. A multi-programmed real-time system must use this technique with caution, and the restrictions on it depend upon the structure of the Supervisory Programs.

Suppose, for example, that an Application Program segment contains a WAIT macro. Control is taken away from this segment, while a random-access seek or some other time-consuming action is completed. At some time in the future control will be returned to this program, but in the meantime another transaction may have started to use it, itself having reached the WAIT. This is possible on some Supervisory Programs but not on others. If it is possible, then the Application Program must not modify instructions or set program switches before the WAIT that will be used after the WAIT; otherwise one transaction will interfere with the processing of another transaction.

If it is to be permitted to modify across a WAIT, then the restriction must be imposed that no transaction can use a program segment until the previous transaction has finished with it completely. In some systems this restriction may mean that the same program will be in core in many places at the same time, and this may be too inefficient to be tolerable. Suppose that in a large real-time system twelve similar inquiries occur at once and are processed in parallel. Then either all twelve transactions use the same program segment, in which case modification across a WAIT cannot occur, or else there must be twelve identical program segments in core at one time.

From a knowledge of the message mix and the programs required, the core storage taken up by programs that are duplicated in core can be found. Depending upon the application, this may or may not be too much. If it is too much, then the restriction must be imposed that no modification across a WAIT can occur.

A similar problem may arise in the use of subroutines.

On some systems priority interrupts do not return control to the instruction at which the interrupt occurred. It may then be possible for one trans-action to use a subroutine before the interrupted transaction has finished with it. Here, also, program modification is not permissible.

When a program requires to set a switch to be used by another pro-gram, a subroutine, or a part of the same program on the other side of a WAIT, or to store any information for use of later programs, it must store it in the Message Reference Block as this is the only area which remains allocated to a specific message for its entire life in the system. There is, then, an area in the Message Reference Block for the transfer of infor-mation and logical linkage between Application Program segments.

INTERRELATION OF APPLICATION PROGRAMS If the relationship between the Application Programs is complex, care is needed in the specification and control of the use of this area. The size of the area needed varies from one system to another and is de-pendent on the nature of the Application Programs.

In some systems there is a need to suppress certain functions of the system when a given program is at work. An example of this is the up-dating of file records. When one Application Program has read a file record and is going to write back an updated record, the other transactions must be prevented from starting to update this record. Otherwise the first updating will be overwritten by the second, and false results will be ob-tained. The first transaction indicates, possibly by means of a bit on the record, that the second cannot use it. It may be a function of the Super-visory Programs to check that it is not used.

Similarly, a system with a complex priority structure may need to stop the scheduling routine transferring control to certain programs at certain times. The use of suppression indicators, C, D, etc., in Fig. 54, Chapter 18 illustrates this. One program sets a suppression bit to prevent another program from being used. Each Application Program registers its status in a priority table which is inspected by the scheduling routine. This is done by means of "Suffixes" and "Prefixes" at the beginning and end of each Application Program. The danger in using such devices for sup-pressing programs is that with a larger number of Application Programs the logical interaction between the programs can become very complex.

DEBUGGING PROBLEMS There will be many other interactions such as these between the various programs. This creates a prob-lem when testing and debugging these programs. One program can be checked out on its own in the normal way; it may work perfectly under all conditions. But when it is interfaced with many other programs, all of which work well on their own, their interactions will probably cause many new logic errors. Some of these errors will be very difficult to pin down without special techniques.

Errors can be especially difficult to trace on a multi-thread system as they may occur only infrequently. They may be triggered off by a rare coincidence of events that is difficult to repeat.

The problems of program and system testing with multi-thread operation are discussed later in the book.

22 EMERGENCY PROCEDURES: THE TREATMENT OF ERRORS

This chapter and the next three deal with the circumstances when the system is unable to process in the normal fashion the messages that are reaching it.

Because an on-line system is operating as far as possible without human intervention, it must conduct its own emergency procedures rather than rely entirely on its operator. It will notify the operator when something goes wrong that he can help with, but, in general, it gives by itself the best possible service to users.

There are, however, many different types of errors or malfunctions that can occur. All of these must be thought about in the planning of the system. The system analyst must think of all the various types of error that are reasonably likely to occur, and for each of these he must ask: "What will the system do when this happens?" If a high measure of system reliability is needed, the answers to this question may be quite complex. If the "mean time to system failure" is not required to be too long, and the "mean time to system recovery," when a failure has occurred, is not required to be too short, then the techniques used may be simpler or less expensive.

TYPES OF
FAILURE

Three types of emergency must be considered in the design of a real-time system. First, a component may develop a failure that puts it out of action. A non-duplexed system may develop a fault that puts the entire system out of action, such as a fault in the core drive circuitry or power unit of the main computer. However, most of the failures will be in components that are not vital to the functioning of the whole, such as a terminal, a communication line, one out of several files and so on. A duplexed system may be designed so that no single failure puts the entire system out of action. As long as a computer in the system remains active, it can take some sort of emergency action if programmed to do so.

Second, there may be an error which is not caused by a permanent failure of part of the system. It may be a noise pulse on a transmission line, a mistake by a terminal operator, a program bug or a transient parity error in the computer circuitry. In a computer of the past a transient parity error would probably have caused the machine to stop. A real-time system should stop only if the error is permanent and there is no way of circumventing it.

Third, certain real-time systems can become overloaded. This may not be possible in a simple single-thread system or in a system which acquires its own input by scanning instruments. However, in a multi-thread system, with random input of different types, an overload is possible. The computer starts work on a set of messages which it will not be able to complete. Unless emergency action is taken, the Application Programs will demand core blocks when there is no core for them. The Supervisory Programs must be able to find a way out of this dilemma as will be described in the next chapter.

This treatment of overloads is needed only for a fairly complex system. The question of *errors,* however, affects all real-time systems from the largest to the smallest and simplest single-thread system.

The policy towards errors should be to keep the system going if at all possible, maybe in a degraded mode, and to minimize operator decisions. These requirements will be achieved at some expense, and the degree to which errors are handled automatically will depend upon the needs of the system. Some real-time systems must be invulnerable whereas others can be permitted to go out of action for short periods at a time.

**ERROR DETECTION
AND CORRECTION**   To handle errors automatically will involve expenditure, both for hardware and programming. It is necessary always to *detect* errors. The degree to which the system will itself *correct* them depends upon what expenditure can be warranted.

The cause of errors may be *transient* or *solid.* In other words it may be one isolated error which will not, necessarily, occur again, or a component may have gone wrong so that it causes errors all the time. In the latter case some means of circumventing the cause of the error is necessary, such as *switchover* to another computer or another component, or *fallback* to a degraded mode of operation. These will be discussed in the next chapter. The small non-duplexed system may have no means of switchover or fallback, so that a solid error causes it to stop.

TYPES OF   The types of error that a real-time system must
ERROR   handle are as follows:

1. *Communication Line Errors*

Communication lines currently in use are constantly plagued by bursts of noise, drop-outs and stray signals which create errors in the digital information that is being transmitted. Very thorough checks must be placed on the messages to detect such errors. A good quality transmission system will use a *parity check* on each character in addition to a *longitudinal check,* in which one or more characters check the other characters in a word or message. This will be done automatically, with *retransmission* of messages when an error is found. On lower quality equipment the checking and retransmission may not be automatic but may be done partially or entirely by programming. This may not be possible on the out-going messages.

For any given system it is possible to calculate the probability that an error is not being detected. Line test information will indicate the number of errors that may be expected. If this estimate does not give a high enough reliability for the application in question, other checks must be built into the system by programming. In any case, it is desirable, normally, to program such checks on the accuracy of the terminal operators, as will be described below.

When an item has been received correctly, the system should send a *message acknowledgement* to the terminal so that the operator knows his message has reached the computer. In a well-designed system this check will often not be automatic because the computer withholds message acknowledgement until the message is in the core of the main processor or, better, until it is written on a logging tape or file. It may withhold acknowledgement until file records have been updated. Doing this ensures that, if a fault occurs, either the operator will have had no acknowledgement and so will repeat the message, or the computer will have reached a point where it can finish processing the message even if a restart or switchover occurs.

In addition to checking that messages are correct, the main computer or line control computer should check that the lines and terminals are functioning. If the line control unit is receiving on a line, for example, and obtains no characters for twenty seconds or more, some action should be taken. It will probably pass on to the next line and meanwhile attempt to transmit a message to the operator of that terminal. If it can obtain no reply it will notify the computer operator who may then telephone the terminal operator. Similar action will be taken if it can obtain no response from a polled terminal or a terminal it has sent a message to.

Communication line error checking aids are normally provided by the hardware manufacturer. An *input/output control program* is normally provided and this should contain all the checking aids except, perhaps, message acknowledgement. When the system is being planned, it is necessary to check that the aids provided are sufficiently comprehensive for that particular application.

2. *Operator Errors*

Related to the question of communication line errors is that of errors made by the terminal operator. It may, for example, be the operator's fault that a terminal does not respond. An operator may press the wrong key. He may accidentally key in wrong information, such as a wrong account number or an incorrect quantity.

The computer should have built into its Application Programs whatever means are reasonable and necessary for checking the operators. Incorrect keying and internal contradictions will be tested for as far as possible, and the operator will be notified immediately. The *accountancy controls* used on a batch processing computer will also be used on a real-time system. *Self-checking numbers* or codes should be used to rapidly detect invalid keying. In these, the last character or characters will be derived from the others in such a way as to check that no wrong key has been depressed. Thus, bad keying of account numbers or other checkable fields will be picked up immediately after it occurs, and the operator will be notified. This on-the-spot detection is likely to reduce the number of mis-keying errors.

In a system in which transactions are sent to the computer for the updating of records, *batch totals* of the transactions should be accumulated for each terminal or each operator. Off-line, at the terminal, transactions will be totalled on an adding machine. A hash total may be produced of account numbers or other items. The computer will similarly total the items that it processes and print out the batch totals. If these disagree, means must be available for tracing and correcting the error. The error will normally be found by comparing the log printed at the terminal with original documents. In exceptional cases it may be necessary for the computer to print out its log.

Not all systems require such rigorous controls. Where inquiries are being made the computer may print an *alphabetic description* to reassure the operator that it is referring to the correct items. For example, if inquiring about the stock of a given part number, the operator may key in a wrong part number by mistake, perhaps 16049 instead of 16409. He detects this quickly when the computer prints back "16049 Hexagonal bracket 5 inch, 125 dozen," instead of "16409 Electric motor ¼ HP. . . ."

In general, if good error detection procedures are used, the entry of transactions on-line should give rise to less errors than similar keying off-line into cards or paper tape, or the writing of documents. The entry of transactions at their source with immediate checking enables errors to be controlled and minimized.

3. *Instrumentation Errors*

The input to some real-time systems is from instrumentation such as thermocouples, pressure gauges, flow-meters and so on. Here it is usual to apply *limit checks* to make sure, first, that the reading is not above or below preset limits, and second, that the change since this reading was last taken is not too great.

If either of these checks is violated the program may transfer control to *violation subroutines*. The action that these take will depend upon the nature of the application. The reading may indicate that an instrument, a line or analogue-digital converter, has become faulty. It may be possible for the system to notify an engineer and continue without that reading. In some cases the violation may be caused by a fault in the plant or the apparatus that is being controlled, in which case the computer must quickly take corrective action.

4. *Computer Input/Output Errors*

The transfer of data between the computer and its input/output units and files will occasionally be subject to errors. The treatment of these will be much the same as on a non-real-time system, except that, if possible, the system will not stop. After a read or write operation in which an error has been detected, the operation will be repeated. If, after three or four attempts, the error persists, there is obviously something wrong with the unit or with that particular area of tape or disk. The program will then branch to an exception routine for dealing with this condition.

There are various types of action that the error routine may be able to take. It is possible that the unit is not faulty throughout. For example, there may be a fault on a magnetic tape. Skipping over this portion of tape and writing again may solve the problem. It may be that one track on a disk surface is scratched and the others are readable. Possibly a disk or tape unit has become faulty, but the disks or tape can be moved by the operator to a spare unit so that work may continue.

Basically, input/output errors may be transient or easily circumventable, or they may be "solid." If an irreplaceable unit fails, the system has three possible alternatives. It may be designed so that some form of *switchover* is possible between the units, since vital data have been duplicated. Second, it may be able to continue operating in some *degraded mode,* possibly executing only a portion of its functions. Third, if these devices are not built into the system, it has to *stop*.

If the system is forced to stop it should execute an *orderly close-down.* This ensures that a restart can be made in an orderly fashion and that no messages are lost. All records are updated that should be updated, and no records are accidentally updated a second time when the restart is made. All incoming and outgoing transmissions should be completed, and an administrative message should be sent to the terminals to notify their operators of the close-down. The lines are then placed in idle condition. Non-processed or partially processed transactions should be tagged and recorded. They may be written on files or tape, printed or punched into cards, depending upon which units are operative.

When the system is restarted the unprocessed transactions will be completed. Restart procedures will then be executed, and administrative messages should be sent to all the terminal operators saying that operations are restarting. These may be followed by the messages replying to those interrupted transactions which have just been completed. The operators should check that the last message they sent has, in fact, been processed.

A complication arises if a record is found to be unreadable or invalid on a file that is otherwise working correctly. Some means must be devised of reconstructing the damaged record. It is possible that a disk surface has become scratched, or, more probable perhaps, a program error has caused a record to be overwritten.

File reconstruction procedures must be devised as a safeguard in almost all real-time systems which use random-access files of data. These are likely to differ with the nature of the application. Some systems will use duplicate files, and as each record is updated the duplicate copy is also rewritten. This considerably increases the file reliability but is a very expensive method. Otherwise it is necessary to dump the files periodically onto tape or some other medium. A log will also be kept of modifications to the file. Every time the file is updated some detail of this will be stored, perhaps again on tape. From these two sets of data the file may then be reconstructed. This will take some time, and normally it will have to be done off-line, or when the system is not doing real-time work. The more frequently the files are dumped, the shorter will be the reconstruction process. To spend twenty minutes every night dumping the file data onto tape would, for most installations, be a reasonable insurance policy.

5. *Errors in the Processing Unit*

All modern computers detect the majority of errors in their operation almost as soon as they occur. As with input/output units, such errors may be transient or solid. Some errors will be catastrophic so that the computer can do no further processing. Others will be such that it can carry on processing, provided it does not use the afflicted piece of circuitry.

All processors used for real-time work should have an *automatic interrupt* when an error is detected. The priority routine which the interrupt transfers to will, if it can, analyze the cause of the error. It will carry out one of the following actions which are listed in order of increasing seriousness:

(i) Re-execute the faulty instruction and continue processing.
(ii) Restart the program in question.
(iii) Transfer to an exception routine characteristic of the program in question.
(iv) Initiate switchover.
(v) Initiate close-down.
(vi) Halt.

Whether a restart or an exception routine is used may depend on the nature of the program in question. Each Application Program may specify whether, in the event of an error, it requires a restart at a certain address or the execution of a specified exception routine. Details of this might be stored in a table in core for each program.

Some errors in the processing unit will cause the computer to stop abruptly. Unless the system has more than one computer this will cause an abrupt interruption in the functioning of the system.

In this case an orderly close-down is not possible. Even if the system has another computer which can take over, it is still likely that the functions of the afflicted machine cannot be taken over in an orderly manner. This situation presents a more challenging problem for the system designer.

Formal procedures must be laid down for the terminal operators and the computer operator to ensure that every message is processed when an interrupt occurs, and that none are processed twice. Methods must be laid down for updating the file, so that every record that should be updated is updated, and that none are updated twice.

When an abrupt interruption occurs in the processing it will probably not be possible to tell how far the Application Programs had gone in handling their message or messages. They may or may not have updated the relevant files. It is, therefore, necessary to put an indication on the file records whereby subsequent restart programs can tell whether a file record has been updated due to a specific message or not. The messages may, for example, be given a sequential number. This might be put on by the operator or by the programs which receive the message from the communication lines and initiate the processing. The sequential number is written temporarily on the file records which this message causes to be updated. If the question then arises in the restart procedures, "Has such-and-such a record been updated by message No. XXX?", this can be answered. The message that is numbered in this way should be logged on tape, drum or a separate file before it updates the file in question. It may not be necessary to log the entire message but only those fields used in updating the record, so that a smaller volume has to be stored.

Schemes such as this, but differing in detail, must be worked out for each system that updates vital files in an on-line manner.

Another possibility that will complicate the error procedures is that some computers may not be capable of detecting *all* of their own errors. Circuitry susceptible to undetected errors on some computers includes the arithmetic circuitry, conditional transfers, and so on. This circuitry can be tested very quickly by simple programmed *diagnostics*. It may be advisable to use simple diagnostic routines of only a few instructions when the central processing unit would otherwise be idling in its scanning loop. If an error is found (which should be a very rare occurrence), orderly close-down or switchover can be commenced, and more thorough diagnostics can be brought in.

6. *Program Errors*

In some of the most complex, multi-thread, real-time systems, program errors, sometimes caused by unforeseen combinations of events, have been more troublesome than any other form of error. Combinations of events that occur very rarely may cause errors, not foreseen in the testing, long after the system is installed. Modifications to working programs may cause unforeseen errors. Errors may occur if data arrive in an unexpected form because of a mistake at the terminals. A data field or an analogue input with an unexpected value may cause an unanticipated divide overflow. It should be assumed when the system is being designed that the programs, even when operational, will be plagued with bugs of varying degrees of virulence.

Program errors may cause various types of malfunction. They may, for example, cause the processing unit to "run wild," destroying perhaps programs other than the one which caused the error. The Supervisory Programs might be damaged and a temporary *close-down* of the computer necessitated while new programs are loaded. It may not be possible to execute an "orderly close-down." Much the same criteria apply as when a fault arises in the processing unit.

It is possible to limit the damage done by a program "running wild" by means of a hardware device for "Memory Protection." This is greatly to be recommended on a multi-thread system. In ways which vary from one computer to another, the device limits the area of memory which a program can access. It would thus be impossible for an Application Program to damage the Supervisory Programs or other Application Programs. If it attempts to refer to an area outside its own limits it will be stopped, and an interrupt will occur. The interrupt subroutine will detect the miscreant and take appropriate action.

In a typical Memory Protection mechanism, the computer has two registers which define the bounds of a program's activity in core. One register defines the upper core address and the other the lower one that it can have access to. The program starts its work by loading these registers, and it is then bound by them until it reloads them or inhibits their action.

Other program bugs may cause the processing unit to loop continuously. This locks up the computer so that other Application Programs cannot operate, and other messages are not processed. Again, a hardware feature can prevent this from rendering the system inoperative. A "Watchdog Timer" allows no program to operate for more than a set period of time— perhaps 500 milliseconds. This is reset by the Main Scheduling Routine. If the time period is exceeded an interrupt occurs, and again the miscreant is caught.

Many other types of program error may be caught in this way because they trigger an interrupt of some type. The more interrupts that the computer has for this purpose, the better its suitability for real-time work. The wrongdoing program should be surrounded with burglar alarms.

When a program is caught going wrong, in this way, the Supervisory Programs may give it a second chance. If it goes wrong a second time, the computer operator should be notified, and the terminal operator should be told that his last message is unable to be processed.

The worst type of program error is that which is not detected. This may cause a record to be updated falsely or other types of undetected error to occur. Later, when there is no evidence of what caused it, the invalid record may be found, or may itself cause trouble.

There is no substitute for elaborate program testing procedures as described later in this book. But, when errors do occur, file reconstruction techniques must be available. However carefully the system is programmed, it would be folly to operate without these.

In conclusion, it is repeated that all possibilities of errors must be seriously considered when the system is being designed. This is an essential part of the system analysis work.

This can be better done if the probability of various errors is known. Hardware and communication line reliability figures should be sought. Figures for *mean time to failure* and *mean time to repair* of parts of the system should be obtained or estimated. The availability of machine engineers should be known.

As errors occur on the working system it should be programmed to keep a log of these, and this should be examined by machine engineers and system engineers to help keep the system carrying out its function as efficiently as possible.

23 EMERGENCY PROCEDURES: THE TREATMENT OF OVERLOADS

A transient emergency condition that can occur on some real-time systems is an overload of the central processor.

A simple system with "single-thread" processing may know no such condition as an overload. It processes one message at a time and ignores any excess. If a hundred operators press keys on their terminals at the same instant, the majority of them will be ignored for the time being. The computer will attend to them as soon as it has time. The line control unit keeps scanning the lines but can probably only accept one message per line.

A more complex system with a faster computer attempts to process more than one message at once, and it is then that an overload can occur. It is possible that when a number of messages of certain types are read into core there may not be enough core blocks to complete all the work the computer has started. This is a situation that can occur on a multi-programmed system with random input. It will get itself into difficulties from time to time, with certain mixes of messages in process. Every message is demanding more core and cannot be processed without it, but no more core is available. None of the messages in process can be completed and no new messages can enter the system. Possibly, file read operations already started cannot be completed as there is no core left into which to read the record when it is located.

In a multi-thread real-time system there may be occasions when such an instantaneous overload occurs. The Supervisory Programs must have some means of handling this dilemma.

A sudden flood of messages into the system may cause a channel overload, an overload of the random-access file "seek" or read mechanism, a temporary overload of the processing unit time, or a core storage overload.

As the effect of the first three is to cause a buildup of queues within the core, all these types of overload will result in the storage becoming clogged. Assume that a message already in the system needs a certain number of core blocks to complete its processing and that, at that time, a new message arrives. If processing is allowed to begin on the new message there will be insufficient storage for either message to be processed to completion. There is therefore a blockage in the system.

When the new message arrives, however, there may be no obvious indication that trouble is ahead. The Supervisory Programs cannot at that stage tell how much core the new message will consume, or indeed how much those already in the system will demand.

AVAILABLE STORAGE CHECK

To prevent a blockage from occurring it is necessary to anticipate trouble and take action when the available core storage sinks below a certain level. If an *Available Storage List* is used, a count of the number of blocks in this is kept. This count is compared with preset limits whenever blocks are requested. This is rather like a storekeeper who has to reorder stock when the quantity in his store drops below a certain level, and who has to take expediting or emergency action if the stock falls to a lower danger point. In a real-time system the levels at which actions are taken depend upon parameters of the systems such as maximum throughput and quantity of core needed to process one message.

TYPES OF CORRECTIVE ACTION

Possible types of corrective action that may be taken are:

(a) The communication lines are sealed off so that no more input can be received. It may, however, still be necessary to admit messages of very high priority, such as danger signals on a process control system. If the system has a separate processor to handle the communication lines, this can be programmed to stop feeding messages to the main processor for the time being. It will stop polling the communication lines, and operators wishing to initiate new actions must wait a few seconds (or less) until the current overload has been dissipated.

This type of action may, however, be too late. It is possible that the messages already in the main processor are enough to cause a blockage of the type described. There may be a small number of messages which are exceptionally greedy in their use of core. The number of available core blocks may thus sink further, and a second level of emergency action is needed:

(b) Those Application Program segments which are temporarily in core, but which are not in use at the moment, may be abandoned. Blocks containing these segments are chained to the Available Core List. The Programs will have to be read in again when they are required.

In some circumstances this can be a dangerous device. If it increases the number of program read-ins from file it will increase the queues waiting to use that file or its channel. This may worsen the core shortage.

(c) As a final and extreme measure, if the system becomes blocked as described above, the computer may destroy items in the system and send a message to the terminal from which they originated, asking for a repetition of the previous message. Random fluctuations in the message traffic are likely to cause overloads which will be depleted in a second or so. The operator may therefore be able to repeat the last message straightaway. If the overload is not yet past he should not be able to repeat it as no new input will be accepted.

(d) If the system is constantly operated at a level near its maximum throughput, the latter solution may not be satisfactory, as there will be too many requests to "Repeat Last Message." An alternative may be to have the line control computer regulate the input so that it does not allow too great a flow of work into the system. It may, for example, allow not more than three messages to be in the main processor at one time. The maximum flow permitted by the Line Control Computer may be fixed or may be governed by the count of available storage blocks.

Figure 58 shows a block diagram for a system using methods (a) and (c) above. Two levels of emergency are triggered by the number of available storage blocks, C, falling below levels C_1 and C_2. C_1 and C_2 can be adjusted according to the needs or the behavior of the system.

DANGERS OF OPERATING TOO CLOSE TO THE MAXIMUM

A well-designed real-time system should have overload conditions only very infrequently. They are an exception that must be catered to, because there is nothing to stop a number of operators sending messages at the same instant which will lock up core in the manner described. However, if the system is constantly overloaded, this is a sign of trouble. It is operating too close to its maximum. A further increase of traffic would have disastrous results.

Some real-time systems have programs designed in such a way that they *degenerate* badly from the timing point of view as their maximum load is approached. On others the timing is roughly proportional to the load. The former is likely to be true in a complex multi-thread system which calls in many programs from backing files. As the load increases, core

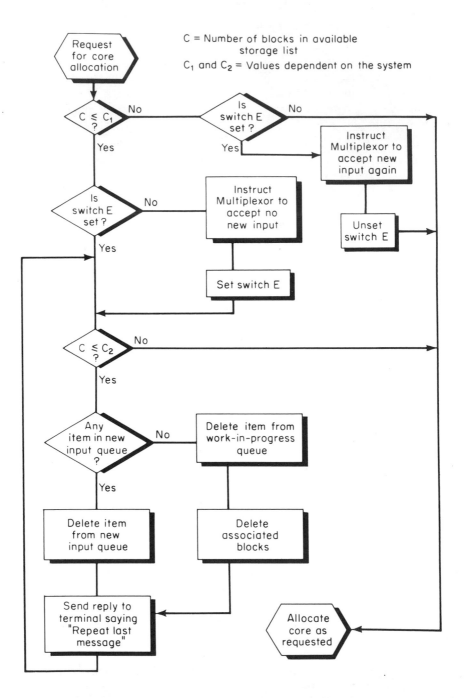

Fig. 58. Possible emergency procedure for handling overloads.

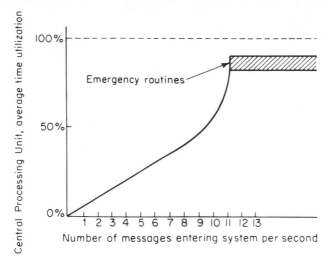

Fig. 59. Variation of the central processing unit's time utiliza-tion on a system that degenerates as it approaches maximum throughput.

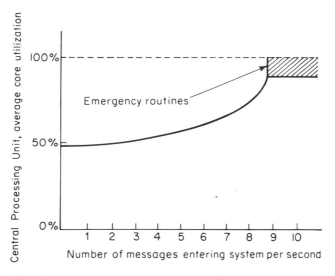

Fig. 60. Variation of the central processing unit's core utiliza-tion with load on a system that degenerates as it approaches maximum throughput.

can rapidly become used up, or the processor time can become fully used. This is illustrated in Figs. 59 and 60. In a system like this it is dangerous to operate too close to the maximum load as a slight increase will cause the system to be constantly taking emergency action.

The load on many real-time systems increases as time goes by. More terminals are added, functions are increased or more people make use of the system. It is desirable in these circumstances to know how close the system is to overload conditions. Simple *system utilization loggers* may be built into the Supervisory Programs. The Main Scheduling Routine may contain instructions which add to a counter during idling time. The counter contents are stored every time a clock interrupt occurs so that the proportion of idling time may be measured. Similarly, the count of Available Storage Blocks may be logged every time a clock interrupt occurs, and these figures are statistically analyzed later on.

24 EMERGENCY PROCEDURES: FALL-BACK

The last two chapters dealt with emergencies in which the computer can normally put matters right or, at least, continue with its work. This chapter and the next are about emergencies in which some permanent fault develops in the hardware, and where the system does what it can to patch the hole in a temporary manner. The computer cannot correct the fault by itself, and the system may have to work in a degraded fashion.

The computer will notify the operator that a fault exists and may need the operator's help in switching to a modified mode of operation.

There are three methods of reinforcing computer reliability. These are *load-sharing, duplexing* and *fall-back procedures.* If several computers share the load, the others can still handle all but the worst peak conditions when a failure develops in one of them. Rather than shutting down, the system runs "slow." A back-up or standby computer costs less in a system using several small computers than in a system with one large one. A multi-computer system may be planned so that one of them is normally "off the air" for preventative maintenance. However, several small computers may be more expensive and less powerful than one large one. The processing in such a system may be difficult to organize and may be prohibitively difficult if all the computers must share the same data files. When one computer is updating a record another might change it, and so logical errors occur. This is difficult to prevent.

"Duplexing" means that two computers are used and when a fault develops in one, a "switchover" occurs to the standby machine. This is an expensive approach. Less expensive is the use of a "fall-back" procedure by which the machine modifies its mode of operation to circumvent the error. In so doing it may give a degraded form of service but still carry out the urgent part of its job. "Fallback" is discussed in this chapter. "Duplexing" and "switchover" are discussed in the next.

GRACEFUL
DEGRADATION

One real-time system may have many different types of fall-back. With many different units in the system the question must be answered for each of these: "What will the system do when this unit fails or is taken out for maintenance?"

The type of fall-back that is needed for each of the units will depend very much on the nature of the system. Generally, the reason for a "real-time" system is that it is meant to provide uninterrupted service to its users; fallback routines are devised to circumvent an interruption of the more important functions of the system where possible. The term "fail softly" is used to mean that, when a component goes out, the system continues by using an alternative method of processing rather than failing completely. It may then have to give a degraded service, but this is "graceful degradation" rather than a total collapse of the system. The degradation will be planned so that the more vital parts of the real-time response will be maintained whenever possible.

Figure 61 shows a typical real-time configuration and indicates some of the failures that can occur. This system uses a Line Control Computer with a stored program to feed transactions to the main computer. The main computer has two channels with drums and disk files. The Line Control Machine also has a disk file—largely for fall-back reasons. If the main computer fails, the Line Control Computer can still answer the most vital messages from a limited set of data which is maintained for this purpose on its disk file. This service would, of course, be a very small part of the normal work, but it may make a big difference to the practicality of the system. In an airline reservation system, for example, answers to one type of query are vital to selling seats on the planes, and this is "Are so-and-so many seats available on such-and-such a flight?" The number of seat availability data needed to answer these queries is small and may be kept on the file attached to the Line Control Computer as well as in the main computer files, so that the Line Control Computer can answer these queries. A Line Control Computer may also log other types of transactions on its files so that these can be dealt with as soon as the main computer comes into action again.

If the Line Control Computer fails, a by-pass procedure is needed to get the more vital transactions into the main computer. The main computer may be able to accept one, or a small number of lines, directly, as shown, perhaps via its console. This permits a small amount of input to be

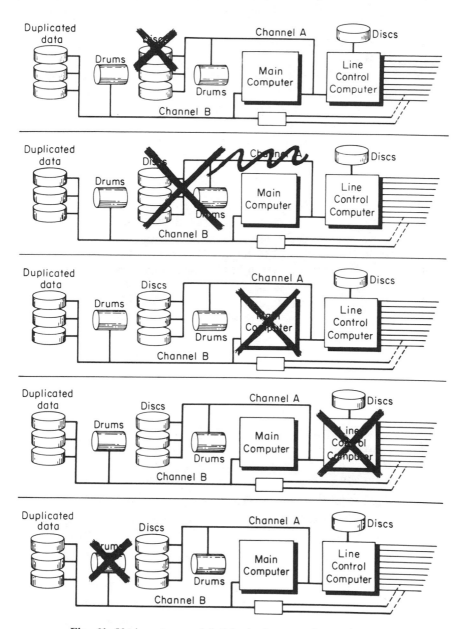

Fig. 61. Various types of fall-back that may be needed.

processed. The lines may be switched frequently so that different terminals have access to the computer.

Alternatively, the lines may have a teleprinter or other device attached to them at the computer center which is continuously printing messages that arrive. Any vital messages will be manually punched into cards and fed to the main computer via its card reader. Similarly, paper tape punches on the communication lines and a paper tape reader on the computer may form a more direct linkage. A similar by-pass will be used for output.

The telephone may also provide a by-pass procedure. A distant operator with a disabled terminal may telephone the computer center. The staff there will feed the query to the computer through a keyboard. The reply will be printed in the computer center and will go back verbally on the telephone.

The random-access files or drums in a real-time system will occasionally fail. The system will then be unable to read the data it needs. Certain parts of these data, and in some systems all the data, may be duplicated on separate files or on drums. If in the system in Fig. 61 a file or a channel goes out, the system will operate in a fall-back mode, reading and updating the duplicate copy. It may at that time start to produce for itself another duplicate copy of the vital file data in case a second failure occurs. Some programming problems associated with file fall-back are discussed below.

CATEGORIES OF FALL-BACK   There are, in general, four categories of failure for which fall-back procedures must be devised in various emergencies. These are:

1. *Failure of an input or output unit* such as a card reader, printer, tape unit, and so on. In this case the sick unit may be temporarily replaced by an alternative unit. For example, if a card reader fails, the input may be keyed in manually or sent in via a paper tape reader.

2. *Failure of a file or drum.* An alternative file or drum will be used where possible. This means that two copies of key file data should normally be kept updated.

3. *Failure of the multiplexor or line input device.* Unless switchover to a duplicate multiplexor can be made, this drastically curtails the performance of the system. Key information may still reach the computer through alternative input/output units or through line connections directly to the main computer.

4. *Failure of the main computer.* There is much to be said for designing the system with a satellite computer, possibly for line control, which

prevents total failure when the main computer goes out. Some systems switch to a duplexed or off-line computer as described in the next chapter.

ROBBING
A BANK

In a system for commercial work clerical by-pass procedures must be devised to come into operation when the most drastic failures occur. If a real-time system used in a Savings Bank goes completely "off-the-air," for example, this will not stop customers at the bank counter asking for money. A customer may ask to withdraw $1,000 when his account record in the computer is quite inaccessible. The bank teller must have some means of knowing whether he has that much money in his account. A by-pass procedure here would be for the bank teller to have access to a listing of all accounts that contain more than, say, $500. The listing would be printed out by the computer periodically. Every night details of major changes to these accounts would be printed and sent to the branches of the bank.

There is less chance of embezzling a bank which has a well-designed real-time system than one which uses other accounting methods. However, unless the fall-back and by-pass procedures are carefully designed, the bank becomes vulnerable when the computer occasionally fails.

Many banks are installing, or have installed, configurations broadly like that in Fig. 61 and in Fig. 17 in Chapter 5. Some of these, especially in the large European banks, have many distant branches on-line to the system. It might be an amusing exercise for the reader to work out methods of robbing the bank when the system or some of its components fail, and then to devise fall-back and by-pass procedures that would prevent this ingenious type of crime.

FALL-BACK AND
THE SUPERVISORY
PROGRAMS

In a system that is operational 24 hours per day, as some real-time systems must be, fall-back procedures are needed to permit preventative maintenance operations as well as emergency maintenance. It will be desirable, for example, to take the files off the system one-by-one to service them. The question must be considered "How is a unit removed from the system while it is maintaining contact with the real world?" How does the system maintain the illusion that a normal configuration still exists although it has actually been modified?

This is in fact a question for the designers of the Supervisory Programs. When the configuration of the system is changed, either because of a breakdown or because a unit is taken out for scheduled maintenance, the Supervisory Programs must modify their actions to suit the new arrangement. Normally, they are not merely maintaining the illusion to the terminal operators that the normal configuration exists; they are also maintaining it in respect to the Application Programs.

FILE
FALL-BACK

Let us consider a system in which one copy of the *vital* part of the file records occupies five physical modules of whatever files are used. This may mean five drums or five sets of disks, and so on.

In order to safeguard this essential part of the data, the system uses the philosophy that there will always be two copies of it on-line. To do this, twelve physical modules are used, making the assumption that not

Fig. 62. File fall-back. The black bands in each file represent that vital part of the data which must be duplicated. The vital data is distributed evenly between the files and channels as far as possible. File 4 has failed, so the duplicate copy of the vital data is being copied from File 12 to File 5.

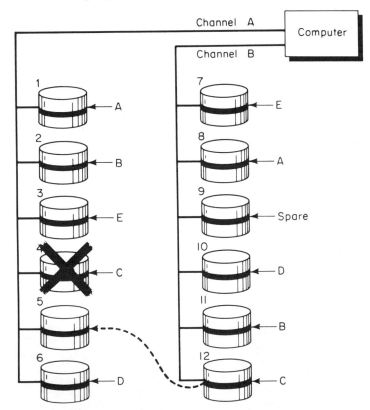

more than two will be out for scheduled or emergency maintenance at any one time. This is shown in Fig. 62.

The Application Programs refer to a set of data without knowing on which physical module it is kept. They refer in fact to "logical" modules A, B, C, D and E, related to the nature and volume of the data and not to the mechanical consideration of where they are kept. The Supervisory Programs have a table which gives the physical locations of the first and second copies of each logical module.

Thus the Supervisory Programs maintain the illusion with respect to the Application Programs and to the terminal operators of having five logical modules. To the computer operator, however, they present the reality of having twelve physical modules as in Fig. 62, some of which may fail or may be taken out for maintenance.

Figure 63 gives an example of the type of status table by which the Supervisory Programs will obtain the machine address of files containing a given logical module. When a physical module fails or is taken out for maintenance, this is indicated in the table. The duplicate copy is then used

Fig. 63. Status table for cyclic file fall-back.

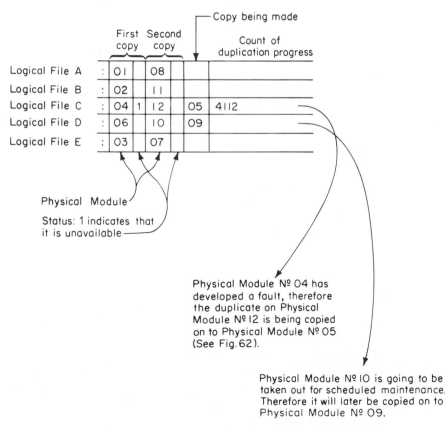

Physical Module № 04 has developed a fault, therefore the duplicate on Physical Module № 12 is being copied on to Physical Module № 05 (See Fig. 62).

Physical Module № 10 is going to be taken out for scheduled maintenance. Therefore it will later be copied on to Physical Module № 09.

by the Supervisory Programs, and this itself will be copied onto a spare module.

The physical module onto which it is copied is given in the status table.

The copying may take place at the same time as messages are being processed in real-time, or the processing may be stopped for a few minutes while the copying is done. In the former case, a problem arises when records are updated. Should the original be written alone, or has it been copied onto the new file yet? In the latter case both copies of it must be updated. To indicate this a count is kept of the rewriting process. This count is stored in the status table (Fig. 63). It must be inspected whenever this logical file is updated to see whether the duplicate is also to be updated.

PSEUDO FILE ADDRESSES   The Application Programs will give a *pseudo file address* to the Supervisory Programs, which is in effect an address for the logical file, not the actual physical file. The Supervisory Programs will convert this to the machine address needed for reading or writing the record in question. This conversion may be very simple. The address within a disk module or drum may be correct, for example, and only the number of the disk module will have to be changed. If two duplicate files must be updated, this will be done by the Supervisory Program. If there is a choice of duplicated records that may be read, the Supervisory Program will read the most convenient one so that access times and queues are minimized.

When a disk unit or drum that has been unavailable is replaced in the system, this does not involve any moving of data since programs always address logical modules. A logical module may at any given time refer to any physical module in the system. When a file is replaced in the system, it simply becomes a spare for the next time file fall-back is needed.

File throughput should not be affected by this fall-back scheme, except when the duplicating process is running in parallel with real-time work. Even then it will only cause a slight delay as the duplicating may be given very low priority and will take place only when there is time available.

MULTIPLE FALL-BACK   If the vital data occupy only a small portion of a file, one file may be used as the fall-back area for more than one other file if the need arises.

There are in general two fall-back conditions to be considered: *single fall-back* when one item has failed and *double or multiple fall-back* when more than one has failed. Planning for multiple fall-back conditions can involve much extra programming, and there is a limit to what is worthwhile.

FAILURE OF
INPUT/OUTPUT
UNITS

Just as the Supervisory Programs modify their action when a file fails, as described above, so they will modify their action also when an input or output unit fails. A fall-back routine for an input/output unit may be entered when that unit is found by the programs to be unavailable or to give continual error conditions.

Examples of alternative actions that may be taken when such a condition is detected are:

1. *Console failure.* If the computer is unable to send a message out on the console, as normal, it may send it on an output printer.

2. *Paper Tape Reader failure.* For a fall-back condition on this unit the normal interrupt routine may be modified to ignore interrupts from the unit. Alternative means of input such as a card reader or a keyboard may be used for vital messages.

3. *Tape or Card Punch failure.* As an alternative output to a punch, a magnetic tape unit may be used. The output may be punched into cards off-line or may be punched on-line later when the punch is in use again.

4. *Printer failure.* Similarly, if a printer fails the output may be written on tape for off-line printing or later on-line printing. Vital messages may be sent to the console typewriter as an alternative.

5. *Tape Unit failure.* An alternative tape unit will be used as a substitute, and the Supervisory Programs will modify the output address as required.

RECOVERY
FROM
FALL-BACK

Recovery from fall-back, that is, restoring the system to the condition that existed before fall-back occurred, must deal with any output that was written on an alternative unit during fall-back. This may be done on-line or off-line. The operator will normally be given the choice which may depend upon how long the system has been in fall-back mode, and how much output has been written on the alternative unit. Small amounts of output will usually be dealt with on-line while real-time operation continues. Large amounts will be handled off-line. The Supervisory Programs may print a note to the operator saying how many records are on the alternative fall-back unit.

25 EMERGENCY PROCEDURES: SWITCHOVER

Real-time systems which must have a high degree of reliability because of the nature of the application sometimes use two duplexed computers. Only one of them is on-line. The other is standing by, ready to take over when a fault occurs in the on-line machine.

This, of course, is very expensive, but a surprising number of applications have found it economically justifiable. It is easier to justify the standby computer if it is doing lower priority off-line work which can be interrupted when a switchover occurs. In many applications there is a need for off-line computing as well as the real-time work, and a good systems analyst can take advantage of this fact in designing a duplexed system.

It is the responsibility of the systems analyst to study the reliability requirements of the application. Some fallback procedure such as was described in the last chapter may be sufficient, but if not, it may be necessary to duplex the main computer. Using three computers would, of course, make the system still more reliable, but only systems with a very exceptional reliability requirement can afford this, such as the system for monitoring the first manned moon shots in the U.S.A.

COMPUTERS OPERATING IN PARALLEL Some special applications use the two computers operating in parallel. The results of the two machines are compared. If they differ, then the decision must be made which is in error. This decision would probably be made by an operator with the help of diagnostic routines. This expensive technique was used on Project Mercury for monitoring the early manned space shots and on BMEWS, the Ballistic Missile Early Warning Systems.

242

STANDBY COMPUTER A commercial installation is unlikely to use a parallel
DOING OTHER WORK approach of this type. Here the standby computer will
normally be doing other work. Typical of such configurations are Reference Systems 5 and 6 illustrated in Chapter 5. These
two systems have a programmed Line Control Computer as well as a main
computer, and two types of switchover may occur, main computer switchover and line computer switchover. A system in which the lines go indirectly
into the computer has only one form of switchover. If a line control computer is used separately from the main computer, certain procedures can be
built into the switchover process which help to prevent loss of data during
switchover. This is illustrated later in this chapter.

THE OFF-LINE The off-line computer, while it may be carrying on
COMPUTER work of its own, may be programmed to keep watch
KEEPING WATCH on the on-line machine at the same time. For example, a clock interrupt in the off-line machine may
cause it to make a check on the functioning of the on-line machine once
every 500 milliseconds or so. The on-line machine may send a signal to the
off-line machine every time the Main Scheduling Routine of the on-line
computer is entered. If the off-line computer does not receive this signal
between its periodic interrupts, it will investigate. It will send a message to
the on-line computer, interrupting it. The on-line computer may take one
of three alternatives:

1. It may reply telling the off-line machine to initiate switchover.

2. It may reply telling the off-line computer that it knows of the situation and can take corrective action itself.

3. It may fail to reply. In this case, the off-line computer initiates
   switchover.

This procedure is illustrated in Fig. 64.

Such a technique increases the alertness of the system, but gives the
off-line machine freedom to carry out any other form of computing. Coupling
the computers in this way is not very expensive.

MANUAL Many real-time systems, however, do not have the
SWITCHOVER computers coupled. The on-line machine itself, or
its operators, must detect any catastrophic malfunc-
tioning in the system. This may be apparent at the terminals. The computer operator will then initiate switchover.

If manual switchover is used the operator must be sufficiently alert to

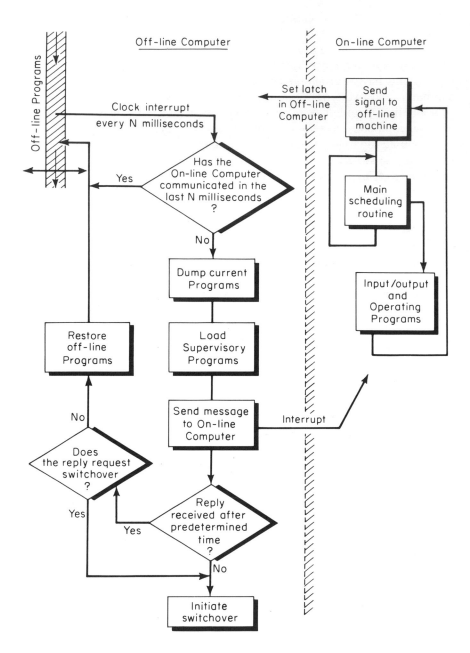

Fig. 64. The Off-Line Computer keeping watch on the health of the On-Line Computer.

execute it quickly. The computer may be equipped with a horn which it blows to alert the operator.

The system may be designed so that the operator can initiate switchover immediately, or it may be necessary to make the standby computer ready before switching.

There are thus three levels of speed in the switchover process:

1. Automatic switchover   Typical time: 1 to 5 seconds
2. Manual switchover, immediate Typical time: 10 to 50 seconds
3. Manual switchover, after readying Typical time: 1 to 5 minutes

If the process of making the standby computer ready involves switching it on, this may be very slow. A typical "second-generation" computer with transistor circuitry may take about 2 to 4 minutes for the power-up process in a room at a temperature of about 70°F. In a colder room it will take longer—10 minutes or more at 50°F. If drums or disks have to be started, this may take 10 minutes or more.

Normally, the standby machine will be switched on with real-time programs ready for loading from tape or disk. When an unscheduled switchover occurs, the standby machine will then have to continue its current work until a suitable checkpoint is reached, or else interrupt its work and dump its core onto tape or files. This done, the new Supervisory and Application Programs will be loaded, and the operator can switch the line control equipment and the necessary files and tapes on the computer which now becomes on-line.

ERROR DETECTION   The on-line machine will detect and analyze its own errors as indicated in Chapter 22. The diagnostic procedure will tell it whether the error was transient and solid, or perhaps that it was a program error. In the event of a catastrophic error this routine will indicate to it, if it can, that switchover is its only course of action. This knowledge will be typed out for the operator, and either the operator or the computer will initiate the switchover process.

The computer may, however, be too sick to diagnose its own illness. It may be unable to initiate switchover because the circuitry which would enable it to do so is faulty. One computer cannot, therefore, be relied upon to initiate switchover. A system which uses automatic switchover must have a standby machine capable of detecting when the on-line machine is faulty and taking matters into its own hands.

If the lights stop flickering on one of these two consoles in American Airlines' SABRE System because a failure has occurred in the on-line machine, the standby computer will immediately take over. In designing a real-time system this switchover procedure can be manual or automatic, depending upon how fast it must occur.

The fault that triggers off switchover may be a hardware fault or a program fault. The on-line computer will commonly have a watchdog timer which must be reset every so often. If a given period of time elapses without its being reset, it interrupts whatever program is being run and restarts it. This program may have a logic fault which under the current circumstances causes it to go into a closed loop. If it persists in going into a loop, the Supervisory Program will either decide not to process the message in question, or else will initiate switchover. Similarly, other program faults, such as attempting to transfer to an invalid location, will cause the Supervisory Program to make the same decision. Error interrupts of the type that these faults cause may interrupt the off-line computer as well as that in which the fault occurs. The off-line computer may then interrogate the on-line machine to determine its condition.

Once switchover has occurred a second switchover, i.e., back to the original equipment configuration, should not be allowed to take place until a service message is sent by the operator to indicate that the machine in question is capable of resuming its duties. This prevents continuous switching back and forth.

EFFECT ON TERMINAL OPERATORS The effect of the switchover on the terminal operators must be considered. Where possible they should not be left in confusion, not knowing why there has been no reply to their last message. If the switchover is a scheduled one, so that the engineer can work on the on-line computer, for example, a message can be sent to all terminal operators saying that the system will be inoperative for two minutes or so.

If it is an emergency rather than a scheduled switchover, it may or may not be possible to notify the operators. However, some message may be sent to the operators by the machine which takes over, such as "Repeat last message and check."

NO LOSS OF TRANSACTIONS It is vitally important in most systems that no transactions should be lost when the switchover occurs. With an enquiry message this consideration is not too important because the operator will naturally send the enquiry again if he does not receive a satisfactory reply. However, if the message is one which updates vital data in the files it is important that, when switchover occurs, the files do indeed become updated and that no record is updated twice by the same transaction. In a banking system, for example, such an error might result in a sum of money not being paid into an account or being paid in twice.

SEQUENTIAL
NUMBERING
OF MESSAGES

The best technique for avoiding this situation usually involves adding sequential numbers to the messages. The number of the last message to update a record on the file is put on that record. In the event of switchover the message number may be compared with the number on the record to see whether that message has in fact updated the file or not.

The sequential number may be added by the operator of the terminal, by the computer or by a programmed line control computer if there is one. It may be regarded as undesirable for the operator to add the number because it gives him extra work to do. A very convenient means of sequential numbering would be to build a terminal which adds such numbers automatically, though to the author's knowledge no such terminal is in use.

If the system has no intermediate link between the terminal and the computer which can add sequential numbers, such as a line control computer, then the computer itself may give a number to the messages. The sequence of events would be as follows:

1. The terminal operator sends the message.
2. It is received by the computer which adds a sequential number to it.
3. The computer sends a message to the terminal giving the number in question.
4. The computer updates the files and writes the number on the record.
5. The computer again sends a message to the operator when the file updating is completed satisfactorily.

If a fault occurs between the first message to the operator and the second and switchover is initiated, the operator will not receive the second reply. He will, however, know the message number. A check message may therefore be sent to the computer that has taken over, and this is programmed to examine the relevant file record to see whether it has been updated or not.

If the fault occurs before the first message or after the second there is no need to worry.

This process may be automated further if the system uses a separate programmable Line Control Computer as with Reference Systems 5 and 6. The line control computer may then add the sequential number and keep a transaction table, giving the numbers of all the messages in process, with the terminals from which they came.

As shown in Fig. 65, the message number is also stored in the computer, probably in the Message Reference Block. It is not deleted from the computer storage until the files have been updated and the computer has sent a reply.

In such a system two forms of switchover might take place: the line

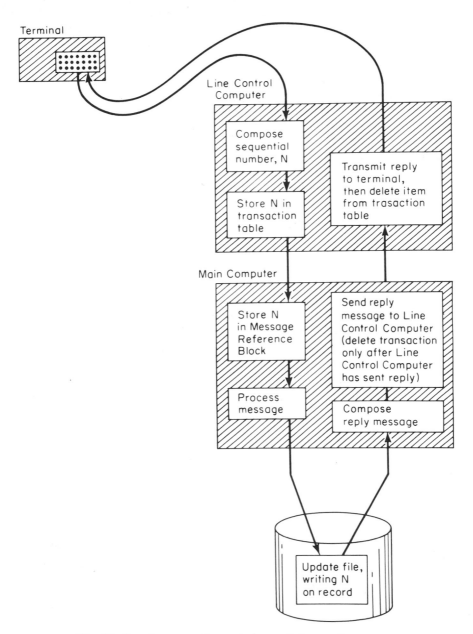

Fig. 65. Security precautions during switchover. Every message is stored in the transaction table of the Line Control Computer until the system sends a reply. If Main Computer switchover occurs, the items in the Line Control Computer's transaction table must be checked to see if the records they relate to have been updated. If Line Control Computer switchover occurs, the Main Computer sends reply messages again to all the transactions in its core. If a terminal does not receive a reply to a transaction the operator must re-send the transaction.

control computer may be switched to a standby line computer, or the computer may be switched. If the computer is switched, the one that takes over must examine the transaction table in the line control machine and check whether each item in it has in fact updated the appropriate files. If line control computer switchover takes place, the main computer must transmit all its items again to make sure that the operator receives a reply. At this time it will notify the operator that line computer switchover has taken place. The operator must then make certain that he receives a reply to every message. If he does not receive a reply, this will indicate that the transaction in question has not updated the files, and it must be sent again.

In the unlikely event of the main computer and line control computer failing at the same time, uncertainty may exist. However, if either of these preserves their core contents it is still possible to recover. Sending the sequential number to the operator does, however, give the facility for a manual check when an emergency occurs.

One other circumstance can lead to uncertainty about the updating of a record. If a failure occurs in the file writing mechanism, this may possibly take place between the time the sequential number is being written and the time the field in question is being updated.

This is an unlikely event if the sequential number is written next to the field in question, though it can happen. If very high reliability is needed on certain records, this uncertainty can be overcome by writing the record twice on different files. When a file breaks down the seconding field will be compared with the first and, knowing the sequential number, this will reveal which one is correct. If the critical field is written twice in the record with the sequential number in between, this will also enable a program to discover how far the writing has progressed when the failure occurred, and so the correct value of the field may be ascertained.

DESIGN AREAS AFFECTED   It will be seen that if reliability is to be maintained during emergencies such as switchover, procedures must be devised which affect many areas of system design. They affect the Supervisory Programs, some of the Application Programs, the file layout, the line control programs and the discipline at the distant operator sets.

Discipline at the operator sets is especially important because no computer programs can prevent data from being lost in emergencies if the operators do not obey the rules of the system.

Reliability considerations and emergency procedures must, therefore, be thought about from the start in the design of a real-time system. It is wrong to plan these procedures as an afterthought when the main programs have already been designed.

REAL-TIME PROGRAM
TESTING TECHNIQUES

26 DIFFICULTIES OF REAL-TIME PROGRAM TESTING

There is a tremendous difference in complexity between the programs in a small single-thread real-time system, for example, in a Savings Bank, and in a large multi-programmed system for airline booking. Hence there is a big difference in the testing techniques required for their program.

In the large real-time systems that have been installed to date, program testing has proved extremely difficult. The crises and delays associated with the testing have been considerable. It is apparent that this is one of the fundamental problems of real-time and that more advanced techniques than those for conventional systems are required.

The purpose of this section of the book is to look at the difficulties encountered in testing real-time programs and to draw up a plan that may help future systems to pass more smoothly through the testing phase. Program testing aids that are necessary for this are outlined.

It is important in a real-time system that testing should be included in the plans for the design of the system. It cannot be separated in any of its phases from the design, implementation and maintenance of the system. This is probably the most important single principle for success in real-time testing. A design policy that aims only at the perfect running system and ignores its suitability for testing is unrealistic and will lead to chaos at installation time.

Accordingly, the Supervisory Programs and other parts of the system must have aids built in for use in testing. These must be designed into the system from the beginning.

Program testing aids may take several man-years to write for a large system. Different aids are needed for different phases of testing, and it is vital that those for each phase should be available and debugged before the phase begins. For this reason the writing of testing Support Programs must be scheduled from the beginning and must be given high priority. One of the causes of delay in some systems that have been installed was that the aids were not ready on time.

Even with adequate aids the time taken to test a program for a complex system may be as long as the time required to write the specifications and coding. Some major systems have used unrealistic schedules because of an underestimate of the time needed for testing.

It is recommended that each system should have a team to handle testing. The team should cover the Supervisory and Application programming areas. It should be responsible for writing the testing aids and for surveying all programs in the system to assess their adequacy for testing.

It is hoped that the following chapters will provide a guide for the preliminary work of such a team.

The difficulties of real-time program testing are caused by six factors not found in conventional systems:

1. The use of terminals and lines for input and output.
2. The use of specially engineered equipment that is not on an "off-the-shelf" computer.
3. Multi-programming and multi-processing.
4. Unpredictability.
5. An added reliability requirement.
6. A very complex interrelation between the programs.

These factors are considered below.

INPUT AND OUTPUT   The input will be from many terminals or remote devices. When testing, it will be necessary to use predetermined input to the programs being tested. However, it would be too slow to use actual terminals; moreover, the terminals will probably not be available in the early testing phases. For this reason the input must be *simulated*. For example, it may be stored on tape and fed to the programs being tested by means of a *Test Supervisor Program*. For a scientific application, input signals from radar or other devices must be simulated.

Terminals, displays or other remote devices are also used for output. The same reasons that apply to input make it impractical to use actual displays or terminals. Some means of replacing these is required, such as recording the output on magnetic tape and later printing it.

The input rate of conventional systems is fixed by a computer which reads cards or tape as required. On real-time systems the input rate will fluctuate. There will be a finite probability of the system becoming overloaded. When an overload occurs the system may have to take emergency action. A means of varying the input rate must be found, and means of feeding enough messages to the system to test its overload action must be devised.

SPECIAL   Equipment especially engineered for an application
EQUIPMENT   is commonly used on real-time systems. This may not
                       be ready for the early phases of testing. A machine
with adequate files may not be ready, or a specially engineered computer
may not be delivered in time. For this reason the first testing may have to
use a specially written program to simulate the system on an existing computer configuration.

The required line control equipment also may not be available for the
early phases of testing. A computer program may be used to simulate this
and its input and output.

MULTI-PROGRAMMING For a complex system specially written Supervisory
AND   Programs are likely to be used. It is probable that
MULTI-PROCESSING these will not be completely debugged when they are
                      used with the Application Programs. A small number of subtle errors usually escape the early testing. Controversy will arise
as to whether an error resulted from a fault in a Supervisory Program or
from a fault in an Application Program. This may be especially troublesome if one team writes the Supervisory Programs and another writes the
Application Programs, as often happens. Or it may happen if the interface
between the Supervisory Programs and Application Programs is not very
clearly defined. Means are required for determining whether an error lies in
the Supervisory or the Application Program.

In a similar manner, when two Application Programs are in core at
the same time, it may be difficult to tell which caused an error. One may
write incorrectly on file records used by another and so cause trouble at
a later time without giving an indication of the cause of the trouble.

When more than one computer is used there may be difficulty in finding out in which processor the error occurred. For example, when a
message is processed by a multiplexor program and by the main computer,
it may be difficult to determine whether the error is in the multiplexor or
the main computer.

When Supervisory Programs are written especially for an application,
it will probably be desirable to start testing the Application Programs before the Supervisory Programs are fully developed. Macro-instructions

which simulate Supervisory Program macro-instructions in a simple manner will be required.

In a duplexed system, switchover between processors may need to be tested. Some means must be devised to feed messages to the system and to receive replies when switchover is being tested.

UNPREDICTABILITY   In a large real-time system, messages will enter the system at random and many partially processed messages will be in core at one time. Whereas in batch processing the sequence of events follows one of a small number of preplanned routes, in a real-time multi-programmed system there is an almost infinite number of possible combinations. It is, therefore, very difficult to remove the last traces of errors from the system. This has proved a tremendous problem in some "multi-thread" systems.

The Supervisory System is designed so that interrupts (or traps) occur frequently—more than a hundred times a second in some large systems. The exact time when an interrupt occurs cannot be predicted before the test, nor can it be easily ascertained after the test. Because of the interrupts the sequence of events in the test is not repeatable. The file interrupts alone would prevent exact duplication of a test because the "end-of-record" or "record-ready" signals may be many milliseconds off the timing of the previous run. This means that some errors will not be "solid." An error may occur once but defy further investigation. Furthermore, an attempt to pin down such an error by using techniques for logging interrupts will probably destroy the timing relationship that caused the error.

Another "non-solid" error will be caused by errors on transmission lines. In some cases it may be difficult to differentiate between a random transmission error and an unrepeatable program error.

In the later stages of testing, when the input is from remote terminals, an error may be discerned only very infrequently because of the slow rate of input. An error which only appears once a day at unpredictable times could be very difficult to track down. Yet a number of such errors in the operational system could cause much trouble, especially if there is a risk that they might damage file data. In practice, the last traces or errors have lingered on in systems now working, long after the program testing phase was ended.

**ADDED
RELIABILITY
REQUIREMENTS**   In batch processing systems it is possible to begin operational running before all the most remote errors are removed. If an error occurs during operational running it is possible to stop the run and look for the cause of the error. The day's work will end later than scheduled.

This is not possible in a real-time system, and because of the changing time relationships more subtle errors will exist which show up only infrequently in a real-time system. In general, if program errors occur after operational cutover, they will be much more difficult to find than on a conventional system and cause much more trouble. The pre-cutover debugging must therefore be very thorough in a real-time system.

However thorough the advance testing, it is virtually certain that there will be some requirement for testing during operational running. Some errors will slip through, and program modifications will be demanded thoughout the life of the system.

Testing during operational running will be difficult because the real-time system must demand all necessary time for accomplishing its purpose. Only such time as is left over could be made available for other functions such as testing, and then only in small installments.

A program error may cause the program to "run wild." In ordinary data-processing this risk may be tolerated since the loss of time or data can easily be repaired. In real-time systems the risk is much more serious unless the functioning part of the system can be protected by rigorous hardware measures.

A program error may cause damage to a disk file or drum that may contain vital records for the customer's business. Means of file protection and reconstruction are required. Because of this problem, testing after cutover will be difficult. It is not practical to have an off-line machine with, for example, ten disk files which are used only for testing.

In view of these problems it may prove impracticable to have a system which operates 24 hours a day and does not have additional hardware for testing purposes.

ADDED COMPLEXITY   The programs for systems at the top end of the range in Fig. 12 have more than 100,000 lines of coding. This means that many different programmers must contribute. When such a large number of programmers are involved, the work of coordinating what they write is extremely difficult.

The work of one programmer must interface with that of many other programmers, perhaps in different physical locations. Invariably, the specifications change, so that when the programs are finally executed together at the testing phase they do not combine exactly. Discrepancies are discovered; parts have to be rewritten.

Because of the difficulty of combining the work of so many people the program testing effort is not directly proportional to the size of the system. For a very large system, testing will be a very major effort.

The large numbers of programmers required for a large system also create major recruiting problems, and managers almost always resort to hiring personnel with little or no programming experience. Many of the programs in an enormously complex system are thus the first programs these programmers write. Most programmers anywhere make many errors in their first programs, and this adds further to the difficulties of program testing in complex real-time systems.

The catalogue of difficulties above should convince the reader that careful attention is required for system testing. The following chapters attempt to indicate what may be done in tackling the problem.

27 TYPES OF PROGRAMMING AIDS REQUIRED

In order to facilitate the testing of real-time programs and systems, a number of Support Programs are needed. Most complex systems have needed a formidable array of such program testing aids.

These are likely to fall into the following categories:

A. Testing the Application Programs

1. Loaders
2. Librarian and Maintenance Programs
3. Data Generators
4. Test Supervisor Program
5. Simulation of the Supervisory Program
6. Error Detection Aids
7. Overload Simulators
8. Off-Line Post-Edit Programs
9. Off-Line Pre-Edit Programs

B. Testing the Supervisory Programs

10. Pseudo Application Programs
11. A Macro Exerciser

C. Testing the Multiplexor Programs

12. A Program for Simulating the Multiplexor
13. A Multiplexor Dump
14. Aids for Feeding and Logging Messages

This chapter describes briefly what these programs are. The subsequent chapters will explain in more detail how the key program testing aids may work and how they are utilized.

A. TESTING THE APPLICATION PROGRAMS

1. *Loaders*

Two types of loaders are required for testing:

(a) Core loaders which load the core with data records, input test data, programs to be tested, Supervisory Programs and debugging aids. The initial conditions for the test may be set up by the loader.

(b) File loaders which load files with data records and programs.

2. *Librarian and Maintenance Programs*

A Librarian system will be required for the creation and maintenance of program and data tapes. This will have the ability to patch, add, delete or change any subroutine, division or package on the tapes. This may run on a small off-line computer. File maintenance programs will also be required. In the later stages of testing the files will be kept permanently loaded. A program to add, delete, or change any records will be required.

When a test takes place certain file data records may be changed. File program records may also be temporarily changed by patches. It will be necessary to reverse these changes after the test. A program may be used to note all records that are changed and rewrite these after the test. A program will also be needed to originate and change addresses on a file loading tape. This may also run on a small off-line machine.

3. *Data Generators*

The input to the test runs should come from a central authority rather than from the programmer himself. Only in this way can sufficient standardization be imposed to make sure that all programmers are using *exactly* the same message and data formats.

There are two methods of producing the required input messages. In the later stages of testing, actual messages and data should be used as far as possible. These might, for example, be produced from collected paper tape or from actual input to an agent set. However, in the earlier stages programmers will need to devise logically arranged batches of specified data. For this purpose data generator programs may be helpful.

On a commercial application descriptions of data records and input messages, in a format such as the Data Division of COBOL, may be stored on a *Pilot Tape*. The descriptions should be submitted only by qualified personnel. The required messages and data will be generated from this and stored on file or tape.

For a scientific application the same form of generator will be needed which produces data as they will appear in core when they arrive from analogue-digital converters or whatever the input is.

Messages or input data of the appropriate format are stored on tape or possibly disk, and are read into the computer at appropriate times in the testing by a *Test Supervisor Program.*

On an application with a complex set of file records, it will be necessary to produce file data before testing. Generators can help in this but cannot do the whole job. There has to be a logical linkage between records, and much of this will have to be built up by hand.

4. *Test Supervisor Program*

The function of reading in the above generated input data, and similarly writing the output on tape, is here described as being a function of a Test Supervisor Program. In different applications this has been called a variety of names such as the Test Loader, the Terminal Simulator, Simulated Input/Output Control, and so on.

It is suggested that a Test Supervisor Program should also be used to enter control cards and patches for testing. The prime reason for tape input/output is increased speed. Manual entry of test input messages through terminal sets would be time consuming.

The function of the program is illustrated in Figs. 68 and 69 in Chapter 29. It reads input messages, patches and control cards from tape. It sets up the test and introduces messages to the Main Supervisory Programs, so that they appear as messages from the terminals of the system. Outgoing messages are similarly handled by a routine which logs them on tape.

In early phases of testing, messages are entered directly into the New Input Queue before the testing. Testing then takes place, and the output, instead of going to a multiplexor, goes directly to the Test Supervisor Program, which writes it on tape. No queuing will occur. In a later phase the Test Supervisor may send the input messages through a multiplexor.

In Fig. 79 in Chapter 33, the multiplexor treats them as though they were output messages, but the line on which it sends them out is "wrapped around," and hence it reads them and sends them to the computer as if they were messages from a terminal. The reverse process applies to the output from the computer.

The Test Supervisor must be designed so that it can handle both the early and later phases of testing as described in subsequent chapters.

5. *Simulation of the Supervisory Programs*

If the Main Supervisory Programs are being written specially for the application, then the testing of Application Programs will probably begin before the Supervisory Programs are complete. Testing must then proceed with simulated Supervisory Programs rather than with the actual ones. This may also enable a standard existing computer to be used rather than a configuration not yet built. The Supervisory Program Simulator should include the macro-instructions that the actual Supervisory Programs will use. It will create any records to which the Application Programs refer by using the Data Generators. Any records or messages which the Application Program attempts to write will be written on tape. No queuing will occur. There will be no multi-programming at this stage.

6. *Error Detection Aids*

In order to help the programmer find his errors, various aids are needed such as dumps, traces, snapshots and logging programs. A compromise must be reached between providing the programmer with insufficient evidence to locate an error and giving him too much, in which case the system is slowed down excessively and too much paper is produced. It is often desirable to define various modes of test running which differ in the quantity of print-out produced. Three possible modes are described briefly in the next chapter.

The possible types of print-out are as follows:

(a) *Core dumps*. Three levels of dump may be used. First, a complete core dump is possible—a Utility Program. Second, a dump of changes in core has been useful in some systems. Core is dumped onto tape or disk before and after a test, and only changes in core are printed out. This is not considered worth implementing in systems such as an airline reservation system, in which the work is mainly the manipulation of data between queues and files, but in a process control system, for example, where change is less frequent, it may be worthwhile. Finally, a dump of Working Storage, accumulators, and so on could be used. This might be the most common type of dump. Dumps of the latter type will be incorporated in the tracing and snapshot programs. In some systems, dumps which give symbolic addresses have been printed. This might be regarded as a luxury.

(b) *File dumps*. A program may be required to read the contents of certain specified file records.

(c) *Tracing*. Three levels of trace are possible—an Instruction Trace which operates on every instruction executed, a Branch Trace which records only transfers, and a "Macro Trace" which records pertinent information when certain macro-instructions are executed, or possibly only when entering and leaving an Application Program via the Supervisory Programs. It is suggested that a reasonably good programmer should not require the Instruction Trace or Branch Trace. The Macro Trace, however, will be extremely valuable. Without it, it would be very difficult to follow what happened on some programs in a multi-programming operation.

There can be several levels of Macro Trace, depending upon how much information is printed out. It is suggested that two levels might be used, one which merely records the macro-instructions, and the other which records them and also dumps working storage and pertinent registers on each occasion.

(d) *Message logging*. Where the multiplexor is used and where there is a possibility that errors may occur in the computer or the multiplexor or the lines, it may be necessary to log input or output messages as they enter or leave the computer in order to determine where an error occurred.

(e) *Interrupt logging*. When testing in a real-time mode of operation, interrupts will occur at random times. Errors will probably arise due to the fact that Application Programs have been interrupted and control returned to them after priority routines were executed. It is therefore essential to know what priority interrupts occurred during the execution of each Application Program segment.

A trace for interrupts, similar to the Macro Trace, would be useful. However, as there are many different types of interrupt this would require many instructions in core. Furthermore, the timing relationships would be upset by the duration of the trace routines. Instead, it is suggested that each priority routine should contain one instruction which sets a bit in a core location characteristic of that routine.

The area where the bits are set is then dumped by the Macro Trace program above. This method is simple, quick to program and does not upset the timing relationships. However, if the same type of interrupt occurs twice during the execution of one Program Segment it will give no indication of this.

A slightly more complicated variation might be to store the return address for that priority routine, thereby indicating that such a routine has occurred. However, it is thought that merely setting a bit will be adequate and that this one instruction might be left permanently in the program, even during operational running.

(f) *Snapshots*. When an error occurs in the logic of an Application Program the programmer may require a dump at a specific instruction in order to find out what is happening. This facility may be written into a simulated Supervisory Program so that it is requested by means of a control card. The instruction in question is replaced by a transfer to an appropriate subroutine which executes the instruction and then dumps the required data.

It would be more difficult to use this aid in later phases of testing when the actual Supervisory Program is used.

(g) *Debug Macros*. The Macro Trace, Message Logging and Interrupt Logging routines described above would be built into the framework of the

Supervisory System. It is possible to allow the Application Programmer to build some aids into his programs if he wishes.

By using Debugging Macros at a predetermined point he might be able to take such actions as dumping core, working storage or registers. Debug Macros may be inconvenient to use because of the difficulty of fitting them into a fixed-length segment of program, and reassembling this. Most of the errors that are introduced by progressing from unit testing of programs to a higher phase of testing could be detected by using a facility to dump core areas when entering or leaving the Main Scheduling Routine.

(h) *Priority error dump.* When an error occurs in a real-time system, it is normal to interrupt into a priority error routine rather than to stop the machine. It would be advantagous to make this priority routine dump all information required for debugging.

The error detection aids listed above are likely to give rise to a large quantity of print-out and to slow the system down very considerably. As the demand for time in a large system under test will be heavy, it is desirable to moderate the use of these aids. A system may, for this reason, use different modes of testing which vary in the amount or type of data they record and print out. The modes may be switched on by control cards, by certain messages entering the system, or by other factors. This is described in more detail in the next chapter.

7. *Overload Simulators*

Most multi-thread real-time systems have a Supervisory Program which takes some form of emergency action on overload conditions. It is vital that the system should be tested under overload conditions, and this may be done in one of two ways. The system may have enough messages fed to it to cause an actual overload, or an overload may be simulated. In a system with a very high rate of input the former may be difficult.

An overload may be simulated in two ways. Application Programs may be used which utilize computer and channel time, or adjustments may be made to key words in a Supervisory Program so that it thinks it has an overload and takes the appropriate action. For example, when available core storage becomes low it takes action; hence, if the word telling it how much core is left is modified, it can be made to behave as though a genuine overload condition existed.

8. *Off-Line Post-Edit Programs*

The tapes which are produced on a test run may be printed out off-line. It will be of value to edit, format and sort this print-out. It will also be advisable to print selectively to cut the excessive quantity of paper produced and the long print time for a test run with many transactions and elaborate dumping.

For example, the Macro Trace may contain bits set by interrupt logging. Indications such as these may be translated into easily understandable messages saying what interrupts have occurred.

Where dumps are made by macro-instructions, these may be numbered and the numbers used to print selected dumps only. It may be convenient for the programmer to have dumps associated with the passage of a message through the system printed in sequence for that message, or alternatively, to have dumps in the sequence of macro-instructions. This can be achieved by an off-line sort.

If Input and Output Messages are logged it will be convenient to edit these tapes so that Input and equivalent Output Messages are printed together. This will be useful for constructing a *Test Results Tape* which can be referred to when a test is repeated with the same data in a more advanced phase of testing.

9. *Off-Line Pre-Edit Programs*

It is desirable to find as many errors as possible before the test run occurs by careful checking of the program. A computer pre-edit run can assist in this checking. This is normally done by a compiler processor. In addition, however, an off-line run could check those features that relate to the Supervisory System. It could scan the program for disobedience of rules relating to Supervisory System macros; it could check, for example, for illegal operation codes, incorrect segmentation of programs, disobedience of core utilization rules, invalid relationships between macro-instructions, and so on. This could save much difficult error tracing later on when the macro-instructions are performed incorrectly.

B. TESTING THE SUPERVISORY PROGRAMS

10. *Pseudo Application Programs*

Data for testing individual segments of the Supervisory Programs will probably be written by the programmers as needed. For testing the Supervisory Programs as a whole, Application Programs are needed. Simple Pseudo Application Programs should be written for this purpose.

11. *Macro Exerciser*

A more thorough test of the Supervisory System should come from a macro exerciser. This is a program designed like a diagnostic, to execute repetitively all the Supervisory System macro-instructions. It may be self-sustaining, continuously generating macros and multi-thread operations in a random fashion. Such a program can test overload conditions and all types of Supervisory System timing relationships. Many of the other programs described for testing the whole system will be useful in testing the Supervisory Programs.

C. TESTING THE MULTIPLEXOR PROGRAMS

12. *A Program for Simulating the Multiplexor*

A program which simulates the multiplexor on a conventional computer may be needed. This would read in the required messages from tape and send the output to tape.

13. *A Multiplexor Dump*

If a stored program multiplexor is used, it will be necessary to dump its core. This may have to be done by means of a program in an attached computer. The multiplexor itself does not have a suitable printer or tape unit.

14. *Aids for Feeding and Logging Messages*

(a) *Use of terminal set to feed messages.* When a terminal set, or sets, send testing messages to the multiplexor, it is necessary to either log these in the associated computer or to return the messages via the multiplexor programs to the same, or a different, terminal. A program is needed in the computer for logging or returning the message.

(b) *Use of a second computer to feed messages.* A faster way of feeding messages to the multiplexor, and a way of increasing the number of lines for testing, is to use a second computer and multiplexor for feeding messages, and possibly also for logging the replies. This might be a good solution in a duplexed system. It would require another program in the second multiplexor which could be the same as the program that is being tested.

28 THE INTROSPECTIVE SYSTEM

A real-time system is normally designed to conduct many operations continuously in an asynchronous fashion. If errors occur it will take corrective action, as far as it is able on its own, without stopping.

One of the main difficulties of testing such a system is that so many programs are being executed so fast in an unpredictable sequence and that these programs interrupt one another more or less at random. There may be an almost infinite number of patterns of events, depending upon when the interrupts of various different types happen to occur.

It is quite impossible to test a system like this manually. The system needs to be able to inspect its own actions as far as possible and to log significant data that may be analyzed later. The programs need to be *introspective*.

To make the programs introspective the entire operating system needs to be planned from the beginning, so that the introspective process can be switched on by various key conditions. This is largely a matter of designing the Supervisory Programs so that they can capture the relevant facts when required; but in many cases the Application Programs also can be written to take certain actions that will indicate to the program-testing team what was going on.

To add this sort of aid to the Supervisory or Application Programs will take extra core and will mean that the system takes more time than it would during normal running. The aids should be written so that they can easily be removed. Indeed, some should be written so that they can be *dynamically* removed or brought into core while the system is running. It will doubtless happen that these aids are needed suddenly when the system is operational because a certain set of circumstances will have caused program errors. For a system with dynamic core allocation it is possible to design the programs so that certain blocks of core may be used for monitoring or debugging aids when required.

Some real-time systems have been designed so that they can run under a type of *Analysis Mode*. When "under Analysis," the necessary monitoring or debugging programs are brought into core. This may mean that modifying versions of some of the Supervisory Programs are loaded which log any information required.

It will be necessary to have an area of core into which the required Analysis data are written. Into this *Analysis Area* a log of interrupts, program identifications, or Macro Trace data may be written.

In a multi-thread system it may be desirable to have an Analysis Area for each transaction. An *Analysis Block* may be chained to the Message Reference Block. When a new message arrives and the Supervisory System sets up a Message Reference Block for it, it also sets up an Analysis Block if the system is "under Analysis."

The Analysis Block will be dumped onto tape or onto a file when the message leaves the system, i.e., when an EXIT macro-instruction is given, or else, when the Analysis Block is full.

By using Analysis Blocks the number of messages that can be held in core is reduced to less than half of the normal number. This is no serious disadvantage as the system will not be tested in this way when operating under near-peak conditions.

Many modifications will be made to the Supervisory Programs to enable a system to monitor its own actions. The key times at which the Supervisory Programs can take dumps or log key factors are, first, when transferring from the Main Scheduling Routine to an Application Program and, second, when control returns from the Application Program to the Main Scheduling Routine (See Fig. 20).

These times are referred to below as *Entry Time* and *Departure Time* —times when entry is made to, or departure made from, an Application Program.

The segment of a program in core, for example, may be dumped onto tape when it is entered and when it is left.

A test of this type means that modifications must be made to the linkage by which the Main Scheduling Routine is entered and left. Precisely what action might be needed at those times is discussed below.

Some means is also needed of recording interrupts. A simple way to do this is to make each priority routine contain one instruction which sets a bit characteristic of that routine in a permanently located *Interrupt Log Word*. The Interrupt Log Word would be cleared at Entry Time and recorded at Departure Time if required.

A means of recording output messages may also be built into the Supervisory Routines. If the system is being tested, then a macro-instruction that normally causes an output message to be sent will also cause the message to be logged on tape. This is done by a modification in the output routine of the Supervisory System.

When errors occur and a Priority Error Routine is entered, this routine should also take a modified course of action. It will normally print out, for the operator, details of the error; but now it should take further action, such as dumping appropriate areas of core onto tape.

One of the dangers of building these elaborate, but necessary, debugging aids into the system, is that they may dump too much material or take up too much time. It is desirable to design the aids so that they operate selectively and only take lengthy action, such as dumping areas of core onto tape, when this is positively required. They should not, for example, dump at every Entry and Departure Time. This applies particularly to a complex system with a high throughput of transactions. Such a system may have a hundred or more Entries and Departures per second.

In the later stages of testing it is necessary to run a number of transactions which approach the number in the fully operational system. Sufficient transactions must be run to thoroughly "exercise" the system, testing as many as possible of the combinations of circumstances that will occur in real life operation. This is referred to as "saturation testing." As saturation testing is approached it is to be hoped that the detailed debugging aids will be required only very occasionally. But some criteria for selecting them when needed must be determined.

In the PANAMAC Airline Reservation System of Pan American Airways three modes of Analysis operation were defined. These were:

Mode I

This logs on tape all input, output and error messages only. It is used when retesting debugged threads.

Mode II

This does the above and also uses the Analysis Block for recording a simple Departure Macro Trace and a simple Interrupt Log.

Mode III

This does the above and also dumps any areas of core helpful in debugging, such as the program segment in use, the working storage area, input/output area, and so on.

The criteria which determine the mode can be as follows:

1. Count

After a specified number of Departure macros, Mode III testing is switched on. After another specified number it is switched off again. This may not be necessary if Criteria 2 and 3 below are sufficient.

2. *Program*

For any one of a number of specific Applications Programs, Mode III is switched on. A test may run for a long time without using Mode III, but when a certain program which has been causing trouble is called in, Mode III will be used.

3. *Terminal*

The normal method of selecting between Modes I, II and III will be on a basis of line and terminal number. Thus, some terminals may run in Mode I, others in II or III.

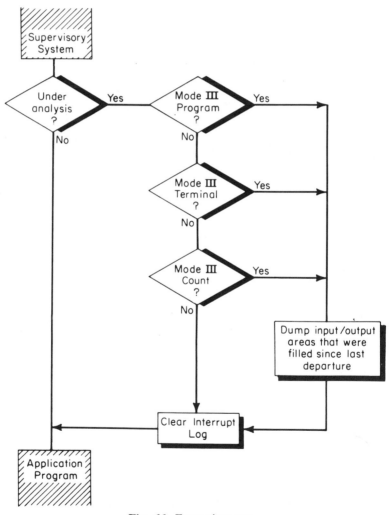

Fig. 66. Entry time test.

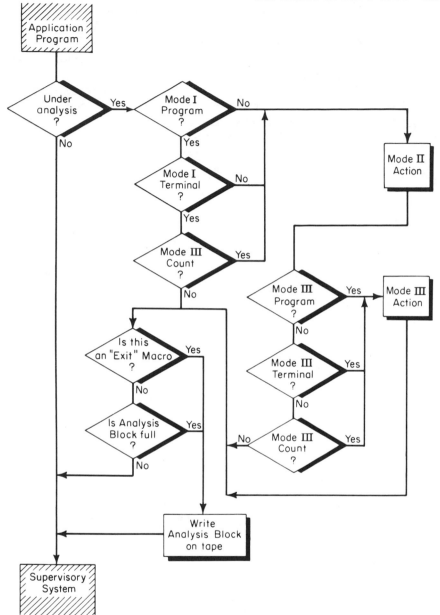

Fig. 67. Departure time test. *Mode II Action:* Place interrupt log in Analysis Block; place type of departure in Analysis Block; place program identification in Analysis Block. *Mode III Action:* Dump on output tape, program blocks, input/output areas, and so on.

An example of the selection of the testing Mode is illustrated in Figs. 66 and 67. The details of the count, program and terminal selection may be specified in control cards which define the test. These would be acted upon by a Test Supervisor Program.

Introspective program techniques such as these, which are here discussed in connection with debugging, may also be used in a simple manner for monitoring the performance of a working system. In a real-time system, with input arriving at random from terminal operators, it is desirable to take statistics now and then. This is especially so if the type of usage of the system is likely to change or increase.

29 DATA GENERATION AND SIMULATION OF INPUT MEDIA

For program testing on a conventional application it is necessary to concoct some input, and perhaps some data, records. The effectiveness of the program testing, especially in a commercial system, depends to some extent on the thoroughness with which this is done.

The same is true in a real-time application, but here two complications arise. First, all but the simplest systems need *saturation testing* to check out all the permutations and combinations of events that can occur. This means that a large number of input messages are needed, and a large number of file records must be provided.

Second, the input does not usually come from a simply reproducible medium such as a deck of punched cards. It may come from a large number of operators keying messages into terminals. Or worse, it may come from instrumentation in a power station, or street traffic detectors, or the output of radar units. It is necessary to simulate these media in such a way that the simulation reproduces exactly what would happen in real life.

These requirements mean that a large quantity of input data must be generated and, for most applications, a large set of file records must be constructed. For a simple application it may be practical to generate all the required data and records manually. Even with a very small system this is a big job. In a complex system it becomes preferable that some form of automatic procedure should be used, such as producing a mass of records by a generator program or capturing data automatically at their source.

Creating the file records for a large system such as an airline is a complex job. There are basically two methods of approaching it, the use of manual methods and the use of programming methods. Programmed generators can produce a mass of file records, but developing the logical linkage required between these records is much more difficult. Producing the addresses for these records may be difficult also, and this demands that file addressing techniques for the application are developed and that these program routines are debugged very early in the program schedule.

It will probably be necessary to use manual methods to some extent in the development of the logical linkage between file records.

The set of records used for testing, form, in effect, a *pilot model* of those which will occupy the system when it is in actual operation. They will relate to a given set of events (during a given period of time) which are smaller than the final working records. The set of records for a warehouse system will, for example, contain only a fraction of the items in the inventory. An airline booking system may have a pilot model in which the records refer to airplanes with only a small number of seats.

The input data that are produced for testing must then relate to the items in this pilot model.

For this purpose a *Pilot Tape* may be set up which contains records, or definitions of records, which may be generated for testing. It will similarly contain input messages or definitions of these. New records or messages will be added to the Pilot Tape as the program writing and testing develops.

Before a session of program testing begins, a Support Program may scan the Pilot Tape to create the required file records and input messages. The messages produced in this way may be augmented by cards containing additional messages which are not on the Pilot Tape.

Correct file addresses must be added to the file records. This will normally require a program which calculates or looks up file addresses by the same methods as the operational programs. It is, therefore, desirable that the methods of file addressing are worked out early in the development of the system, and that the file addressing routines are programmed and debugged, so that these routines can then be used in loading the file for "saturation testing." Usually, the file addresses are added manually in the early testing when not too many records are in use. This is necessary to check the file addressing routines.

The program which loads the file should be able to load not only the data records, but also program segments from the Program Library tape. It should also have some means of making changes, either to the programs in use or, possibly, to the records. This might be done by means of patch cards.

A Test Input Tape will be prepared from the Input Message Tape and other optional data, possibly on cards. Control cards might be used, for example, for controlling what occurs in the test.

When the files are loaded, the Test Input Tape will be read by a Test Supervisor Program which makes the input appear as though it had arrived in the normal manner on communication lines, and so the test run proceeds.

This process is illustrated in Fig. 68.

On a process control system, or a system with analogue input from instruments rather than digital input from human operators, some means may be needed for recording the input at its source.

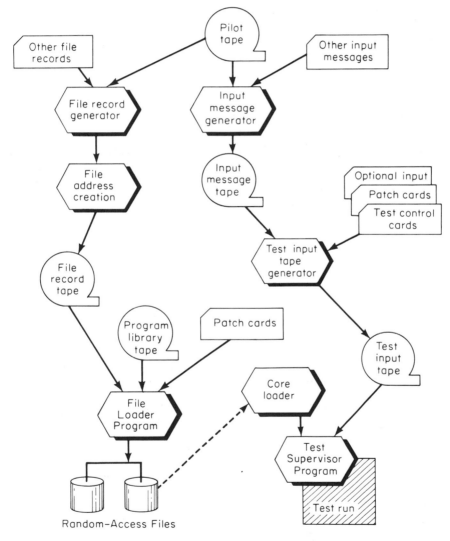

Fig. 68. Preparation of data for program testing on a commercial system.

A system for power station control may be tested, for example, with input from analogue tapes on which actual data from power station instrumentation have been recorded. However, it is also desirable in a complex system to use simulated input to give a thorough test because this is so much more flexible and because all the possible combinations of inputs can be simulated.

Figure 69 illustrates how simulated data might be generated for a missile tracking system. There are four stages:

1. Input to the first program gives details from which possible missile trajectories can be calculated. It also gives details of observation stations with, for example, position and type of radars. The program calculates a complete set of observations that would be made by each site, giving the range, azimuth, and elevation reading that would be taken.

These generated data may be printed out and a tape produced for input to the next program.

2. Only a small number of the readings generated above will be produced on an actual flight. The second program separates the readings that occur at certain specific times from those generated by the previous program. It may add details, such as the teletype channel over which transmissions are to be sent.

3. Messages sent over teletype or other communication lines are likely to contain transmission errors. Similarly, radar sets may generate errors due to random noise while making their reading. There may be other non-random failures which cause the dropping or garbling of bits, words, and transmissions. There may be outright failures in the systems.

The third program adds these "perturbations" to the data, because the testing must check that the computer can handle these conditions. It will also add valid or invalid end-of-transmission codes, start-of-transmission codes, transmission identifications, and transmission delays.

In this way the various combinations of transmission circumstances that occur in real life are reproduced.

4. Finally, a program sorts the messages into the sequence in which they would occur in actuality and merges them with other items if necessary.

A large number and variety of tapes may be produced in this way. They serve as input to the testing run. They are read during the run by a Test Supervisor Program and the messages are presented to the operating programs as they would be in actual operation.

The Test Supervisor Program also logs the output from the test. If the output gives details of the trajectory in question it may be compared with the original trajectory mentioned in the first of the above programs.

The Test Supervisor Program may be governed by a clock which

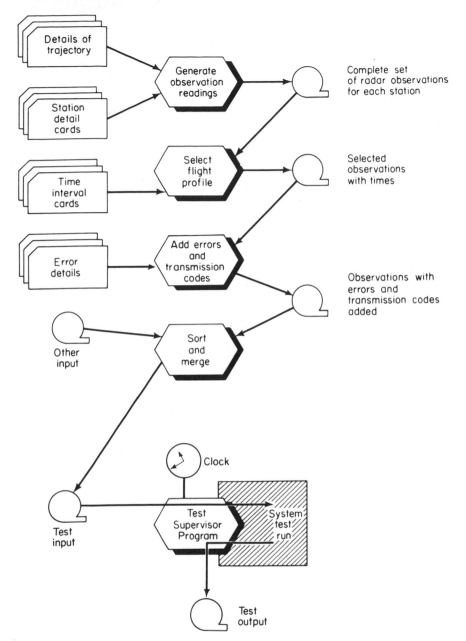

Fig. 69. Preparation of input for testing on a scientific system.

interrupts the system at frequent intervals. In this way it can simulate events in a manner very close to the real-time situation. The Test Supervisor will perform its function, based on its estimate of time. If no input/output interrupts require simulating, a return is made to the location in the program which was interrupted by the clock. If, however, it *is* time to simulate an interrupt, this will be done so that it appears to the main Supervisory Programs as a normal interrupt.

Using this technique, the Test Supervisor may suspend processing when necessary to log test data or make dumps. When this is done the clock interrupts must be temporarily stopped. Time, in other words, may be suspended as required.

To summarize, the advantage of using programmed generators is that, once the programs are set up, an endless and fully variable sequence of system conditions can be produced. These should test the program system far more thoroughly than any man-produced sets of test data. Subtle, infrequently occurring errors are likely to be brought to light. Transmission and other hardware errors can be simulated to test that the program takes the correct action. Also, for a large system, this method of producing data is likely to be quicker than doing it by hand. Higher languages may be used as these needed not be at maximum efficiency. COBOL, with its Data Division, may be a useful tool for generating data for commercial systems.

For scientific systems it will commonly be possible to use programmed data generators such as those described here. For commercial systems it will probably be necessary to generate some of the data by hand or from existing records, and some by program.

30 THE PROCESSING OF TEST OUTPUT

In program testing in a conventional system the test output is inspected visually; it tells the programmers what they wish to find out.

In a real-time system, with an almost infinite variety of combinations of input, "saturation testing" is needed to track down the errors caused by rare combinations of input. The quantity of output is then likely to be too great for adequate visual inspection. Some form of automated processing of the output is needed.

The output from saturation testing will normally be on magnetic tape. This tape may be sorted or processed as required.

The Test Supervisor Program should be written in such a way that it logs output messages against the input message that requested the reply. Error messages or any debugging information, such as core dumps or information recorded by the "Analysis" aids described in Chapter 28, should also be in the same record. An indication or copy of file records used or updated may also be stored. A record will thus be written on tape for each input message, indicating what happened to it in the system.

This may not be sufficient to pin down the causes of all program errors. The sequence with which events happen in core during multi-thread operation may also be significant. A separate indication is needed, perhaps on a separate tape, with data such as a macro-instruction trace and an interrupt log.

The output tape will have indications of message type, of programs used, and of input terminals. It may be sorted into these categories, and selected portions of it may be printed. The behavior of a specific program may then be investigated, or the messages sent from a particular terminal may be checked.

Many messages which have already been used as input for single-thread testing may be used over again in multi-thread. These may be sorted by the Test Output Processor programs and compared, to see that they give the same answer, or the same answer appropriately modified. The comparison may be automatic, so that the program testing personnel are notified only if an error has occurred.

In a warehousing system, for example, all messages relating to a given item may be compared to see whether the inventory record has been modified correctly. During a period of saturation testing it may be arranged that the large number of transactions being sent always bring this item back to a certain stock level. When the output is inspected it will be known that, if the item does not have that quantity in stock, then a transaction has been processed incorrectly.

In a duplexed system, computer A may feed the testing messages to computer B, and receive the replies. In certain systems it may be desirable to modify the messages used, depending upon the status of information in computer B. Computer B may, for example, reorder a given stock item because it has received so many transactions depleting this stock. In this case Computer A may be programmed to send messages saying that more stock has been delivered. In any case, it must log the cause of computer B's exception actions.

Computer A, in effect, can become a real-time system for testing the programs in computer B.

Computer A can modify the testing process according to the conditions generated by the testing. It also analyzes the output and can produce for the testing personnel a quick summary of what is happening.

The test output analysis may thus be on-line while the test is proceeding, or it may be off-line, done at a later time.

To shorten the analysis of test output, the output processor may be capable of giving two levels of print-out. First, it will do a summary of what happened. In the summary it will print index numbers so that any portion of the test print-out may be referred to by these. Punched control cards containing the index numbers can then be used where needed to instruct a second print program to give full details of certain areas.

Where the first output processor is capable of detecting that an error has occurred, it will indicate this. Elsewhere it will give the testing personnel the simplest print-out for them to carry out a visual inspection.

Chapter 28 suggested the use of three modes of testing which differ in the quantity of output. Mode I logs input, output and error messages only. Mode II does the same but also may give a brief log of "Departure" macro-instructions and an interrupt log. Mode III, which is used only on exceptional occasions when all else fails, gives Mode II data and also gives dumps of certain critical areas of core or programs or records that are used from the file.

Various conditions, such as using a certain program, may cause a Mode III dump. Hence a session of saturation testing may cause a number of Mode III dumps to be on the output tapes.

It is necessary to be highly selective with respect to test print-outs in a complex system, especially in the later stages when long runs are performed, and especially when using debugging aids classed here as Mode III. In systems at the top end of the spectrum in Fig. 12, with a high message throughput, testing equivalent to a minute of operational running could generate so much information by using Mode III that it would take several hours to print it out in full on a modern high-speed printer.

When the test output is being processed, it would be edited and arranged into a format that is easy to read. Examples of the first print-outs from Phases I, II, and III are shown in Figs. 70, 71, and 72.

Assume that a programmer requesting the test shown in Fig. 70 knows that after Application Program Segment 124A, the next program should

```
INPUT  MESSAGE
6C  GG00101  CHARLES  SNODGROUSE

OUTPUT  MESSAGE
200101  NAME  RECORDED

ERROR  MESSAGE
NONE
```

Fig. 70. Mode I Testing Output.

```
INPUT  MESSAGE
6C  GG00101  CHARLES  SNODGROUSE

OUTPUT  MESSAGE
200101  NAME  RECORDED

ERROR  MESSAGE
NONE
```

INTERRUPT CODE	PROGRAM ISSUING DEPARTURE	DEPARTURE MACRO
- - - -	SUP	ENTERB
- - - -	124A	ENTERA
- - - -	125B	RETURN
- - - -	124A	WAIT
	SUP	
- - - -	126A	EXIT

Fig. 71. Mode II Testing Output.

INPUT MESSAGE
6C GG00101 CHARLES SNODGROUSE

OUTPUT MESSAGE
200101 NAME RECORDED

ERROR MESSAGE
NONE

INTERRUPT CODE	PROGRAM ISSUING DEPARTURE	DEPARTURE MACRO	MESSAGE REFERENCE BLOCK	PROGRAM ISSUING DEPARTURE	FILE READ-IN AREAS A	B	C	ACCUMULATOR AND REGISTERS D	
----	SUP	ENTERB	094	095	096	097	098	099	101
----	124A	ENTERA	101	102	103	104	105	106	107
----	125B	RETURN	108	109	110	111	112	113	114
----	124A	WAIT	115	116	117	118	119	120	121
	SUP								
----	126A	EXIT	213						

Fig. 72. Mode III Testing Output.

have been 128X. It was in fact 125B as shown. In order to determine what happened, the programmer wants to see:

1. The Message Reference Block after 124A finished.

2. Program 124A at "Departure Time."

3. File Read-in Areas C and D when program 125B was entered.

In order to get these areas printed out the programmer enters a control card to the detailed test output processor program. This would state the identification of the test dump tape that contains his information and index numbers 101, 102, and 109 (taken from the print-out in Fig. 72).

These records would then be printed in a readable format. The Message Reference Block, for example, may have each character or bit defined.

Techniques such as these involve much work and should be planned early in the development of a system. If the system is of such a nature that saturation testing is needed, then some means of automatically processing the test output as indicated here will be required.

FITTING THE SYSTEM TOGETHER

31 BUILDING UP A SYSTEM

If program testing is to be successful and to move rapidly it must proceed in small, logical steps. If too large a step is attempted at one time the program testers become lost in complications, and progress slows down. This is true in simple batch processing. It is very much more important in real-time processing with multi-programming and more than one processing unit.

A complex system needs to be built up piece-by-piece. Different programmers or groups of programmers will write different programs, with varying degrees of independence. As the programs are produced they always drift away from their original idealized concept. Each segment of the programs will be debugged by the person or group who wrote it until, on its own, it is logically correct. When all the various segments are put together, each tested by itself, there will be new errors because the segments do not interface together exactly. Part of the work of system testing is to straighten out these interface problems and to make sure that the component parts of the programs fit together.

The various sections of programs should be put together one at a time so that the system is built up stage-by-stage.

Where several program segments are used in the processing of a message, these segments must be tested first singly and then in sequence. Where several programs interface to form a system, these programs must be tested first individually, and then linked together stage-by-stage. Where several processing units are involved, these must be tested one at a time and then jointly. Finally, where multi-programming is used, the programs must be tested first sequentially or single-thread (where one thread contains all actions associated with one input message) and then in parallel or multi-thread.

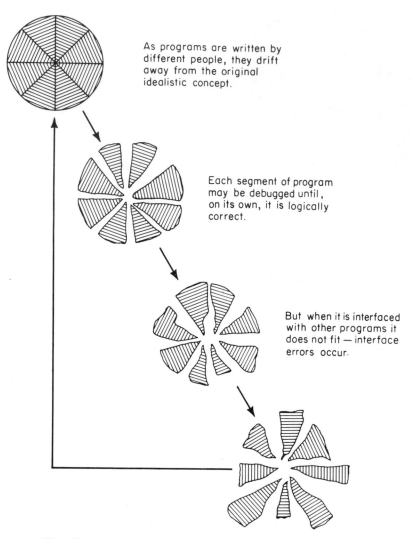

As programs are written by different people, they drift away from the original idealistic concept.

Each segment of program may be debugged until, on its own, it is logically correct.

But when it is interfaced with other programs it does not fit — interface errors occur.

Fig. 73. System testing is the job of making programs and components fit together, so that the system as a whole works as was intended.

Figure 74 illustrates this. For a system with Application Programs and a set of Supervisory Programs in the main computer, and a separate program in the multiplexor, the stages shown would be required.

There may be more stages in the testing than are shown here. For example, the system consists of two multiplexors with different programs, handling different types of communication facilities. One multiplexor might be a standby which monitors the work of the other for security reasons.

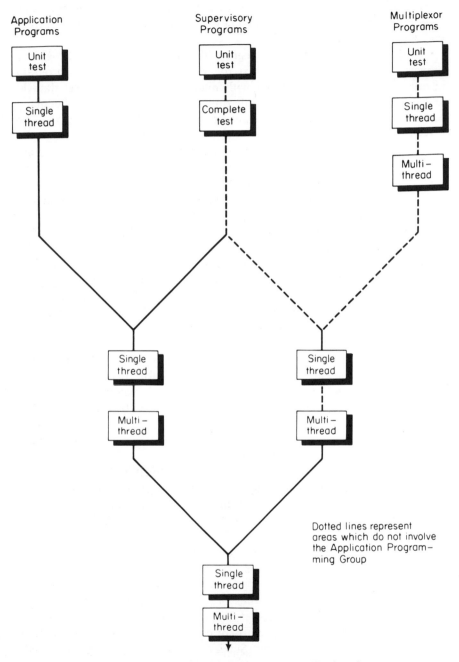

Fig. 74. The breakdown of System Testing, I.

There might be fall-back programs to be tested, which the system uses when a component fails. This is shown in Fig. 75. If multi-processing were used between different processing units, the diagram would be further complicated.

Each phase of testing should begin with small batches of data, logically designed by the programmer to test the various functions of his program in easy stages. Thus, a program with many paths may have test data in which the first items take one path only and the later items take many paths. This will show up the obvious errors. Less obvious errors may be brought to light by using a large quantity of data that were not logically planned by the programmer. The programmer may have neglected certain types of data or combinations of data. For this reason, data should be used before the completion of testing that was designed by a person other than the programmer. There may be a large miscellaneous batch of generated data, a set of real-life data reproduced by actual operations, or data originated at the terminals by operators experimenting at random after their training period.

In general, it is necessary to progress from simple short batches of input designed by the programmer to bulk data for saturation testing.

Similarly, it is necessary to progress from generated data to actual data, and from a simulated environment, i.e., input and output on magnetic tape using a special program, to a real environment, e.g., terminal sets in remote offices.

When a very complex system is designed it is difficult to install the entire system in one cut-over. It would be much easier if the system could be split up into a succession of models. A relatively simple model would be installed first. At a later date this would be replaced by a more complex model, and in this way the system would develop to its final concept. It is extremely difficult to install a system of, for example, 100,000 instructions of real-time coding in one cut-over.

The modular growth of a system would be by function, by area covered, or by both. An initial system may handle only a few operator terminals. When this is working without error more terminals are added, and the throughput is increased. If this works, then, as confidence builds up, more and more terminals are added until the entire network is on-line. In a banking system, for example, that is ultimately to handle a large number of branches, one branch may be on-line in the initial system, perhaps the branch in the same building as the computer. When this is operating, other branches are added. As other branches are added the number of account records in the system increases. Larger files may be needed. As the throughput increases the system may have to switch from single-thread to multi-thread processing. Some Supervisory routines may be changed. And so the system is allowed to grow steadily.

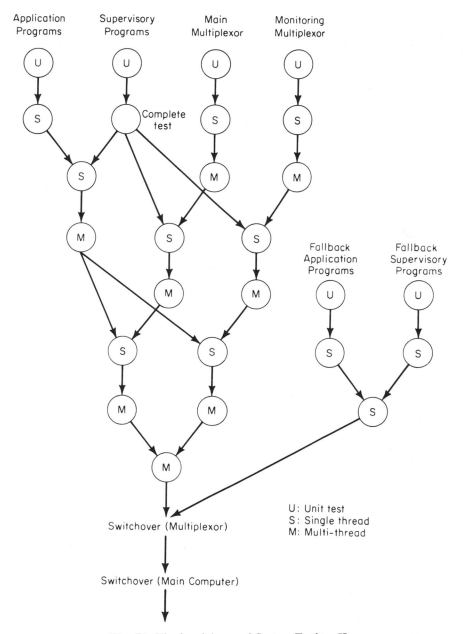

Fig. 75. The breakdown of System Testing, II.

As the system is tested in operation it is necessary to check out not only the programs, but also the way the system interfaces with its environment. The installation of a real-time commercial data-processing system will cause vast changes in the administrative procedures that surround it. Difficulties in the new flow of paper work must be straightened out. It is as important to debug the man-machine interface as the interface between programs.

If the system grows by *function* rather than by area or volume covered, completely separate models may be required, each being a natural outgrowth of its predecessor. The *design feedback* from one model would be used to improve the next, and so on.

An airline reservation system might begin by handling bookings and availability enquires only, for example. Passenger records and their handling might be added in a later model that is much more complex than the first but uses the experience of the first. Cargo handling and fare quotations might be handled on a third model.

A system which handles enquiries and updates files as well as doing message switching might begin with the former and add the latter in a later model. In the development of a system it may become desirable to rewrite some of the Supervisory Programs, re-plan the files, or make other major changes. These improvements need only be executed if it is possible to install a new model at a later date.

When a new model is installed it will have program errors in it, and certain aspects of its design probably will be worth improving. It is important that each model should be fully shaken down and used for a period of time before the next one is installed. Only in this way will there be sufficient feedback of performance information to improve the design of later models. In very complex systems it may be desirable to pass through one or more models before the system becomes operational; here the design feedback from each model would be used for developing the system.

Figure 76 illustrates the planning schedule of a model-by-model approach. The specifications for each model must be frozen at some point in its implementation and any further changes must be saved for a later model. This diagram shows a period of about 1½ years between successive models. For not too complex systems this period might be shorter. However, to install a major real-time system that handles many functions is a long process and may require a *five-year-plan* for implementation—a longer period than with conventional systems, though even these take on one function at a time. With a real-time system the modular development needs to be planned at the outset.

A difficulty in using the model concept is that when one model is operational it is not easy to test and cut over to the next model. This

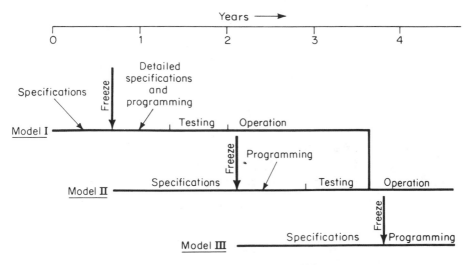

Fig. 76. The model-by-model approach to building up a system.

may not be much of a problem in a large military system such as SAGE where other computers could bridge the gap, or in Project Mercury where the system was operational only for the duration of an orbital flight, but for an airline reservation system operational 24 hours a day, it is a difficult matter. It is probably worthwhile to plan the system so that it has an extra file for use in a model change and for testing. If that is not done it is very difficult to have the system fully operational 24 hours a day.

The following two chapters discuss the phases of system testing that are needed to build up a complex system. The next chapter discusses the check-out of the system used in Project Mercury for monitoring manned space flights which used radars round the world as its input. The following chapter outlines seven possible phases of system testing on a complex commercial installation.

32 LEVELS OF TESTING ON TECHNICAL APPLICATION

This section describes the testing techniques used on Project Mercury in which IBM 7090's were used to monitor the first manned orbital space flight.

The testing of these programs differs from that for commercial applications programs in that a very high degree of confidence is required, but there is plenty of non-operational time between flights for development and model change. The program system is less complex than that in a large airline reservation system, and there are no problems of destroying file data. Input is from a worldwide complex of equipment which includes tracking radars and the Mercury Ground Instrumentation Systems. Elaborate programs are needed to simulate deviations from normal input, such as transmission errors. Prior to an orbital flight the program system, in conjunction with the entire Mercury complex, must be tested in a manner that approximates the actual system operation during the flight.

System testing is performed on the following levels:

1. Simulated tests.
2. Unsimulated tests using simulated data produced locally.
3. Unsimulated tests using simulated data produced remotely by the tracking sites.
4. *Network drills* in which simulated data from the tracking sites are transmitted according to a prearranged procedure and are monitored by the site director.

Among the output requirements of the programming system are the display of quantities such as deviations from the calculated trajectory, orbital capabilities and a GO/NO GO decision for orbit, computed time of retro-fire, computed impact point, and other computed values contributing to a successful mission.

In most cases the termination of the data link is a radar tracking site. Sites are strategically located around the world in such a manner that in a normal mission the capsule passes directly over or within communication range of each site. The computer receives the data, processes them, and displays the required quantities at the Mercury Control Center. Only after developing the operational readiness of the program system is an attempt made to check the data links with the program system. When the program alone has been checked, network components are added level-by-level. To accomplish this a system of simulation programs and techniques is required.

SIMULATED TESTING   The simulated test is the first level of testing and is controlled by the Simulated Input/Output Control Program (SIC). This test is not run in real-time, and there is no dependence on any network components. A Data Communication Channel Clock is used. This is an internal timing device which steps once each millisecond of time and can be interrogated by the program for the purpose of synchronizing time with the operation of the program. The simulated data are read in from magnetic tape. Generating the data is an elaborate procedure as was described in the last section.

Since SIC enters all the data the program system is in an artificial environment. The Data Communication Clock enables SIC to maintain its sense of real-time, thus supplying the simulated data at the corresponding times as which they would normally arrive in a real operation.

The advantages of this simulated testing in a scientific application are:

1. *Repeatability*. It is possible to duplicate exact conditions, timing and data, in case results are not as anticipated and must be repeated.

2. *Controllability*. The testing of the interaction of the various programs is under strict control of the programmer. If a large communication network were used, testing would be very difficult to control.

3. *Recordability*. Intermediate results not displayed in the real-time operation of the program can be recorded for future analysis. The results may be stored for comparison with future tests if required.

4. *Flexibility*. Any combination of input data or conditions can be built into the test.

5. *Low cost*. It would be expensive to use the communications network and actual terminals for all tests.

6. *Reduction of variables.* Undetermined equipment failures outside the computer and line errors would introduce unwanted variables into testing. Simulated testing isolates program errors from network errors.

7. *Time factor can be modified.* The time increment used in processing can be stepped at a rate slower than real-time to allow the dumping of any output data required from the test. It can be stepped at a rate faster than real-time to compress the occurrence of events. For example, a 90-odd minute Earth orbit required only 30 minutes of computer time to test.

UNSIMULATED TESTING WITH LOCAL INPUT Unsimulated tests with input from the computer center form the second level of testing. These tests do not operate under the control of SIC. Input data are in real-time and produce real-time outputs.

Input data to the Mercury Program System are of two main types:

1. High-speed data received at a nominal rate of one message every half-second. These data are received during the launch phase of every Mercury mission. They consist of a telemetry data summary and either position and velocity vectors with their associated time tag, or radar observations reflecting the trajectory of the launch vehicle.

2. Low-speed data received at a nominal rate of one message every six seconds. These data are received during the orbit, re-entry, and high-abort phases of Mercury missions. They consist of radar observations with their associated time tags and messages defining critical pieces of information. A sequence of data contained in these messages is used to refine an already defined orbit.

In order to enter information of this type into the computer system for testing, data that were recorded on earlier orbital flights can be "played back" for the purpose of testing the computer programs. The high-speed data are recorded by a unit called the Operational Data Recorder on Ampex tape. The low-speed data are recorded on paper tape. The Operational Data Recorder and teletype paper tape readers in the computer center play back the tapes when testing, and to the program the input is indistinguishable from live data from Cape Kennedy and the Mercury tracking sites.

The data recorded on the Ampex Tapes consist of time, position and velocity of the capsule. Also recorded is an indication that a number of discrete events have taken place, such as lift-off, staging, escape tower released, capsule released from sustainer, retro-rockets 1, 2 and 3 fired, etc. The initial source of the velocity and position data during a mission would be the radars at the Cape. The source of the discrete events would be:

(a) The capsule via telemetry receivers.

(b) The launch pad.

(c) The vehicle telemetry system.

Many different trajectory tapes can be prepared, and the discrete events can be recorded by manually throwing certain switches after the proper elapsed time. In this way a variable number of test conditions can be produced. These are recorded on the Operational Data Recorder for later playback and testing.

The paper tapes for low-speed input can be prepared from magnetic tapes generated with simulation programs (described in the last section). The paper tape readers are wired into the input lines from the sites so that to the computer programs the data appear to have come from the sites. As there is direct control over the data, the data themselves can be varied so as to provide for any number of possibilities, e.g., word drop-out, interruption of transmission, wrong data, etc.

Certain messages must be fed into the system at specific times. For example, the abort phase message causes the program to think that an abort has taken place and that now the program must go into the operation of computing re-entry data and refining the impact point of the capsule. Since an abort may take place at any time after lift-off, the program must be tested for low, medium, and high altitude abort cases. The time of the entry of this message during the testing creates the above conditions.

UNSIMULATED TESTING WITH REMOTE INPUT   The next level of testing uses the communication network components and tests the interaction between these and the program. The term "remote testing" does not always imply that the entire input is from remote sites. Sometimes only one site (e.g., Cape Kennedy) is the source of data, and additional data, if needed, are supplied locally. The larger the number of sites involved, the greater is the need for coordination, scheduling, and manpower.

The output of tests are:

1. On-line messages.

2. Results and intermediate results logged on tape for later print-out.

3. Local real-time displays.

NETWORK DRILLS   In this last level of testing, data from the sites are transmitted according to a prearranged procedure. At this stage not only the program system but the entire complex of equipment and personnel and all the interfaces are tested. Control over the

Network Drill is exercised by a Network Control group rather than by the group in the computer center. The drills exercise the program in an unsimulated mode impossible to duplicate in any other way. This, in effect, is the highest level of testing attainable and one which comes closer than any other to approximating an actual mission.

33 SEVEN PHASES FOR TESTING A COMMERCIAL SYSTEM

This chapter discusses the fitting together of the Application Programs to build up a complex commercial system.

The testing of the Application Programs starts with the first unit test of one program segment and builds up to testing the fully developed system. It is possible to break this work into seven phases. These are described for a system such as Reference System No. 6:

PHASE I:	Testing segments of Application Programs with simulated Supervisory macro-instructions and possibly with some of the hardware simulated also. No files. No multiplexor.
PHASE II:	Testing single threads of Application Programs with the actual computer and files and the actual debugged Supervisory Programs, but no multiplexor.
PHASE III:	Repeating Phase II, but with multi-thread processing.
PHASE IV:	Testing with the multiplexor, simulating actual operation as closely as possible but without having remote terminals on-line.
PHASE V:	Repeating Phase IV, but with distant terminals on-line.
PHASE VI:	This is the cut-over phase. Files containing actual working data will be built up during this phase.
PHASE VII:	This refers to the maintenance of the operational system and to the adding of additional functions or modifications during operation.

Recycling

Programs being tested will not necessarily pass in sequence through the phases. Programs may drop back to a previous phase. For example, if in Phase III an error is found in an Application Program, this program may drop back to Phase I or Phase II. It is recommended that Phase I *alone* should have debugging aids such as the ability to make selective dump on given instructions. Hence, if the internal logic of an Application Program is incorrect, it will be desirable to drop back to Phase I. If, however, a previously debugged Supervisory Program exists, then selective dumps and other debugging aids may be built into Phase II so that programs need not drop back to Phase I. Phase I might be dispensed with altogether.

Any alteration made to a program in the system may have an effect on other programs. If a program is modified it may then be necessary to repeat previous tests which use this program. Some organized scheme for *recycling* programs which are changed should therefore be considered.

Concurrent Operation of Phases

When testing the later phases, computer time will almost certainly be short. It will be desirable to test more than one phase at the same time on the same computer. This will only be done when all the obvious errors have been removed from the programs in operation. It is necessary to design the testing aids and file organization for testing with this overlap in view.

Phase I will not operate concurrently with other phases because it uses simulated Supervisory Program macro-instructions. Phase II will operate alone as it is single-thread. Phase III should be able to run concurrently with Phases IV, V, VI, or possibly VII. Phase IV might run concurrently with Phase V, but it will probably not be necessary to run Phase IV with Phases VI or VII. Random experimentation by terminal operators, which can find many errors when testing Phase V above, must be restricted because of file organization when running Phases VI or VII.

As the testing proceeds to higher phases, or as the system is put together piece-by-piece, the remaining errors become more difficult to locate. The majority of errors should be found in Phase I. A few will linger on to later phases, and some subtle ones will almost certainly still exist in the system when it becomes operational. These might, for example, be caused by timing conditions which occur very infrequently. They might be errors caused by the coincidental arrival of two messages of certain types, perhaps referring to the same data (Fig. 77).

The longer errors remain in the system, the more trouble they cause. Errors that still exist after cut-over to operational running are immensely troublesome. They may, for example, cause damage to the working files.

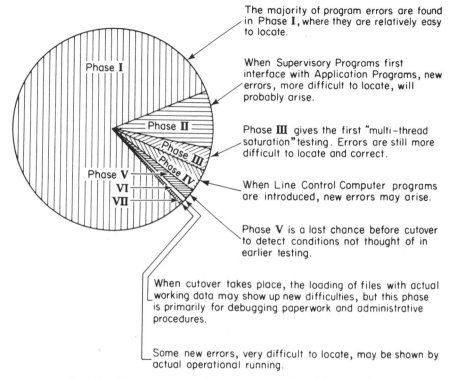

The majority of program errors are found in Phase **I**, where they are relatively easy to locate.

When Supervisory Programs first interface with Application Programs, new errors, more difficult to locate, will probably arise.

Phase **III** gives the first "multi-thread saturation" testing. Errors are still more difficult to locate and correct.

When Line Control Computer programs are introduced, new errors may arise.

Phase **V** is a last chance before cutover to detect conditions not thought of in earlier testing.

When cutover takes place, the loading of files with actual working data may show up new difficulties, but this phase is primarily for debugging paperwork and administrative procedures.

Some new errors, very difficult to locate, may be shown by actual operational running.

Fig. 77. The proportion of program errors found in each phase of testing, on a complex Multi-Thread System. The early phases of testing should be as thorough as possible, because the later errors are detected, the more trouble they cause.

It will ultimately save time and trouble if the earlier phases of testing are done as thoroughly as possible. "Saturation testing" in Phase III, for example, should "exercise" the system as completely as possible.

The following pages explain these seven phases in more detail and indicate what testing aids are necessary and what equipment will be used.

PHASE I   In Phase I, *non-real-time debugging* takes place. It is probable that when the testing of Application Programs first begins, the particular hardware configuration with any special equipment and files will not be available. Probably the Supervisory Programs will not be available either. Therefore, Phase I testing may run on a standard available computer. No disk files will be used. *No multiprogramming will occur.* This phase corresponds broadly to conventional computer testing, except that simulated Supervisory Program macro-instructions are used. It is possible that the computer may have to be simulated with programming on a different, available, machine. The computer in question may not yet be delivered or even built.

Phase I should consist of three parts:

1. Individual program segments will be tested.
2. Complete threads will be tested one at a time.
3. A group of threads will be tested sequentially using the same records.

The Data Generator will create any records to which the Application Programs refer. Input will be from tape and output will be to tape.

Upon successful completion of Phase I testing, programs will be considered debugged and added to the Librarian Tape for testing in subsequent phases. Any errors in Application Programs picked up by later phases may cause that program to return to Phase I debugging.

This phase will need a number of program testing aids.

First, as this is single-thread non-real-time testing, any debugging aids that are used on conventional testing may be used here. This may include trace routines or transfer traces, selective dumps, symbolic core print-outs, snapshots, and so on. As these will be more difficult to use in later phases of testing, full use should be made of them here.

A snapshot technique might be particularly useful. By means of a control card the programmers might obtain a dump at a specific instruction. The instruction in question is replaced by a transfer to an appropriate sub-routine which executes the instruction and then dumps the required data. Accumulators, registers and so on may be dumped as well as selected storage.

In the testing of most programs a trace is probably too long-winded a procedure; however, a trace which logs only transfer instructions might be useful. A trace of macro-instructions is recommended for multi-thread work, but it is probably not needed on Phase I as this is single-thread.

Before any testing occurs at all the programs should be scanned for obvious errors. It is a platitude to say that thorough desk-checking of the coding is invaluable in the difficulties it will save later. The checking can to some extent be automated by writing a program to scan the instructions in the way that an assembly program does. This routine would check the program for, for example, invalid macro-instructions, incorrect segment lengths, obvious logic errors, and other predictable false conditions.

By the time segments of program pass out of Phase I, all the logic errors should be removed as far as possible. Operating on their own, or as a solitary "thread", these segments should then work correctly. When they are interfaced with other segments of program or other threads in later phases, new errors will come to light.

Second, simulator routines will be needed. It may be necessary to simulate the equipment or part of the equipment and to simulate some of the Supervisory Routines.

If a relatively new type of computer is used this will possibly not be available as early as required for the program testing. However, some means may be available of simulating this machine on an existing computer with a simulator program. Instructions written for the new computer will be analyzed and executed on the old machine in a way that imitates the new one. In doing this, the programs will, of course, run much more slowly. The effectiveness of such a procedure will depend upon how thoroughly the simulator is written.

The input/output equipment and files of the final system are not likely to be used at this stage. Input will be fed to the programs under test from cards or tape which have the same format as the data they will receive when working under real-time conditions. Similarly, the output they produce will go to tape or be printed rather than go out in a real-time manner.

There may be no Supervisory Programs debugged and available for testing at this stage. The macro-instructions which would normally generate Supervisory Program routines must generate simple substitute routines which in effect simulate the Supervisory System. For example, a WAIT macro-instruction might generate a link which causes the same program to continue after its WAIT is satisfied. An EXIT might cause a dump of relevant core, and the testing on this transaction then ends. Work begins on the next item using the same program segment or "thread." An output macro-instruction causes the relevant output to be made to tape or printer. A file request causes an equivalent record to be read, possibly from a different type of input unit. The records of this type that are needed must be generated prior to the run.

Third, a means of generating the data and input is needed.

The quantity of data or input needed at this stage will probably be small enough to generate by hand. However, it is important that the data records and input come from a centralized source rather than from the programmer in question. If each programmer produced his own data for testing this would increase the difficulties in later phases, because different programmers often tend to have slightly different concepts of what data should be used. This difference, if it exists, should be found in Phase I so that there is a greater chance of the programs working together in later phases.

As a *Data Generator* will probably be used for later *saturation testing,* this Data Generator may also produce the data, or some of the data for Phase I. The Data Generator requirement was discussed in Chapter 29. As indicated in that chapter, the data and input would be drawn from a *Pilot Tape.*

When a program passes successfully through Phase I, it should be written onto a *Debugged Program Tape*. This tape will contain all the debugged programs, packages and subroutines. It will be used throughout all the phases of testing.

A *Librarian Program* will be needed to maintain tapes such as the Debugged Program Tape. It will have the ability to patch, add, delete or change any subroutine, program or package on this tape.

PHASE II   Phase II can be entered when the actual computer to be used is available with its files and the main routines of the Supervisory Programs.

Phase II no longer simulates the files or the Supervisory Programs. It does, however, still simulate the communication lines and terminals. Input will then still be from a medium such as tape, and output will go to tape (Fig. 78).

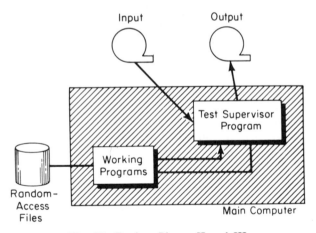

Fig. 78. Testing, Phases II and III.

There will still be no multi-programming. The computer will be set up with the Main Scheduling Routine of the Supervisory Programs running in a loop (Fig. 48, Chapter 16). Messages will be fed to this one at a time.

One of the difficulties of this phase may be in determining whether errors are caused by the Application Programs or by the Supervisory Programs. This will not be so if the Supervisory Programs are fully debugged and proven routines; but if they are written or modified for this particular application, errors may originate in these Supervisory Programs.

To help find out where the errors arose, the Analysis Mode testing aids described in Chapter 28 may be employed. The aids are needed in Phase

III and later, when multi-thread testing takes place. Phase II acts as a dress rehearsal for this.

Phase II will use files loaded with a set of data that is a miniature version of the final operational files, a pilot model of the system. The data must be designed so that they tie together logically and relate to input messages. These may refer, for example, to a certain set of accounts on a certain group of days of the year.

Again, the loading and use of the files is to some extent a dress rehearsal for later phases when the problems of creating, loading and maintaining bulk files occur. Aids such as those discussed in Chapter 27 will be used.

The system will also need a means of loading core with the relevant Supervisory Programs, Application Programs, tables, and so on. These may perhaps be kept on the files now for ease of loading, though it is also necessary to have them on card or tape in case the testing erases part of the file. The core loader will load the required program and data and set up any initial conditions. This program can be the same one that is used in operational running. The program may be used in the off-line computer for switchover.

Input and output in Phases II and III will be to and from tape or disk, rather than by communication lines. The input will be read in by a *Test Supervisor Routine* which presents it to the main programs in such a way that it appears as if it came from the lines. Similarly, output will be logged on tape (Fig. 78).

The functions of the Test Supervisor Routine may be as follows:

1. All input messages for Phase II (or III) debugging are placed on the New Input Queue of the Supervisory Programs.

2. Output messages are logged on tape when the Application Programs give output macro-instructions.

3. The messages read from the test input tape may also be written on the test output tape to facilitate analysis of test output.

4. The phase of the test and the mode for different conditions are indicated to the Analysis Mode routines.

5. Patches specified by the test input tape are made, and the records are written on the files.

6. All file records that are changed (written) by the test are recorded.

7. At the end of the test the changed records are reinitialized by using the file loader tape before the next test is started.

The Test Supervisor Routine will probably be designed so that it can handle later phases of testing as well as Phases II and III.

PHASE III Phase III is a repetition of Phase II but with *multi-thread* input. It will build up to the *saturation testing* needed to thoroughly "exercise" the Application Programs working with the Supervisory Programs.

This phase is defined for systems which operate in a multi-thread manner. For systems which are always single-thread it would not be necessary. Saturation testing could take place in Phase II.

The Test Supervisor Routine, which in Phase II fed messages to the New Input Queue one at a time, now sends them in bursts. Instead of placing one message in the New Input Queue and waiting until this is completely processed, it will now place a batch of messages in the queue. The Supervisory Programs operating in their normal manner will then work on more than one transaction in parallel.

If Phase II testing were completed thoroughly for the Application Programs in question and the Supervisory Programs were thoroughly tested also, there would not be many errors to be found in Phase III. Most of those that do occur are likely to be associated with timing and may be difficult to repeat. It is almost impossible to make a multi-thread run reproducible as interrupts will not occur at the same time on reruns. Disks, for example, may introduce a time factor up 30 milliseconds or more different due to their rotational positions, and interrupts connected with file references will occur at different times. It would be possible to start the test when a specific disk is in a known position by allowing a false disk read operation to trigger off the start of the test. However, if more than one set of disks or if drums are used this will be pointless. For this reason, the Analysis Mode debugging aids are of immense value in Phase III. A print-out of the Interrupt Log, when the system enters a priority error routine, should, for example, be used. A macro-trace and the facility to inspect certain machine conditions at certain times are invaluable.

When errors do occur in Phase III, it may be of value to allow the program causing the error to drop back to Phase II testing or even Phase I. To simplify Analysis Mode it is suggested that no facility for the temporary patching of records or programs should be given in Phase III as it is in Phase II. If a program requires this, it should drop back to Phase II.

If errors pass through Phase II undetected they are likely to be much more difficult to find and to be very troublesome in later phases. It therefore is recommended that Phase III should be done very thoroughly with many messages. However, this presents the difficulty of checking a large quantity of output. Some programmed means of checking output may be desirable.

The output might be sorted, for example, and compared with earlier single-thread output.

Bulk testing with many messages is required at the end of Phase III, but it will be difficult to program Analysis Mode economically so that any message of a large test may switch on Mode III. Some restriction on the use of Mode III is needed in this bulk testing.

With bulk testing a large number of file records will need to be loaded. To avoid having to reload these for each test a *Disk-to-Disk Restore Program* is suggested which notes those records written on by the test; after the test it restores these, and only these, from a duplicate copy. A similar program may be needed by the working system to restore files after a period of fallback operation.

In exercising a multi-thread system it may be desirable to send the messages asynchronously rather than with any preordained timing pattern. For this reason, some systems have stored input messages on disk files, as the variable times for file references made the input asynchronous. This could also be done by padding tape records, by building a loop into the Test Supervisor Programs, or by using a Real-Time Clock. It may be important to make sure that no two messages from the same terminal arrive in the system at the same time in this way.

One of the difficulties to be faced in Phase III is determining what caused an error. When a system with a high degree of multi-programming is running non-stop it may be difficult to tell which Application Program caused an error, or whether it was caused by an Interrupt Routine or by a Supervisory Program. This will be especially difficult to track down if the timing conditions of the test cannot be repeated exactly. It was for these reasons that the Analysis Mode aids were devised.

By the end of Phase III the system should have been thoroughly exercised, and considerable confidence in the Application Programs should have been built up.

PHASE IV   The purpose of this phase is to simulate actual operation as closely as possible without having *remote* terminals on-line. For the first time input and output will be via the multiplexor rather than by using tape alone. The interface between the multiplexor programs and the central processor programs will be tested. Means must be devised of indicating whether an error is caused by the multiplexor or by the central processing unit.

For the first time the queues in the system should be loaded to capacity. Emergency action due to overloads, errors and other causes should be tested. This may possibly involve a new method of feeding in messages, though the queues may be loaded to capacity by programming aids. It may be thought desirable to have one computer feeding messages to another computer via the multiplexors (Fig. 80).

For the first time actual terminals will be used, though the main input will still be from tape or disk. Messages from tape may be fed to one multiplexor, *wrapped around* and fed back into the computer as test input (Fig. 79). The input of very long-length messages should be tested. Invalid messages should also be tested to see that they are rejected correctly.

Now also various types of switchover and fallback may be tested. Computer switchover, multiplexor switchover, tape switching and file fallback may be tested. Scheduled and nonscheduled switchover should be tested.

Phase IV might be divided into the following parts:

1. Testing with input and output via the multiplexor using lines *wrapped around* (Fig. 79).
2. Testing with input and output via multiplexor and terminals.
3. Loading the queues to capacity to test overload conditions.
4. Multiplexor switchover.
5. Switchover of central processing unit.

These are described below.

1. *Testing with the Multiplexor*

For this level of testing, a simple hardware adjustment might be used as shown in Fig. 79, so that messages may be sent out on a line which is *wrapped around*. These messages then appear as normal input to the system and pass through the multiplexor programs to the main computer programs.

When testing in Phase IV, the Test Supervisor Routine must have the

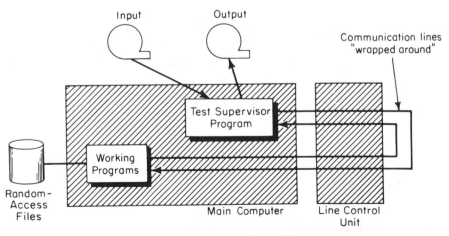

Fig. 79. Testing, Phase IV.

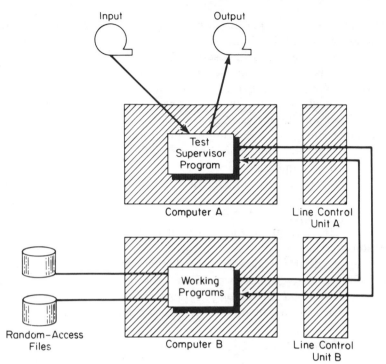

Fig. 80. Testing, Phase IV, using two computers for testing on a duplex system. (Could be used in Phase VII with Computer A handling real-time work while testing takes place on Computer B.)

facility to allow test messages to be sent to the appropriate multiplexor for wrap-around. This may be written, so that the Test Supervisor Routine can operate Phases III and IV tests while Phases V through VII are in operation.

The Test Supervisor Routine might analyze an input message to determine whether it is to be tested in Phase IV or Phase III. The messages on the input tape would be coded to indicate this. If a message is to be tested in Phase IV the Test Supervisor will send the message to the multiplexor. This will analyze the message as it would analyze output to a terminal set. The message is sent out on the line and it will return via the wrap-around. It will now appear to the multiplexor as a normal input message from a terminal. The multiplexor will perform all its functions on this message and send it to the main computer.

Upon completion of processing, the message will be sent out to the multiplexor and again wrapped around. A special program is necessary to catch this message when it returns to the computer. This program places the output message on the test output tape.

This technique will permit switchover to be tested under overload conditions—an otherwise difficult feat.

A set word or register will describe the list of chained available blocks. This contains the addresses of the first and last block in the chain and the count of blocks. The Supervisory Programs use this word to allocate core and to decide when to take emergency action because core is becoming short. They update this word as core blocks are allocated or returned to the Available Storage List. Setting up this word is part of the initialization procedure. This procedure should be modified to change the Available Storage Word as required.

This simple procedure for effectively reducing the number of storage blocks may be used in other phases also. It may be desirable to know whether a programmer is using too many core blocks, for example, in Phase II or III. Cutting down the available storage would impose definite restrictions on him.

It may be desirable also to test what action the system takes when there are an excessive number of file actions or excessive usage of computer time. *Overload Simulator* programs can be devised for this which consume given amounts of processing time or channel time.

2. *Testing with Multiplexor and Terminals*

When the programs work with the multiplexor, the next step will be to introduce terminals. Single-thread testing of single messages from one terminal will be the start; after this comes multi-thread testing, with messages coming from tape with wrap-around and from terminals at the same time.

No extra programs will be required, but the message codes must be such that the different messages are directed by the multiplexor to the correct lines.

When the system is "under Analysis", messages from a terminal are used to determine the mode of testing for all messages from that terminal.

3. *Loading the Queues to Capacity*

When the queues are fully loaded, emergency program mechanisms come into play. These are triggered by the count of available core blocks falling below certain limits. It is thus essential to test the system loaded to capacity before it becomes operational. It could be disastrous if no adequate test of emergency mechanisms was made before a peak in actual operational running brings them into play.

It is, however, difficult to feed sufficient messages into the system to load the system fully. It could be done by using additional hardware. It could also be done by allowing one computer to feed the other computer via the multiplexors as shown in Fig. 80 and to receive its output. This computer would contain an adaptation of the Test Supervisor Routine and would contain a program for logging the replies.

Both these schemes tie up a considerable amount of hardware, and the complications of having so many messages travelling to and fro would slow down testing. If two computers were used this would preclude the testing of switchover at the same time as the queues are loaded.

An alternative would be to produce a false overload condition. One way of doing this would be to fill up the New Input Queue to capacity before starting the test, using up all the available core blocks. This would produce an overload that would last for only a brief period.

A neater and more controllable method would be to effectively remove many of the available core blocks. If this is done the Supervisory Programs are forced to take overload action when only a few messages are in the system. This action can be produced easily and the effects inspected without undue complication because of the small number of messages.

4. *Multiplexor Switchover*

When any form of switchover is tested the Test Supervisor Routines should not be used, as this would complicate the process unnecessarily. Input should be from terminals.

The testing of switchover must perform the following functions:

(a) Test that the machines have in fact switched and continued working.

(b) Check that no messages were lost in the switchover process that should not be lost, and that no errors were caused in messages or file records.

(c) If errors losses did occur, their cause must be located.

A batch of messages should be fed through the system without switchover and then the same batch repeated with switchover and the results compared. If an error occurs or a message is lost, the test should be repeated, varying the input scientifically to determine what conditions cause the error. It may be possible to repeat the error with only one single message.

All the various types of switching should be tested in this manner.

5. *Switchover of the Central Processing Unit*

The functions of computer switchover testing are similar to those of testing multiplexor switchover. Again, terminals might be used rather than the Test Supervisor Routine.

Scheduled switchover should be tested before automatic switchover. When testing the latter some means of triggering the various types of automatic switchover at the correct moment will be required.

When it is found that an error is occurring in switchover routine it will be desirable to find which compter is causing the error. A memory dump should be taken of the computer which is shutting down, after it has shut down. A memory dump should be taken of the new computer when it has initialized itself but before it has started processing. It may be desirable to run the Supervisory Systems on both computers "under Analysis" during switchover.

Close cooperation between the various groups of the programming team will be needed when testing at this level.

PHASE V   This is the phase in which distant terminals are introduced on-line for the first time. It will range from the time when the first city terminal is hooked up for a short single-thread test to the time when many terminals are on-line for the entire day. The purpose of this phase is to remove as far as possible all remaining errors from the system, so that the cut-over to actual operational running will be as smooth as possible. One of the problems in this phase is to cause the most remote errors, which occur only very infrequently, to exhibit themselves.

By the time programs or groups of programs pass into Phase V they should have been largely debugged, though certain very infrequently occurring errors may remain.

Phase V will have three main functions:

1. To test with terminals in the remote offices to see whether any errors are introduced by the use of long-distance lines.

2. To train operators and to familiarize office staff with the use of terminals.

3. To cause the remote errors which only occur very infrequently to exhibit themselves.

The types of error that may be introduced when long-distance lines are first used are, apart from engineering troubles, errors due to line transmission noise. The programs must be able to handle all types of transmission errors and to reject messages when they require to be rejected. It is difficult to generate all types of transmission errors for the purpose of testing this function of the program. Some means of artificially putting noise on the line might be considered.

One difficulty may arise in deciding whether a fault is caused by a program error or a transmission error. If it is a program error, has it occurred in the multiplexor or the computor? The same message may be re-sent, and if then it gives the same error, this indicates that it is a program fault rather than a random transmission error. If the error is not repeated it is probably a transmission error though it could be a transient program error.

It is necessary to train the terminal operators of an on-line system very carefully. Usually it is a good idea to use computer programs to help in this. The computer programs may be used in two ways. First, a specially written *sequential teaching program,* of a simple type, may be used. Second, a *Training Mode* of normal operation may be defined. In the latter the programs run normally, except that a code indicates that certain file records must not be written on.

Training Mode is likely to be used in Phase V to familiarize the operators with the system. It can, however, provide a remarkably effective de-

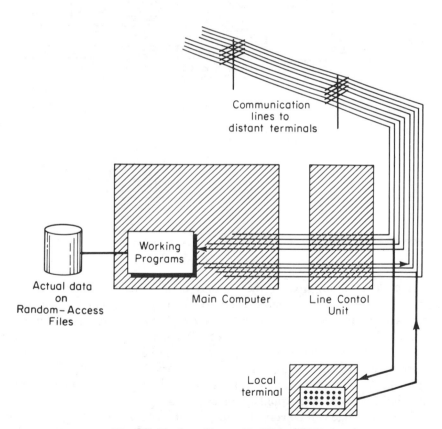

Fig. 81. Testing, Phases V, VI, and VII.

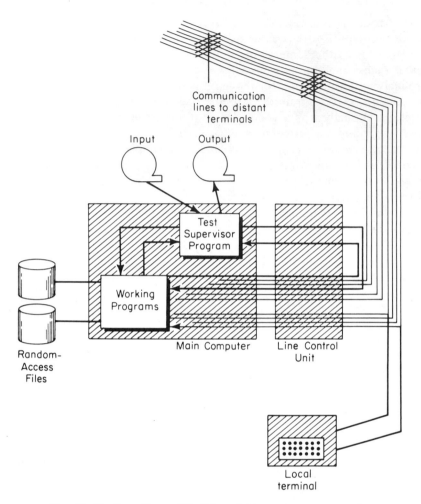

Fig. 82. Testing, Phases III, IV, and V running concurrently.

bugging aid. Certain areas of the file may be allocated to distant terminal operators who would be encouraged to enter all types of transactions. They would progress from normal everyday input to exceptional input: from simple messages to complex ones. When this is done, it is usually found that the inventiveness or randomness of the operators far exceeds the imagination of those who designed the formal test input. Operators would check their results under supervision, and any inconsistencies in the computer's performance would be investigated.

Computer time will be very short in the later phases of testing. For this reason it will be desirable to run tests in Phase III and Phase IV at the same time as Phase V. The file organization must be planned with this in mind. The Test Supervisor Routines must be able to operate while messages from terminals are being answered (Figs. 81 and 82).

PHASE VI   Phase VI is the cut-over phase. For the first time the files are loaded with actual working data. The entries will all be actual messages referring to actual current events.

This phase may begin with only one function of the system in use, only a small number of records and only one terminal location. As the phase proceeds more records are added, more locations come on-line, and eventually the functions of the system are increased.

Parallel operation will occur between the new system and the previous methods of operation. A point will be reached in the operation when sufficient confidence is built up to cut over to actual operations.

With a partially installed system it may be difficult to update all the records as required. Some information relating to a given record may have to come from locations not yet on-line. For example, in an airline booking system, information relating to flights may normally come from cities not yet on-line. Some means must be devised for bridging this gap.

The files in Phase VI will be loaded with actual data and, as in Phase VII, it is important that this should not be accidentally damaged by a program error. This may be difficult to prevent as other phases of testing will occur at the same time as Phase VI, but it is important that means of file protection should be devised because this will be essential in the early days of operational running. This might be achieved as follows:

The files are divided into two areas, an area used by Phase VI, or actual operation, and a scratch area which is used for testing. When macros are given which write on the file, the address is checked by a *File Address Checking Program* to insure that a test program is not attempting to write on the wrong area.

Ideally, the files might be split up, with certain files used for testing and the others for Phases VI or VII. However, to minimize file reference time, operational records may not be split off in this way but rather will be distributed throughout all the files. Therefore, the division must be by area within the file rather than by file. Testing might use the innermost cylinders, and operating programs the outermost on a set of disks, for example.

When the operational system grows to its planned eventual size, the operating programs will require all the files. When this happens it may be worthwhile having a separate file for testing purposes. It may be possible to use files with interchangeable disks or to dump the working data onto tape before testing. In a system on which modifications are likely to be made, and which works 24 hours, or almost 24, a day, a separate file for testing is a good idea.

PHASE VII   However thorough the testing of Phase V, it is virtually certain that errors will occur when the system first becomes operational. For this reason some means must be devised of handling errors during real-time operation.

It is also certain that many modifications will be made to the system while it is operational. The number of changes that will be made to a system can easily be underestimated. Batch processing programs undergo many modifications, but it is probable that there will be more for a large real-time system because the terminals of a real-time system are in direct interaction with the external world. Furthermore, any change to a highly integrated system affects many programs.

The testing requirements are likely to be greater when the system first becomes operational or partially operational. It is, therefore, recommended that when the system is cut over, the following conditions apply until confidence is built up:

1. It is not operational 24 hours per day.
2. Not all the files are used operationally. Some are reserved for testing purposes only.
3. Automatic switchover is not used.
4. If the multiplexors are duplexed, one is used for testing purposes.

When the system is operational and a catastrophic error occurs, there are two considerations which must be weighed against each other:

1. Putting the system back on the air as soon as possible with minimum damage to vital system records.
2. Obtaining sufficient information regarding the nature of the error to facilitate subsequent debugging.

In accomplishing the first objective it may be desirable to investigate queue entries, to see whether there are any incomplete file actions which may cause an error on the file. This must be considered in the specifications of switchover and recovery.

The second objective requires that start-up be delayed to obtain debugging data. At least a core dump will be required. An analysis of this will usually indicate whether any records may have been damaged by the failure.

File protection is essential during operational running. The methods described under Phase VI will be even more important here. It is doubtful whether file protection means can be devised that will insure that file damage will never occur, especially when testing. For this reason, some means of file reconstruction is important. Audit trails should be left, or sufficient information should be logged or dumped nightly to reconstruct the vital records if an error should erase them. The error may not be discovered until some time after it occurs. File reconstruction techniques are a difficult subject requiring much thought and should not be delayed unduly in the development of the system.

One of the most common causes of accidental file damage is likely to be the generation of an incorrect file address. If the indirect addressing or indexing scheme produces an address incorrectly and the program attempts to write on that record, damage will be done. The following recommendations will help to avoid this:

1. All file addressing schemes must be tested before Phases VI or VII with exceptional thoroughness. Very elaborate and complete schemes for testing these must be used, because if file addressing goes wrong in Phases VI or VII it will cause great difficulties.

2. Changes to file addressing schemes should be avoided as far as possible once Phase VI is reached. If a change must be made, then it should be checked out very thoroughly before use.

3. In all cases simple file addressing techniques should be used. Ingenious but difficult randomizing or indexing schemes should be avoided.

4. Insure that all programmers understand the danger of errors in file addressing.

5. Insure that all file addressing is done by standard macros under centralized supervision.

6. When operational programs write a record, make them read the record first and check its contents as far as is possible to make sure that they have the correct record.

When the system is fully operational and modifications are introduced the testing of these modifications will be difficult. It is suggested that the system may have to become non-operational for a short off-peak period on occasions, or that a degraded form of service must be given. When a new overpass is built on a highway a short period of degraded service cannot be avoided.

It will be necessary to test some modifications while the system is operational. If a duplexed system is available as in Fig. 18, Chapter 5, the two computers may be used as follows:

1. They may first be used independently; as much testing as possible should be done on the off-line machine. For Phase IV testing this

will mean that the operational system can use only one of the multiplexors.

2. The on-line computer could be used to feed messages to the testing machine. This would require a simple program in the on-line machine operating on a real-time basis. It would be a real-time variation of Fig. 80.

3. The testing machine in the later stages of testing may have the same messages fed to it as the operational machine via a separate multiplexor. The input would then be live, but the output would be logged on tape.

4. Last, when the modification first becomes operational this might be regarded as testing on the operating system. The off-line machine should be standing by for immediate switchover in case of trouble. This would only be done with programs debugged as far as possible by other methods. It should only be done at off-peak hours.

Because of the difficulties involved in making modifications to the operating system, tight control should be exercised on the frequency of modifications. Where the change is a small one, the effect of which can be completely tested off-line, this is not difficult; but where the change affects many different programs, for example, a change in message format or a change in the Supervisory Programs, this will be very difficult to test during operation. It is desirable to make the latter type of change as infrequent as possible. Modifications might be handled in one of two ways, depending upon their nature. It may be possible to split them up into small, easy changes that are easy to test. If this cannot be done then the modification should not be made until a complete new model of a program or set of programs is installed, which incorporates all such changes. Each of these new models should be carefully documented, and they should be sufficiently infrequent to allow each one to be completely shaken down before the next one is installed.

It is worth taking a lesson from professional diplomats that, if requests for changes are postponed or queued in this way long enough, the desire for the change may in many cases cease.

34 SUMMARY OF PROGRAMS REQUIRED FOR TESTING

This chapter is intended to provide a check list of the programs mentioned in previous chapters that are required for testing.

The hardware involved is mentioned on the right. This may be the complete system, with communication lines. It may be only the computer of the system, or the computer and the files, in which case it may be possible to do the testing on a different computer before the system in question is set up. It may need only an off-line computer such as a peripheral machine normally used for high speed tape-to-printer work. These alternatives are shown.

Another column suggests the language level that the program may be written in. This may be a language of the level of Autocoder in which one line of code generates one instruction, or, with macro-instructions, a set of instructions. Or it may be a higher level language such as COBOL. It may have to be written as an Application Program segment with all the restrictions that bind such segments. It may be a utility program provided with the system, such as a sort or core print-out.

Any specific system is not likely to need quite all of the items on the list, but it may need most of them. There can be a considerable amount of work in preparing these testing aids for a complex system.

	Language Level	Hardware
1. *Creation of Data for Testing*		
File record generator.	COBOL	Off-line computer
Input message generator.	COBOL	Off-line computer
Pilot Tape creation program.	COBOL	Off-line computer
Pilot Tape maintenance program.	COBOL	Off-line computer
File address creator.	Autocoder	Off-line computer

	Language Level	Hardware
File loader programs.	Autocoder	Computer & files
File modification programs (Programs for making temporary or permanent changes to a set of random-access file data).	Autocoder	Computer & files
Program for adding errors or other "purterbations" to input data.	COBOL	Off-line computer
Programs for generating or selecting technical data.	COBOL/ FORTRAN	Off-line computer
2. *Preparation for Testing*		
Core loader and initializer.	Autocoder	System computer
Test input tape generator.	COBOL	Off-line computer
Test Supervisor Program.	Autocoder	System computer
3. *Simulators*		
Simulator of Supervisory Programs	Autocoder	System computer
Simulator of Operator Set input	Autocoder	System computer
Simulator of input from technical equipment	Autocoder	System computer
Simulator of Line Control Equipment	Autocoder	System computer
Pseudo Application Programs	App. Prog	System computer
Overload simulators	App. Prog	System computer
4. *Debugging Aids Built in the Supervisory Programs*		
"Analysis" aids:—		
Entry-time Routine	Autocoder	System computer
Departure-time Routine	Autocoder	System computer
Routine for logging interrupts	Autocoder	System computer
Macro-instruction trace	Autocoder	System computer
Priority routine for logging errors or taking appropriate core print-outs when an error occurs.	Autocoder	System computer
Routine for logging output messages	Autocoder	System computer
5. *Other Debugging Aids*		
Core print-outs.	Utility	System computer
File data print-outs.	Utility	Computer & files
"Snapshots" for taking print-outs of core and registers at specific points in a program.	Utility	System computer
Macro-instruction "exerciser" for checking macro-instruction routines.	Autocoder	System computer

	Language Level	Hardware
Supervisory Program "exerciser" for checking performance of Supervisory Programs.	Autocoder	System computer
6. *Test Output Processing (for Saturation Testing)*		
Output sort	Utility	Off-line computer
Primary Output Processor	COBOL	Off-line computer
Secondary Output Processor	COBOL	Off-line computer
7. *Other Aids Built into the Supervisory Programs*		
"Analysis" mode initializer. (An Application Program may enable control messages to switch on "Analysis" mode in the Supervisory Programs, or modify the type of data it collects.	App. Prog	System
File Address Checking Program for protecting the files by preventing certain addresses being accidentally overwritten by certain types of action.	Autocoder	System
File Restore Program, for logging details of file records that are changed in a test run and restoring the original after the test.	Autocoder	Computer & files
Line Control Program for use with "wrap-around" of lines.	Autocoder	System
Programs for permitting one computer of a duplexed pair to feed test messages to other, and to receive its replies.	Autocoder	Duplexed System

SECTION **VII**

MANAGEMENT PROBLEMS

35 THE PROBLEM OF CONTROL

As has been seen, the programming of real-time computer systems brings many problems and challenges not usually encountered on conventional computers. Perhaps the greatest of the problems lies in the management of a team putting together a complex system with the constraints of "real-time." More rigorous disciplines and a different order of management control is needed.

In the remaining chapters, techniques and disciplines are discussed that have proved successful in the program management of complex real-time systems so far.

Work on the real-time system will usually start with a small and competent group of systems analysts who understand well the problems of the application. These people may be selected from the different areas with which the computer will become involved. When this team has produced a tentative design plan, programmers will be brought in to begin working out the details of the plan. They will draw up programming specifications and block diagrams and eventually will start coding. The programs will be written in separate units small enough for one man to handle. The size of the units is often determined by the size of blocks of program that the Supervisory System can read into core. The system may have many separate blocks written at different times by different people. The blocks of program will be tested individually for logic errors and then, later, will be made to work in conjunction with each other, so that the complete system is slowly built up and tested.

A carefully planned schedule for this is needed, as will be discussed later. Certain programs, e.g., the Supervisory Programs, must be specified before work can begin on the others. Similarly, during the testing, certain programs must be in existence and debugged before work can begin on testing the others. The Application Programs need macro-instructions, Common Storage, programming relocation techniques, and so on, to be defined before work starts on them.

COMPLEX INTER-ACTIONS BETWEEN WORK OF DIFFERENT PROGRAMMERS A large real-time system is likely to have many of its programs being worked on concurrently. These programs are small parts of what will become a tightly integrated whole. The segments of programs that are being written separately must at a later time all plug into each other and work together like a complex piece of machinery.

The work of one programmer thus considerably affects the work of the others. This is illustrated in Fig. 83. The circles in this figure represent the segments of program and other items in the design, such as file records, input transactions, and so on. They could also represent elements in the hardware design. The lines and arrows represent logical interactions between these items. The figure shows only a few circles, but in a moderately sized real-time system, there would be many hundreds of these, possibly thou-

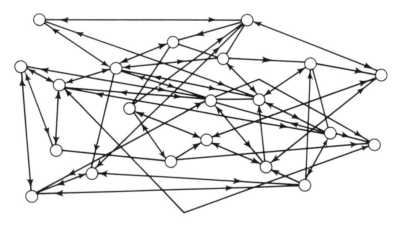

Fig. 83. The problem of control (I). The circles represent segments of Program and also file records, input transactions, and so on. The lines represent logical interactions between these on a system in which they are tightly interdependent. If a Programmer makes a change to his program or to his data specifications, this is likely to affect the work on any of the items indicated by the lines and arrows. In reality, Programmers make many changes, and communicating these to other Programmers who need to know becomes a severe problem on a system with hundreds of segments of program.

sands, and pattern of interactions between them would be very complex. In the eventual system, these items fit together and are closely interdependent. The units of program, for example, could not be written independently as they affect the functioning of each other in a complex fashion.

If a programmer makes a change to his program or to his data specifications, this is likely to affect the work of a number of other programmers, and these must all be notified of the changes. In reality, in the course of his work the programmer constantly makes changes of this type. Programs tend to grow and develop rather like the growth of a city. To communicate all of these changes to all of the other programmers who need to know about them on a large system becomes a severe problem.

The basic problem that this chapter discusses is as follows: *How can the programs that make up a real-time system be developed concurrently by separate programmers when there are so many interactions between them? How can control over the interactions be maintained?*

It is interesting to pursue the analogy between this type of system and a complex piece of mechanical or electrical engineering. Some of the techniques that have become traditional in conventional engineering point the way here also.

DOCUMENTATION   First, the level of documentation used in engineering is very much greater than that normally found in the programming world. Before work commences on the components of a new piece of computer circuitry or a section of a chemical plant, it is planned in fine detail on paper. Elaborate specifications are drawn up for the components and for the overall layout. If, during the construction, any deviation occurs from the specifications, this again is documented in detail and replanned with care.

Without doubt, real-time systems need a higher degree of documentation than is found in conventional systems. Part of the solution to the problem posed above is to draw up detailed specifications for each program segment and data record in the system. The same discipline that is used in engineering documentation should be applied here in programming. Details of the documentation that is needed are discussed in the next chapter.

There is a basic difference, however, between programming and engineering construction. Because of the nature of programming, the programmers constantly find the need to make changes to the mechanism they devise. They constantly invent cleaner and better patterns of logic that mean modifying the structure of data records and changing their specifications. Each time they make a change that affects the specifications, this must itself be documented. Where it affects the work of other programmers, as it normally will, these must read the documents giving details of the change. There will thus be a flow of paperwork as indicated by the arrows in Fig. 83.

The flow of such paperwork can indeed become too great to be reasonably manageable in a large system unless it is controlled somehow. The programmers become deluged with so many tedious documents that they do not read them all or do not assimilate their significance. Programmers almost invariably dislike this large amount of paperwork. Generally they do not like writing specifications. Any means of cutting down the number of interactions should be used so that the paperwork can be lessened. Where interactions of the type described do occur they must be documented, especially in a large system, or serious confusion can occur, bringing in its wake chaos at system testing time.

DIVISION INTO SUB-SYSTEMS The number of interactions between programs, or between programmers, can be cut down by dividing the system programs into sub-systems. This is illustrated in Fig. 84. It is rather like making sub-assemblies in mechanical engineering. The behavior of the sub-assembly is clearly defined and the way it fits into the rest of the machinery is specified in detail. This done,

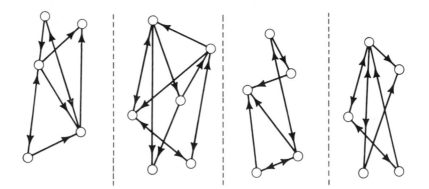

Fig. 84. The problem of control (II). Part of the solution to the problem illustrated in Fig. 83 is to divide the system into largely self-contained units of Program which can be handled by a group of Programmers small enough to communicate with each other easily. The interface between the units of Program must be very clearly defined and documented. These are represented by the dotted lines above. If changes to these interfaces must be made, all Programmers are notified of the changes.

the sub-assembly can be made independently of the remainder. Sub-systems of program might be, for example, the Main Scheduling Routine, the communication line input/output control, message editing routines, self-contained groups of Application Programs, and so on. These units are small enough for two or three men, or even one man, to handle them. The interactions within this unit are then relatively easy to control. The unit is insulated as completely as possible from the other units. The interface between the unit and the rest of the system must be very clearly defined.

Every attempt will be made not to modify the interfaces between the units. This means that, before programming begins, the functions of the units must be very clearly thought out. It will, however, be inevitable that the interface needs some modification as the system develops. When this occurs it must be documented thoroughly, and all programmers concerned must know about it.

CONTROLLING CHANGES   An engineering project, once it has been laid down what is being built, will not normally change from the original plan. In programming, however, it is often thought by those not directly involved that changes can easily be made. Persons often think that the functions can be modified slightly as the programming proceeds, as this is only a matter of altering lines of coding on a piece of paper. This may be a reasonable view for a conventional system for billing, or payroll, or doing engineering calculations. Here changes can easily be made. However, when a complex real-time system is fitted together it causes endless trouble if the requirements of the system are changed now and then as it is being programmed.

Any requirements for changes that do arise should be noted and left for incorporation in a later model. As soon as the writing of operational programs for one model begins, this model and its functional specifications should be *frozen*. When this model is working the programmers may then begin a second version of the system which incorporates any improvements thought of while the first was being developed.

MODEL-BY-MODEL BUILD UP   The changes built into the second model may include additional functions and modifications required by the users of the system, and, sometimes more important, modifications desired by the programmers themselves. It is rare that a good programmer reaches the end of a piece of coding without wanting to rewrite it. He sees ways of cleaning up the logic, speeding up the program, making it perform better. In a large system written with a team of many coders this is much more true. There will be many deficiencies in the first working model, many areas which could be simplified and improved. The testing phase, when the work of several programmers is first made to perform as one system, normally suggests many possibilities for improvement. It is likely that the first model of a multi-programmed system will have a number of elements in the combined logic which slow it down. The second model of most such systems is considerably faster than the first. The Supervisory Programs, in particular, may be capable of being speeded up.

Saving all the possible changes for a new model, rather than tearing the present coding to pieces as soon as improvements are thought of, will enable one model to go "on the air" fairly quickly so that experience can be gained in using it. Furthermore, the second model will certainly benefit from a joint planning of the improvements incorporated in it.

The *freezing* of each model, and the model-by-model buildup, as shown in Fig. 76, Chapter 31, is desirable, then, to protect the system both from external pressures for change, and from its own programmers' desire for change. The programmers will generally be happier if they know that they can incorporate the modifications they invent in the next model.

In engineering development it is common to build a prototype, designed to investigate the functioning of a system, or part of a system, before the final working product is built. Design feedback from the prototype is used to improve the final system. This technique is useful also in a complex programming system. Sub-units of the system may be programmed and tested experimentally, often using simulation, before the coding of the final product begins. The first of the models in Fig. 76 may be designed not to be an operational model but an experimental prototype.

The "models" of the Supervisory Programs may be treated separately from the models of the Application Programs. The Application Programmers need the main part of the Supervisory Programs to be defined before they can start coding, and debugged before they can start testing. A Model 1 of the Supervisory Programs may be handed to the Application Programmers, and they may use this while the Supervisory Programmers develop their Model 2. Functions not immediately necessary for the writing and testing of Application Programs may be saved for Model 2. These might include fall-back programs, switchover, error handling, overload procedures, emergency interrupts, and so on.

Building up the system model-by-model helps to control the use of core, processing time, and, indeed, money. A creeping inflation in these critical factors frequently sets in if piecemeal additions to the programming task are permitted.

A management problem that can become very difficult with an inventive programming team is deciding which of the many features they devise should be incorporated. To add them all could run the system out of core storage or processing time. It can be difficult to decide whether a programming proposal is worthwhile when it is considered on its own. However, when all the various ideas are discussed together in deciding on the features of a new model their relative merits can be compared. The decisions can be made which are practical and economic. The core storage, processing time, and possibly, money available for improvements can be assessed.

CONTROL GROUP

Some decisions must be made as the system is being programmed. They concern changes which cannot wait for the next model. To approve and help handle these it is suggested that a separate Control Group should be set up. For a small system this may be one man. On a larger system the function may need six or eight people full time.

The Control Group would read all Program Specifications before they are handed to programmers to work on. It would thus build up a complete knowledge of the system under development. The Control Group would evaluate the core storage utilization, processor time utilization, file utilization and other critical factors. It would monitor the progess of the program writing to ensure that these figures did not exceed the allowable values. Any changes to the Specifications that programmers need to make would be referred to the Control Group. The Control Group would modify the specifications as needed and so relieve the programmers of a task they generally dislike. It would communicate all changes to the persons who need to know about them. This is illustrated in Fig. 85.

On a large and complex system a Control Group of this type has proved very valuable in directing the progress of what can otherwise be a most unwieldy monster. It monitors what is happening, as described in Chapter 39, and channels it down the right paths. The Control Group needs to be planned in such a way that it will not itself become a bottleneck. If it is unable to read, assimilate, and approve of specifications fast enough a queue of work builds up which can become an annoying delay.

This central authority, planning and monitoring the development of the system, should also oversee the program and system testing. The data for program testing should come from a centralized source rather than from individual programmers. This should be seen to by the Control Group which should also inspect the results of the testing, again being the one group that has an overall view of the system.

The programs, as they are written, should be checked by the Control Group to ensure that they do not exceed any of the critical factors of the system, such as core or time utilization or lengths of input/output opera-

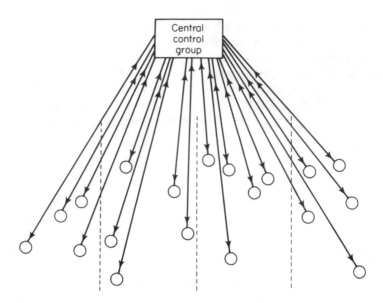

Fig. 85. The problem of control (III). Tight control may be maintained over the changes in an evolving system by using a central group to approve of specifications, and of all changes to these that may become necessary. The control group has an overall knowledge of the system and insures that all changes it agrees to are adequately documented and details are sent to Programmers who need to know about them.

tions. After unit testing they should be signed off ready for higher levels of testing.

It is important that there should be only one Control Group for the whole system, and, indeed, one overall management. Some systems have suffered from split management, with part of the programs being done by one group and part by another, and no one person of overall authority. For example, in some cases a computer manufacturer or consultant has specially written the Supervisory Programs and sometimes also the Support Programs, while the system user has written the Application Programs. Sometimes the groups, with no combined management, have even been in different countries. Not to have an overall Control Group and an overall manager with power of veto is to impose a grave difficulty on a system that is already difficult enough. Tight management and very tight overall control is needed on these systems. Split management is a grave and unnecessary hazard.

To return again to Fig. 83 and the problem of interactions between programmers, some of the methods above represent a *formal* means of control of interactions. *Informal* contact between the programmers must also be encouraged to the full. It should be a point of pride with programmers to know as much as they can about the system as a whole. They should know exactly how their own work fits in with other parts of the system. They should understand the nature of the interactions represented by errors in Fig. 83, as fully as possible.

Parochialism is a fault that occurs only too easily on a large programming team, especially if parts of it are in different locations, as is sometimes the case. A programmer can become so immersed in the problems of his own program or sub-system that he tends to lose contact with the rest of the system and its environment. Regular exposure to the problems and viewpoints of other personnel is essential. This may be done by periodic seminars which the whole programming team attend. Selected programmers or systems analysts should speak to the group about their work, or aspects of the system.

An external consultant or person not connected with part of the system can be of value. Programming groups may periodically discuss their approaches with such a person. Exposure to a completely external or overall viewpoint can improve their work or remove deficiencies that result from shortsightedness.

To a large extent the understanding of the interactions with other programmers requires good *teamwork*. The members of the programming team must recognize each other's problems. They should be encouraged to strive for careful cooperation and should be made to understand the importance of the separate elements meshing together cleanly. Simplicity of individual programming mechanisms is often a key factor in fitting together a complex system. As good team members the programmers should know that the ease with which the components fit together is more important than individual brilliance.

36 PROGRAM DOCUMENTATION

Experience of implementing real-time systems has shown that the conventional methods of program documentation are inadequate for a complex system. More exact and detailed specifications and descriptions are needed.

Good documentation is, of course, essential for all data-processing, but in many "conventional" systems the documentation is done largely as an afterthought when the programs have been completed. On an elaborate real-time system the documentation should not be regarded as something to be done after the programs are written. It is a tool without which the development of a tightly interrelated set of programs will run into endless trouble.

This chapter discusses why documentation of a different degree to conventional systems is needed. It suggests what levels of specifications should be planned, and it gives guidelines for preparing these.

There are several reasons why detailed specifications are essential; they can be summarized in one word: *constraints*. If a complex piece of machinery is being built and different components are being made by different people, the specifications for these components must be drawn up very carefully so that they fit together when the machinery is assembled. Once the specifications are drawn up they must be adhered to exactly or the parts will not fit. A relatively simple piece of mechanical engineering has this type of discipline, and yet many highly complex pieces of data-processing have been attempted without it.

One of the difficulties of writing programs is that, as they are being written, the logic which underlies them is likely to change or develop. A programmer improves the logic of the system, thinking as he works. He discovers complications that were not foreseen at the outset. He invents refinements that improve the performance of the system. He will sometimes reach a stage in his thinking when he wants to scrap a section of coding and start again on a cleaner, more logical basis. He constantly makes changes. In view of the *constraints* that apply, because his work must fit in with all the other parts of the programming, he must be careful in the changes he makes. He must not modify items that will upset the work of other programmers without consulting them, and the changes must be documented very carefully; otherwise the whole system will get out of hand, and one programmer will not know what the others are doing. In this environment of constant change there must be careful control of the documentation; otherwise there is no hope that the parts of the machine will fit together when the time comes to assemble it.

The documentation, and the channels of flow for documentation, must therefore be designed so that changes, where essential, can occur and be communicated easily to the programmers who need to know about them. However, the volume of documentation can become so overwhelming and unreadable on a large system that a planned effort should be made to keep changes to a minimum, once programming is under way.

A conventional data processing system may have as many lines of program coding as a real-time system, but it would not require the same order of documentation because there is little interaction between the programs. Many of the programs run on the computer at separate times. They are independent except, perhaps, in some of the data they use. In a real-time system many of the programs are in the machine concurrently, sharing the same storage and peripheral units, and often fitting into a tight timing pattern. A better method is needed to define individual program boundaries. Usually the programs cannot all be in core at the same time, and so they must be artificially segmented with a well-defined linkage between them. On multi-programmed real-time systems an almost infinite number of combinations of program segments can be in core together, with control switching constantly from one to another. The input is often unpredictable and variable in its rate and message length and type. Queues of different types and varying lengths will build up in the system. To construct such a complex piece of machinery the necessary *constraints* must be very clearly defined and documented.

One of the most difficult aspects of building up a complex real-time system is the program testing, discussed at length in Section V of this book. When the mass of programs are finally being run together, errors will occur which are caused by the juxtaposition of programs. These will often be very difficult to trace and correct. Good documentation is essential to help in this. It has been estimated that in one airline reservation system using about 140,000 lines of real-time coding, there are 250,000,000 possible paths through which the input may go before a response is obtained.

The consequences of errors in real-time systems are usually severe. The system is normally designed not to stop, and there may be a danger that undiscovered errors may damage the data files. When an error occurs in a conventional system, it can be detected by means such as batch totalling, and the machine can be stopped while the matter is put right. If a program has to be patched the batch can be run again at a later time. This is not so on a real-time system. The errors must, as far as possible, be found before cut-over to actual operational running. Again, detailed specifications of programs and data and thorough testing to ensure that they meet their specifications are needed to help eliminate errors.

When errors do occur, switchover or fallback to a degraded form of operation will take place. The programs used in the fallback mode will, to a large extent, be modified versions of those used in normal operation. These also need to be carefully specified.

The degree of documentation will depend upon the complexity of the systems being programmed. A large system with, say, 100,000 lines of real-time coding or more will need careful and elaborate specifications as described in the following pages. Smaller systems with, say, 5,000 lines of coding may not need such elaborate program specifications, though they need data specifications and, of course, must have careful documentation of the final product.

CROSS-INDEXING THE SPECIFICATIONS   In a complex system with, perhaps, 500 or so specifications, a well-thought-out means of cross-indexing the specifications is necessary. The specifications might be thought of as being the circles in Fig. 83. With 500 circles the diagram will be much more complex. Each of these should be numbered. Changes in the specifications will be made throughout the development of the system, and when a change is made the other specifications which may be affected by it must be thought about. These are indicated by the arrows in Fig. 83. Each specification should be given a unique code number which as far as possible indicates what type of specification it is. It should contain the code numbers of other specifications indicated by the arrows in Fig. 83, so that when a change is made these can be referred to.

The team developing the system needs somebody assigned, not necessarily full time, as a librarian to maintain control over the documentation and changes that are made to it. Some large projects have used punched cards or a simple computer program for maintaining control of their specifications. This gives a powerful analytical tool by means of which all programs that may need modifying in certain circumstances can be pinpointed. It is, however, a tool that is only justified in a very large system.

The specifications are likely to keep changing as the system thinking

develops, and therefore the means of filing them must be designed to ac-
commodate this constant change. The distribution to individual programmers should be minimized as the programmer can quickly become deluged
with too much to read and assimilate.

SPECIFICATIONS
OF THE
SPECIFICATIONS

Fairly early in the development of a system several
people will be writing specifications for file records
and Application Programs. As the system design
progresses, a larger number will be working on the
specifications. It is necessary, before this work begins, to define what specifications are needed for this particular system; in other words, to write
specifications for the specifications.

The remainder of this chapter indicates what documentation is likely
to be needed and what it should contain. There are basically four types
of documentation.

1. *Functional Description of the System*

In the beginning, the functions that the system is to perform will be
written down. This document will describe how the system affects its users,
what the input and output will be, what records the computer will maintain, what the volumes of messages will be, and so on.

A general system flow chart will be drawn up in the preliminary planning
to show the overall flow of work through the system. It will indicate which
functions are to be performed by the computer and which manually. It
will show where all the input transactions and documentation come from,
and how the output from the computer is utilized.

2. *Data Specifications*

When the functions of the system have been agreed upon it is necessary
to begin working out the details and to draw up specifications for the program and for the data that will be used and referred to.

The Data Specifications will describe in as much detail as possible what
information is kept in the file records, what is in the input and output messages, how the files are laid out, how the core is laid out, and so on.

The Data Specifications will be used by the programmers to manipulate
and use these data. At first it will not be possible to describe the data in
full detail saying what the significance of every bit or character is, but as
the system is developed the Data Specifications must be added to, to contain such information in detail.

3. *Program Specifications*

Once the general flow chart of the system is completed, the next step will probably be an attempt to list all of the programs that are needed in the system. The list will, of course, be added to as the system thinking develops. Having listed the programs, the next step will be to write down the functions of each program.

More detailed specifications for the programmer to work from will then be developed. These will contain details of the input to the program and its output, what file records it will refer to, and any restrictions there must be on the program, such as restrictions on timing and restrictions on the use of core storage. It will list cross-references to other Data Specifications and other program specifications to which this one is related. A specification of this type written for an Application Program will be a document which can be given to a relatively inexperienced programmer, to enable him to write a program that will fit in with all the other programs that make up this system.

In addition to Application Program segments specified in this manner, the system will contain macro-instructions, Common Subroutines and Supervisory Programs which are likely to be used by any of the Application Programmers in this system. These must be defined in detail before coding begins on the Application Programs that use them. A manual should be provided which is as explicit as the computer programming manual. It should tell the programmer exactly how to use the macro-instructions, Common Subroutines and Supervisory Programs that are available.

4. *Documentation of Completed Programs*

When the programs are completed it is necessary to write full documentation on them, to facilitate program testing and to enable modifications to be made to them at later times. The programmers should draw a detailed block diagram with notes written on it, where necessary, to explain the functions of various blocks where these are otherwise not clear. An outsider who has read the Data Specifications and Program Specifications relating to this unit of program should be able to understand how the program works by looking at this block diagram.

Some or all of the blocks on the block diagram should be numbered, and these numbers should be used in the labels of the program coding lists. As the block diagram will be used when debugging the system, it should be clear which lines of coding relate to which parts of the block diagram. As a block diagram will sometimes be used by a programmer other than the one who developed it, it must be done in a manner sufficiently clear for him to be able to understand it easily. During system testing, programmers must be able to make cross-references between the various block diagrams and Data Specifications which define the system.

The coding which must be clearly related to the block diagram should also contain sufficient comments to enable a programmer, other than the one who wrote the program, to understand the coding and to make modifications to it at a later date.

As the completed system will contain many separate segments of program, it will often be difficult to know what segment has branches to what other segment. To avoid the immense confusion that can occur a *Skeletal Flow Diagram* should be drawn of the entire system which presents the interconnections between all the program segments and also major data blocks. This diagram should show simply, for each segment of program, all other program segments entered by this program, all programs which enter this program, and all major data files and records which are either entered or changed by this program.

It is the Data Specifications and Program Specifications that give instructions to the programmers and place the necessary restraints upon them. It is these documents that are used to ensure that the various parts of such a complex machine all fit together when they are completed. The rest of this report lists what these documents should contain to enable them to carry out this function.

DATA SPECIFICATIONS Data specifications are needed to give details of the overall usage or layout of a file or core area, details of logical files with their header tables, if any, means of access, and so on, and details of individual records within the files or individual messages.

There may, thus, be five sets of data specifications as follows:

1. *Bulk Storage Layout Specifications*

During the planning it is essential to think about the backing storage as a whole, deciding what records will go where, how additions and deletions will be handled, where indexes will be kept, and so on.

The specifications for this should contain information such as the following:

(a) A map giving the types of record in each part of bulk storage and saying how large an area is set aside for these.

(b) A list of each type of file (i.e., category of records) saying how many records are in this file, average and maximum.

(c) A list of each type of record, giving its average and maximum size, and the average and maximum size of the complete file of these records. This will include programs kept on the files.

(d) A statement of where in the storage each record is kept.

(e) A description of the means of addressing and locating each record.

(f) A statement of the access times for each record, average and maximum.

(g) Statistics relating to overflow areas where these are used, including size of location of overflow area, percentage of overflows, average and maximum and times of overflow seeks.

Some of this information may be tabulated for ease of reference and planning.

2. Core Layout Specifications

(a) A map of the core utilization should be drawn up to show how each area of core is to be used. If it is used differently at different times several maps will be needed.

(b) The map should allocate space to various functions and differentiate among fixed data areas, variable data areas, fixed programs, and areas for relocatable program segments.

3. File Specifications

A specification should be written for each logical file, or category of records, such as bank customer account records, airline flight records, audit trail, index records, and so on. The detail of individual records within a logical file may be described separately as indicated below, or it may be part of this document. If there are many types of record within the logical file, some of the information which is common to each is better written once only in an overall file specification.

This may contain the following:

(i) *Identification.* A number which identifies this specification and indicates its content. Name of author. Space for authorization signatures.

(ii) *Abstract.* A brief statement of the purpose, functions and contents of the file in non-technical language. This and other abstracts of specifications are intended first, to give a summary without reading in further detail, and second, to be read by a staff who examine, review and approve the *functions* of the system but who do not necessarily have any detailed programming familiarity.

(iii) *Assumptions.* This paragraph should state any assumptions that have been made in planning the records. When the specifications are reviewed it will be possible to check whether the assumptions are still valid. Assumptions might include such items as: a file reorganization run will take place nightly; a 3000 word index will be available for addressing; records updated will be dumped for file reconstruction purposes; and so on.

(iv) *Details.*

(a) The location of the file in the system.

(b) The size of the file, including facilities for estimated expansion.

(c) The concepts underlying the file layout.

(d) The technique for addressing and accessing file records.

(e) The number and frequency of probable overflows and details of the overflow area.

(f) Header and trailer labels if the file is serial. Means of identification if it is random.

(g) Details of index tracks, file addressing tables, tables of available space in a file with additions and deletions, and so on.

(h) Any restrictions that may apply, for example: no programs except . . . may write on this file.

(v) *Cross-references.* Numbers of the specifications that relate to this category in such a way that they might change it, or *vice versa.* These will include specifications of programs that update the file and use the file, and so on.

4. *File Record Layout Specifications*

(i) *Identification.* A number which identifies this specification and indicates its content. Name of author. Space for authorization signatures.

(ii) *Abstract.* A brief statement of the purpose, functions and content of the record in non-technical language.

(iii) *Assumptions.* As above.

(iv) *Details.* A record layout chart will be given which contains full details of record contents. If the record is made up of several sections several charts may be needed. The chart and description accompanying it must contain details of every field, word and bit in the record. It will describe all fields, saying whether they are fixed length or variable length. The length will be stated if they are fixed length. If not, the range will be specified and, if necessary, the specification will say how the programs ascertain the length.

The specification will state the type of coding, i.e., binary, BCD, BCC numeric, and so on, or mixed. It will state what each field is. It will give maximum or minimum values if necessary. It will give the meaning of all coded characters or bits. It will quote any restrictions on the use of fields. It will specify headers, trailers or means of identification if these are used.

In general, it will describe the record unambiguously so that several programmers can write programs using it, quite independently of each other.

(v) *Cross-references.* Numbers of the specifications that relate to this category in such a way that they might change it, or *vice versa,* that it might change them.

5. *Data Record Layout Specifications*

In the same manner that specifications are written for file records, so they must also be provided for any other records. This includes input messages, output messages, and any records which may reside in core such as the Message Reference Blocks.

The same amount of detail as above must be provided.

6. *Program Specifications*

If the Application Programs are divided into segments which can be read into core in relocatable positions, it may be desirable to describe these in two documents. One of these should describe the entire program and its functions and the other its individual segments. It may not be possible to see far enough ahead to specify the breakdown into segments until the coding begins. In this case it may be left to the programmer to plan this breakdown and document it. However, in the complex system careful control of this is needed.

After the functional specifications have been put together and agreed upon, detailed program specifications may be drawn up for the programmer as follows:

(i) *Identification.* A number which identifies the specification and indicates its content. Name of author. Name of programmer. Space for authorization signatures.

(ii) *Abstract.* If a functional specification has already been written, an abstract might be in this and hence would not be needed here.

(iii) *Assumptions.* Details of any assumptions that were made in drawing up this specification. This might include assumptions such as that certain off-line programs will exist and be run daily, certain fixed subroutines will be in core, other programs will make adjustments to the file, and so on.

(iv) *Input.* The input to the program should be specified in detail. Commonly the input will be a data record or message for which a Data Specification exists. It may, however, be an item in core or in a register which does not have a separate specification. It may be part of the linkage to the program. In any case, a description of it must be made available to the programmer in fullest detail, specifying each bit and the location of the input. These considerations apply also to intermediate input which the program obtains in the course of its running.

(v) *Output.* The output of the program should be specified in detail. Commonly the output also will be a data record or message for which a Data Specification exists. It may however be an item placed in core or in a register. It may be a file request. It may be a linkage to another program. In any case, a description of it must be made available to the programmer in fullest detail, as with input.

(vi) *Storage and timing requirements.* At the time of drawing up this specification, an attempt should be made to estimate the number of instructions needed as accurately as possible. This judgement should be based on a close look at the program logic.

A budget for program core storage utilization and program time should be made. These should be fitted into the overall core and timing budgets of the system. An estimate of the number of file accesses and other input/output operations should be made, along with their average and maximum timings.

Core storage utilization estimates should be divided into core that is permanently taken up, and core that is used on a temporary basis because the program is read into core from the files when it is needed. Besides program storage in core, storage for data will have to be considered. This will include input and output areas that might be allocated by the Supervisory Programs, or it may include tables or alphabetic messages in core, and so on. These also might be temporary or permanent. These figures may be tabulated for easier reference.

(vii) *File accesses.* The specification should list all accesses to files, random-access and tape. It should quote the relevant file specifications. Estimates of average and maximum access times should be given.

(viii) *Environment.* The means of *entry to* and *exit from* the program must be specified. The circumstances under which the program is entered should be detailed, along with any information the program needs other than the input specifications. The various types of exit the program may have must be similarly specified.

Any *error* or *exception action* must be specified. *Validity* or *error checks* that the program is to make should be stated, along with what action it takes when it finds something wrong. Details of any *restrictions* there may be on the program should be stated. For example, the program may not be used during peak hours because of the time or core it consumes.

(ix) *Logic description*. A description of the logic the program is to use should be given. This will frequently be done with the aid of a general block diagram. This diagram should not go into too much detail as this is the job of the programmer. A one-page diagram will often suffice, with narrative to assist in its understanding where necessary. Any techniques or approaches which the programmer should use on grounds of efficiency should be specified, and similarly, any techniques which the specification writer thinks undesirable. For example, the programmer may be told not to hold a file access arm between reading and updating certain records.

(x) *Cross-references*. The numbers of any specifications should be given which relate to this specification in such a way that they might change it or it might change them. These include the Data Specifications of the data used, the Program Specifications of the program this program is entered from and that which exits to, and so on.

Certain parts of the programs need to be designed and documented in sufficient detail so that other programs can incorporate them directly into their work. This applies especially to the Supervisory Programs and the macro-instructions that are used. These need to be documented in an exceptionally clear fashion, so that they are easy to use and so that there is no ambiguity in their use.

Programs of this type which are needed in the development of other programs must be produced at an early stage. Careful scheduling of this work is needed, as will be described in Chapter 38.

37 PERSONNEL

In the development of a large computer system, it is essential that an adequate number of suitably skilled men are available where and when they are needed. For a real-time system this may be still more critical than in a conventional system because the various parts of the system are highly interdependent, and delay in one can hold up the others. To ensure smooth installation of the system the completion of the different elements must be scheduled tightly, and the schedule must be continuously re-evaluated. In drawing up the schedule, manpower estimates must be adequate to ensure that no holdup occurs.

The main difference between the programming effort for a real-time system and a batch processing or conventional system of similar complexity is that the former must be a tightly integrated piece of *teamwork*. The programming group must be built up as a team and managed as a team. They are building a cathedral in which each piece of craftsmanship fits exactly with the rest to contribute to the overall effect, not a housing estate in which the efforts of individuals can be quite separate.

Each programmer must see his role in the system clearly and understand the concept of teamwork in constructing the system. He must understand the roles of the other programmers and how he fits in with them. General system education for all programmers will pay dividends. The specifications and interface documents described in the last chapter will help them to understand this and must be available.

Not all programmers work well in close teamwork. Some of the best programmers are creative persons who feel they need more freedom than such work offers them. Careful consideration should be given to this in recruiting and building up the team. Being a member of a real-time programming team may not be the right place for a programming *"prima donna."* Highly skilled and fast-working programmers who enjoy fitting into a team and seeing an excitingly complex system develop, are needed.

To install such a system on time the various specifications and segments of program must be phased in on schedule. Certain elements must be specified or coded before work can begin on other parts of the system that use these. To maintain a tightly planned and probably PERTed schedule it is necessary to recruit and train the requisite number of programmers, so that they are ready at the time they are needed to make their part of the schedule come to life.

On complex real-time installations it has often become necessary to recruit a large programming team in a short time. This is likely to be a much worse problem than on conventional systems for which the programming team grows over a relatively long period.

In order to plan the manpower requirements it is necessary to make estimates at a fairly early stage of how many men will be needed at what time. These estimates should be obtained by projecting the size and complexity of the programs in question and then applying a manpower factor based on past experience.

In preparing the material for this chapter various projects in the U.S.A. were surveyed in an attempt to indicate what relationship should be expected between the numbers of lines of coding and the manpower requirements for various types of program. There seems no reason to suggest that the figures obtained in America should not also apply in Europe and other parts of the world, although in Europe the programmers are somewhat less expensive.

Programmer experience is an important factor in making estimates. The productivity of a new, inexperienced, and poor quality programmer may differ from that of a good, experienced man by a factor as high as ten. A very sharp increase in efficiency of the programmer is evident in the first six to twelve months of programming. In almost all cases studied in preparing this chapter, the number of programmers required by large real-time systems has been so high that a large proportion of inexperienced programmers have been recruited especially for the Application Programs.

It is important to take education into account when making programming estimates. New programmers will require training. Some will have programmed before and will need to learn the machine and the system. Others will not have programmed before and will need to learn the basic techniques involved. A period of time representing the education should be added to the estimates.

The number of instructions per man-year varies considerably with the *complexity of the programs* being written. In real-time systems, for example, the number of Application Program instructions written per man-year might be four or more times as high as the number of Supervisory Program instructions.

Another factor affecting productivity is the question of how much of the program requires basically *new thinking*. Frequently the Application Programs have to be thought out from the beginning, as they are unique to the application in question. The Supervisory Programs and some of the Support Programs may be more likely to follow the pattern of similar systems of the past for which documentation or recommendations from a computer manufacturer exist. Parts of these may be provided with the computer's standard package programs, around which the user builds the remainder of his Supervisory Programs. The more specifications and routines from previous systems can be used the better from the manpower point of view.

The *efficiency of programming required* also affects the speed at which programs can be written. The program may have to be written so that it operates in the shortest time possible, or perhaps so that it consumes the smallest amount of core possible, or a combination of these two. This tight programming will take longer to code than programming in which efficiency is of no great importance. In real-time systems high efficiency is vital in parts of Supervisory Programs and, possibly, in those Application Programs which are most frequently used. Infrequently used Application Programs, which will be the majority in most systems, and Support Programs need not be coded with great efficiency.

It is possible to fall into a trap by comparing a system with another half its size, and estimating twice the time for program writing. The relationship is not proportional. It is not true to say that a system will take thirty man-years because one half the size took fifteen man-years. With larger systems the logic is usually more complex and programmers will spend more time in examining the overall system. The problem of inter-actions between programmers will be worse. Actual production will there-fore be slower. This argument applies especially to the Supervisory Programs. A set of Supervisory Programs for a large system requiring 8000 instructions is likely to take 16 man-years of skilled effort for specifying from the beginning, coding and debugging. A set for a much smaller system requiring 2000 instructions might take only two man-years if the men are skilled.

This argument may be less applicable with the Application Programs. Given Supervisory Programs with similar basic functions, the individual Application Program segments can be written separately and have about the same degree of complexity in a small real-time system as on a large one.

The *time taken in testing* the overall system, i.e., the time taken from the completion of individual unit tests to the completion of the complete system test, is likely to be disproportionate for the size of the system. In a small system with, perhaps, 10,000 lines of coding it is relatively easy to fit all the parts together so that they work in unison. In a system with 140,000 lines of coding such as American Airlines SABRE this was a large job requiring manpower and computer time running into thousands of hours.

Programming language is another factor which affects the productivity of programmers. Most real-time coding has been done in a one-for-one assembly language with macro-instructions of the level of IBM Autocoder, for example. Where a language of the level of COBOL or FORTRAN is used the number of instructions generated per man year rises sharply. However, because of their inefficiency these languages are only likely to be used for programs such as off-line testing aids or the mass of non-real-time programs that is often needed to back up these systems. One typical large system produced about 500,000 instructions of off-line coding with a language of the level of COBOL in about 8 man-years.

On the basis of this study the figures in Table 4 suggest manpower estimates for the programming of real-time systems. The figures give the average number of line is of code per day per programmer and include the time taken for specification, coding and unit testing, but not system testing

Table 4. SUGGESTED MANPOWER PRODUCTIVITY ESTIMATES

	Number of instructions written per man per day (averaging over the whole period of program writing)
Average figure for general data processing:	12 to 15
Application Programs	
For producing detailed specifications (only):	20
For producing the coding and testing from good detailed specifications:	20
Supervisory Programs	
For specifications, coding and testing,	
overall size 1000 to 2000 lines of code:	3 to 5
overall size 2000 to 4000 lines of code:	3 to 4
overall size 4000 to 8000 lines of code:	2 to 3
Support Programs	
For real-time testing and monitoring aids (e.g., Macro Trace, "Analysis" aids, etc.)	
Specifications, coding and testing:	4 to 8
Off-line Support Programs,	
Specifications, coding and testing:	10 to 20
Ditto, coding in COBOL:	20 to 50

or multi-thread testing. The figures assume that a one-for-one assembly language with macro-instructions will be used, except where stated, and that not more than fifty per cent of the programmers are inexperienced. Programmers with less than four months training are not included.

Some programming managers regard these suggested estimates as being on the optimistic side.

The figures should be adjusted for the following five factors:

(a) *Experience in programming.* If all the programmers are either inexperienced or are known to have high productivity the figure may be adjusted.

(b) *Education.* An appropriate amount of time should be added for the education of new programmers or programmers unfamiliar with this machine or system.

(c) *New thinking.* The figures in the table were for programs for which the concept had not been previously worked out in detail. If specifications of a previous program can be used it may be possible to add 50 per cent to the estimated number of lines of code per man-year.

(d) *Efficiency.* Supervisory Programs must be written with a high efficiency. This is one reason why the number of lines of code per man-year is lower for these types of programs. Some of the Application Programs will also need this degree of efficiency because they are very frequently used. For these programs the above suggested estimates may be too high.

(e) *Higher Languages.* FORTRAN or COBOL coding of Application Programs is possible in some cases. This may increase productivity greatly. In process control systems, for example, FORTRAN has been used to good effect.

HOW MAY MANPOWER BE REDUCED? The manpower requirements calculated as indicated, may seem large, but it could be dangerous to use more optimistic estimates. It is, however, worth paying close attention to any means of cutting the manpower requirements or making the best use of what manpower is available. The following means are suggested:

1. *Use Programs from Previous Systems*

As much use as possible should be made of programs and specifications that exist for other systems. It is very tempting to devise one's own

Supervisory Programs or testing techniques, for example, rather than to use existing ones which were "not invented here." Resisting this temptation may save much manpower.

Specifications from other systems may be brought from other computer users or obtained through the computer manufacturer. On many systems it is possible to take Supervisory Programs written for a different application and modify them. If this is done, much work of specification will be saved. The testing of the Supervisory System will be quicker, and it will probably be available at an earlier date, thereby making the testing of Application Programs easier. Better computer software will probably be developed in the years to come to help with parts of the Supervisory System. Similarly, many of the Support Programs such as testing packages could be taken from one system and used on another if this is planned from the outset.

Only the Application Programs need be unique to a system, and even here, if a similar application has been programmed in the past, the use of its specifications will make the specification writing easier.

2. Use Skilled Manpower

In systems analysis and programming work, there is a great difference in output between a good experienced man and a poor inexperienced one. It is more economic to use highly-paid skilled manpower than to use a larger number of inexperienced or low caliber men. One of the great difficulties in the development of a large real-time system is the control of the interactions between the work of different personnel. It is constantly necessary to make changes as the system is specified in more detail and as the specifications are coded. Each change made by one man may affect the work of many others, and many of the changes will not be appreciated in time by those who need to know of them. The smaller the number of people, the smaller this interaction problem will be. A small group of high productivity can be much more efficient than an army of inexperienced programmers. The reason for hiring inexperienced personnel should be the unavailability of anyone else, not the cost.

This is especially true in the area of Supervisory Programming where tight, efficient, well-integrated coding is required. In Application Programming a lower level of efficiency can be tolerated, except perhaps in the most frequently used programs, but here the interactions between different programmers will be more complex and more difficult to control.

In the search for skill the concept of teamwork must be retained, however. A brilliant man who will not be a good team member and work closely with the others, is better for a different type of system.

3. *Split the Work into Self-contained Units*

The extent to which these interactions are controlled will effect the number of man-years used in systems testing and recoding. Any method of reducing or clarifying the interactions will help to save manpower. Separating the Supervisory Programs from the Application Programs in a clear-cut accurately-defined break, is an example of the way in which interactions between programmers can be lessened. A similar break can be made between other parts of the system (Figs. 83 and 84). The Application Programs may be split into small groups. Those groups can be made completely self-contained and independent, with the exception of an interface between the groups which can be as well-defined as that between the Supervisory Programs and Application Programs. This interface would, for example, specify records used in common between two groups and messages passed between groups. A small self-contained group of three or four men, or perhaps even one man, is likely to produce results faster and more accurately than a large group. If the interface between groups is adequately defined, there are likely to be far fewer problems when the programs are finally put together at the systems test stage.

4. *Continuity of Manpower*

A cause of slowing down in some systems has been the lack of continuity of manpower. Key men who participated in the early design have left the project, and thus there is a shortage of men with an overall understanding of what is being done.

Often the large and sudden build up of a team of programmers forces the recruitment and training of many men with no previous computer experience. Many firms installing real-time systems have had to do this; but after two years the programmers, now experienced in a very complex computer system, find their market value higher than their current salary and leave.

As far as is possible, men with experience of the system should be retained until cut-over or after. The gap that they leave is expensive to fill.

5. *Easily-programmable Functional Descriptions*

In some systems the initial functional descriptions have been done with little or no assistance from programmers. This has given rise to specifications which are difficult to program and which could have been considerably more simple.

The participation of programmers in the initial functional descriptions can reduce the manpower requirements later. The specifications should be drawn up with this objective always firmly in mind.

6. *Restrict Complications*

In any computer system there is a tendency for complications to multiply and for unnecssary sophistications to be written into the specifications. Programmers are as guilty of this as non-programmers. In a real-time system this can cause trouble. It will save much manpower and speed the installation progress if the first model is as simple as possible and elaborations are saved for a later model.

7. *Restrict Changes*

There is a tendency on the part of the people who will use the system to have new ideas and to ask for changes. This can slow down the installation progress even if the changes are small. After a certain point in the installation schedule the system should be frozen, and no further changes to its specifications should be permitted. Any requests for modifications should be queued and left for a later model.

8. *Schedule the Program Development*

Fitting together the parts of a real-time system at system test time is likely to be faster and easier if the programs are available in a certain sequence. For example, the Supervisory Programs and macro-instructions should be available early so that Application Programs can be tested jointly with them. Testing aids should be ready before the programs that use them. File addressing algorithms should be available to the Support Programs which create a pilot model of file records for testing, and so on.

If these programs are not ready in the sequence in which they are desired for testing, additional manpower will be consumed. The sequence of program production should be scheduled with systems tests in mind.

9. *Schedule the Recruiting*

A bar chart or PERT chart should be used from the start to indicate the sequence of program development. Use of this chart should be supported by the projected numbers of lines of coding to give an estimate of the manpower requirement at various points in the development of the system. It is important to have first class men in the initial period of designing the system. Only high caliber men can do jobs such as designing the Supervisory and Support Programs, devising an optimum file addressing scheme, etc. Lower quality men can be introduced later when the specifications are written and need to be coded. However, it has proved very wasteful in some systems to have a large number of program coders before the specifications are written and ready for coding. To put men trained only in coding on to the job of finishing the specifications is likely to cause trouble later.

In general, the manpower build up should be smoothly scheduled and the requirements should be continuously monitored. A deficiency in the schedule can result in crisis action being taken later. Sending in a fire-brigade to help meet the installation date will be *very* wasteful in manpower.

10. *Indecision*

In large systems, both real-time and otherwise, one of the main causes of a slowing down of the installation phase is the inability of individuals to solve problems and keep the implementation of the system moving. Once progress slows down in any area, additional problems arise and force ineffectual solutions to maintain a show of progress. It is essential to keep the installation phase moving. When problems arise, technical or political, they must not cause a delay in installation progress. Indecision and delay in taking action can waste manpower considerably. It is normally better to force a decision, even if it is known not to be the best, than to impede progress toward implementation by avoidance and delay.

Let us reiterate the most important personnel consideration of all for large real-time systems. A well-knit *team* is needed which is managed efficiently and which moves fast, as a team, to tackle the problems that confront it.

38 PLANNING THE IMPLEMENTATION SCHEDULE

For any complex computer project it is desirable to lay down a schedule for the work to be done. In a real-time system this is normally more important than in a batch processing system because there are so many interrelated factors which tie together. Furthermore a very large financial investment may be involved.

A schedule is needed, both for the programming and for the other factors such as physical installation, planning the environment in which the system will work, planning deliveries, buildings, communications facilities, and so on. It is valuable to have a check list of points to be considered in planning the installation as seemingly insignificant items have often caused hold-ups. One computer company listed the causes of delays in installing its computers and the seventh most common cause was lack of an adequate electrical earth! This chapter discusses the schedule for programming and systems analysis.

A schedule is needed, both for planning the work and for monitoring its progress. It will indicate how much emphasis should be placed on which items at various points in time. It should be used in planning the manpower requirements and the other resources that are needed such as computer time. By measuring the progress on various parts of the schedule it will help to evaluate the quality of the manpower and so plan its usage better.

In simple computer installations a bar chart is often used for planning the schedule. In a real-time system a bar chart may be too clumsy a tool because of the more intricate relationships between the programs. This is illustrated in an oversimplified manner in Fig. 86. The vertical lines on the chart indicate relationships between the activities, i.e., one program or specification being needed before a certain activity can begin.

354

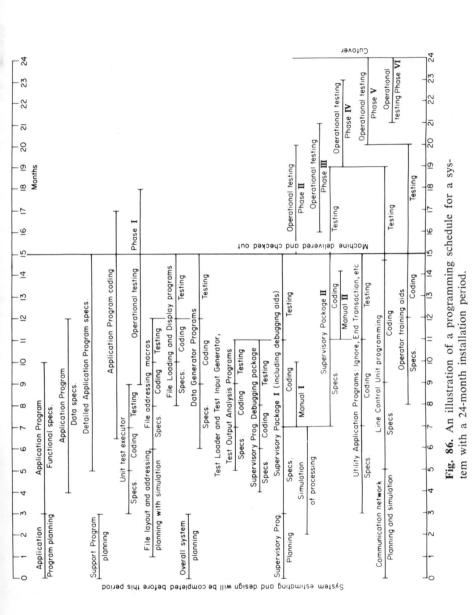

Fig. 86. An illustration of a programming schedule for a system with a 24-month installation period.

For example, the Supervisory Package I must be completed and debugged before Operational Testing Phase I can begin. The Supervisory Program Debugging Package must be completed before the Supervisory Package can be debugged. And so on. This chart shows only broad categories. If it showed details, for example, individual programs, there would be many more vertical interrelations. One Application Program must be specified before another is written. Macro-instructions must be specified in detail before programs using them are written. They must be debugged before the program that uses them. File organization and addressing need to be planned early.

The timing relationships on this chart are typical of a system with a 24-month installation schedule. The chart assumes that the overall system planning and specification of functions are completed before the 24-month period. For some complex systems the period required for system testing is a larger proportion of the whole than is indicated here. *The time for system testing may be as long as that for writing program specifications, coding, and unit testing.* The testing phases referred to in the diagram are the seven phases described in Chapter 33.

Many separate programs must be tested, all working together in conjunction with one another. The work of many programs must be fitted together to form a tightly integrated whole, and the sequence in which the pieces must be fitted together needs to be scheduled. Testing aids for various types of test must be ready on time. Data generators must produce test data in time for the tests. File addressing routines must be ready and debugged before routines that use them. The Supervisory Programs must be written and debugged with appropriate diagnostics before being interfaced with the Application Programs.

For an actual installation the planning chart would be broken down into greater detail in the Application Program area. Individual packages of Application Programs and their interrelation would be shown. A model-by-model approach may be used in producing the system as a whole, as in Fig. 76, Chapter 31, or in producing individual packages, as for example, the two Supervisory Packages indicated in Fig. 86.

A Model I which is fairly simple, may have a low throughput and perform only a portion of the projected functions. This is fully debugged, and when it is working correctly it is changed for a more complex Model II. The mistakes which are made in Model I will be ironed out on Model II as it is being produced. Design feedback from Model I will be used to improve Model II. Additional complexities will be added on Model II and can be debugged with the confidence that the routines they interface with from Model I are now working error-free. This all needs to be scheduled.

A chart such as the one in Fig. 86 will help in planning the manpower build-up. To do this the numbers of lines of coding in various programs will be estimated. Rough figures for programmer productivity such as those in the last chapter will be used to indicate the manpower needs at various points in the schedule.

When planning this, the training of the men must be considered as well as their familiarity both with the computers and with the system concepts.

The manpower used during one of the periods illustrated by horizontal lines on the chart is not likely to be constant over the length of the line. It begins with a small group or perhaps only one man, builds up to a peak of activity and then, as the work becomes completed, it tails off in the manner shown in Fig. 87.

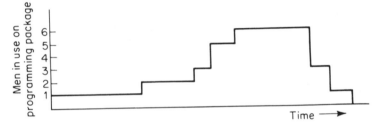

Fig. 87.

CRITICAL PATH SCHEDULING   Rather than use a bar chart, a more flexible and refined method of planning is to use PERT or some means of Critical Path Scheduling. This technique emphasizes the interactions between different events and highlights those parts of the schedule that may become critical if not watched. Unlike a bar chart, the lengths of the lines in a PERT arrow diagram are not proportional to the time taken to complete the item. This is helpful because the initial estimates are often little better than guesswork, and as the work proceeds the estimates will change constantly.

Packaged computer programs are readily available for producing PERT reports. These are simple to run and once the arrow diagram has been drawn they give an easy way of keeping the installation schedule up-to-date. An arrow diagram is described for the computer program by punching a card representing each line on the chart. The card will contain the name of the activity, its estimated duration, and if it has already been started or finished, the actual start or finish date. As the project proceeds this information may be updated, where necessary, perhaps once a month.

The program will produce management reports which highlight any slippages. It will indicate which items are the most critical and list them in order of criticality, taking into account how one item can delay others throughout the project. This should be a useful guide for telling management where extra effort is needed.

It is not always possible˙ to advance an element of a programming project by pouring additional effort into it. It may already have as many men as it can usefully employ. Thus, a critical item in the schedule can be taken care of with extra manpower only up to a certain point; beyond it nothing can be done. If any item on the arrow diagram reaches this degree of criticality, it will delay the completion of the project.

The question who in management receives the PERT reports can be an important one. For self-monitoring they are invaluable, but to higher management they may be misleading. It is not easy to lay out the schedule in detail at the start of a project. The more detail there is in the initial schedule, the less likely is it to agree with the facts as they unfold. However, for internal monitoring it is desirable that the schedule be as detailed as possible and be changed, when necessary, as the picture becomes clearer.

Unfortunately, higher levels of management who need an account of how closely the schedule is being met are rarely former programmers. They will have difficulty in understanding the apparent delays and constant changes. For this level of management it may be worthwhile to produce a different report showing fewer sub-tasks. This will have less guesswork and be less misleading to them, so that less justification will be called for.

In determining how much of a program remains to be done, so that the PERT reports can be realistically updated, close contact with the programmer is necessary. The programmer often has an unrealistic attitude. Like an engineer he likes to tinker with his creation and adjust it until its operation is highly tuned and sophisticated. While this is, in general, an excellent trait, there may not be time for too much adjustment in the rush to get a real-time system "on the air." Furthermore, if the tinkering results in increased use of core or processor time, it may be undesirable for this reason. There is always a tendency among good programmers to over-engineer.

It is sometimes difficult for management to know exactly what the programmers are doing, especially in the early stages before segments of coding become ready for testing. The programmers sit at their desks all day, presumably working, but little that can be easily assessed emerges. On some systems, the programmers have been made to fill in daily activity reports, but this is generally unpopular with the programmers and does not help the problem of assessing the quality of what they are doing.

The best way of tackling this, and of guiding the programmers generally, seems to be to have close personal supervision, with one man supervising not more than six programmers. The man would have detailed familiarity with what they are doing. He would decide what tinkering with a program is needed and what is not. He would help to settle the many controversies as to whether additions and elaborations are needed or not. And he would provide all the information required for the formal monitoring of the programming progress.

SCHEDULING
TEST EFFORT

Determining how much time and effort remain necessary for package and system testing is likely to be more difficult. Dividing the number of lines of coding by a fixed factor will give no valid indication of this.

The technique used on one large project was to allocate complexity point values to the various programming packages. A package usually included several blocks of program. It frequently contained between 1000 and 5000 lines of coding. A group of experienced programmers, familiar with the system, allocated an arbitrarily assigned value of 10 to a complexity point relative to a package with which they were all familiar. The complexity point value was intended as a measure of the difficulty of testing the package and making it work successfully.

American Airlines used eight steps through which each package would have to go, each being a landmark in the progress of making the package work. These were first, for single-thread, non-real-time testing with simulated hardware in a normal Data Center and with simulated Supervisory Programs:

Step 1. All programs have been punched onto cards ready for running.

Step 2. All test data necessary to test the package are ready.

Step 3. At least one non-trivial test case works properly.

Step 4. All test cases work properly.

and second, for real-time testing on the actual system, with the actual Supervisory Programs using real terminal sets or terminal set simulators:

Step 1. All programs necessary to run the package have been introduced into the system and recorded on the drum.

Step 2. All test cases to prove the package have been prepared and the files loaded with all necessary records.

Step 3. At least one non-trivial case works properly.

Step 4. All test cases work properly.

Saturation testing will normally be needed in a multi-thread system as well as the above test steps.

39 MONITORING THE IMPLEMENTATION PROGRESS

The functions of the new system are agreed upon. Estimates of computer requirements are made, and the computers, with a galaxy of attachments, are selected and ordered. A programming team is recruited and sets sail on its hazardous journey.

The progress of the team must be charted, and where it deviates from a course that is likely to take it to its objective on time, corrective factors must be applied.

Here are a few of the things that can go wrong:

(a) The consumption of core storage may become higher than anticipated so that, when the programs operate together, they will not fit in the available computer.

(b) The programs may take more time than anticipated so that, when they work together, the available computer is not fast enough.

(c) The channel utilization may become too high, perhaps because too many program segments are being read into core or because of core shortage.

(d) The utilization of random-access file "seek" mechanisms may become too high, possibly because of file addressing or overflow problems.

(e) The Line Control Unit may become overloaded.

(f) The functions of the system may not have been too well understood at the outset. As they are worked out in detail they may prove to be much more complicated than originally anticipated.

(g) The schedule may slip so that the programs cannot be completed in time to meet the installation date.

(h) Certain vital programs may have been neglected and hold up implementation progress, for example, testing aids.

The cause of any of these troubles may be inherent in the initial design or schedule of the system, or it may be brought about by trends in the programming work. In either case there are means of correcting the fault, but the trend away from the desired course needs to be discovered as early as possible. The progress in implementing the system needs to be carefully monitored to detect any undesirable features as soon as they become apparent.

However carefully the initial design estimates for a complex real-time system are made, systems implemented to date show that inaccuracies, even gross inaccuracies, are liable to appear.

The deviations between the original estimates and the final system may be inherent in the estimates, but, more likely, the system may drift from its original design assumptions. In the two years or so in which the system is being programmed and its functions worked out in detail, it is difficult for all concerned to have the design assumptions in mind.

When the estimates are made there are always many factors which are not known in as much detail as would be desirable. These may be program factors, factors concerned with the way data are routed through the system, or factors involving details of the system functions or the Application Programs. As the system begins to take shape, block diagrams are drawn and program specifications are written, and the factors that were not known well enough when the estimates were made now come more sharply into focus. It is possible to recheck the estimates with much greater accuracy. The more specifications and programs are written, the greater will be the certainty of the estimates.

As the system implementation is progressing it is essential to monitor its development by continually rechecking the design and schedule estimates. If this is done, poor estimates will be detected in time to make changes. A drift away from a workable system, which can so easily occur, will be observed in time to take corrective action. The types of corrective action that might be taken may include: reworking certain program routines, for example, to save time instead of saving core; trimming the specifications of the system functions; changing the Supervisory Program mechanisms; or, in extreme cases, adding extra hardware such as core, drums or channels, or changing the processing unit.

It is very desirable that any changes such as these are made at the earliest possible time. The longer they are delayed, the more program rewriting and specifying they will necessitate. In particular, any change in the hardware, such as adding drums in addition to disk files, will cause a big upheaval in parts of the Supervisory Programs. As the availability of the Supervisory Programs is critical in the implementation schedule this could hold up other work. Furthermore, the delivery time on the new hardware may be high.

By continually monitoring the system's progress a feedback loop of design information is set up so that the development is controlled. If this is not done it is likely that drifts from the original estimates will occur. In complex systems these may be large drifts, and when they are detected a crisis situation will usually result.

The following pages indicate briefly the methods recommended for monitoring a system's progress.

In general, there are two aspects of the system that need monitoring. First, the progress in programming needs continuous checking to make sure that nothing is slipping behind schedule. Second, the various technical aspects of the system such as core utilization, channel loads, queue sizes, and so on, need to be monitored to ensure that the programs or loads are not outstripping the capability of the hardware to handle them.

MONITORING THE PROGRAMMING PROGRESS   This was described in the last chapter. A detailed PERT analysis of the programming schedule, updated at least monthly, and computer runs producing management reports to indicate any slippage, will help to retain a tight control. Computer reports in which the jobs to be done are sorted by allowable "float" will indicate which are the most critical items. Items on the "critical path" should be at the top of the list, with the least critical jobs at the bottom. This will help focus the attention of management on those areas where more effort or attention may be needed. Some managers question whether the work entailed in running PERT programs for the system is worthwhile. The package PERT programs that are now available, however, are so easy to run that, once the initial arrow diagram has been prepared, the work involved in using this tool is not great. Many of the complex systems that have had serious slippages could probably have avoided them, at least in part, if they had had this discipline imposed upon them.

The information for updating the PERT reports best comes from the programmers' group leaders who are supervising not more than six programmers. These men are in the best position to monitor what the programmers are doing. It is necessary that they provide the information needed for formal monitoring and also check the quality of performance of the persons they supervise. They should, as far as they can, make sure that the emerging programs will indeed do the job that is intended, and that the more ingenious programmers are not consuming excessive core storage, processing time, or effort in building intricacies and sophistications that could be dispensed with.

MONITORING THE TECHNICAL ASPECTS OF THE SYSTEM Whereas inadequate control of programming progress may result in a slippage of the date when the system goes into operation, failure to monitor the technical aspects may result in an unworkable system. So perhaps the latter is the more vital of the two.

If the monitoring is inadequate on conventional systems and the programs take more time or core than was initially estimated, the system can usually still carry out its functions though it would take more time to do so. In a real-time system, this latitude does not exist. The messages will flood into the system at a rate largely independent of the programming. If the estimates were too low, then the system may not be able to process these messages. It may be incapable of doing the work it was intended for, without expensive additions to the hardware such as an increase in core storage or processor speed.

In making the estimates for a real-time system, eight factors may become critical. These are:

1. Utilization of core storage on the computers.
2. Utilization of processing time on the computers.
3. Peripheral file storage space, e.g., drums and disks.
4. Channel utilization.
5. Utilization of file arms or heads.
6. Utilization of the line control unit or multiplexor.
7. Line utilization.
8. Terminal utilization.

These eight factors are the potential bottlenecks of the system. In designing the system each of these factors must be estimated with care, and the relationship between the factors must be examined. In some systems one of these factors may be more critical than the others. In other systems several of them may be critical. But whether the system is large or small, these eight factors must be checked carefully in its design.

In a real-time data processing system there is to some extent a pay-off between these eight critical factors. If one of them becomes too tight it may be possible to relieve it at the expense of some of the others. Designing a real-time system is then to a large extent a matter of obtaining a balance between the factors involved.

The estimates for the system are initially made with considerable uncertainty, especially with respect to the size of the programs. The estimators often think they are generous in their allowances for sizes of programs because of the uncertainties. Nevertheless, in many of the systems tackled so far the program sizes and other critical factors have climbed way beyond what was originally allowed for when the equipment was ordered.

There are basically three possible causes of wrong estimates. First, the data collection carried out for the system may prove incorrect. There may be more messages sent to the system than originally counted. This is probably the easiest of the three causes to control when designing a system. However, with certain types of systems it is possible that terminal operators may tend to use the system merely because it is there and send transactions or make inquiries that would not have occurred on a manual system. This needs to be forseen and carefully controlled.

Second, functions that the system must perform may be ill-defined. Frequently a proposal must be made without knowing all the details of all the functions the system is to perform, or all the operations that are necessary to carry out a certain action. This is very dangerous as it will almost certainly lead to underestimating the Application Programs. Complications in the functions of a real-time system can often not be seen until its operation has been specified in considerable detail.

Third, given a set of functions and a set of throughput figures, the system may be designed inadequately. This may be because of inability to foresee all the complications that will arise in the processing, or inability to estimate the number of program steps required. Often it is very difficult to estimate the core or time required for programs without actually writing part of them, and this is not possible in the time available when a computer is ordered. The best method may be a critical comparison, if this is possible, with similar programs on another system. A likely cause of inadequate design is insufficient understanding of the mechanisms for routing work through the system, such as the Supervisory Programs, file addressing routines, and so on.

As progress continues in implementing the system there will be more and more evidence on which to base estimates.

It is therefore desirable to recheck the estimates periodically and to have available means of detecting any trend away from a workable design while there is still time to do something about it. *System design check times* should be planned in the schedule so that when certain phases in the planning and programming are complete the overall system design can be reevaluated.

As the programs are being written and more detail is being obtained in this area, a study of the input data to the system may be also begun.

Determining the traffic that will go to the system from various locations can involve a very long study.

Of the eight critical factors mentioned above, the two most likely to cause trouble are the core storage requirements and the processing times. It is a good idea to have some kind of *budgetary control* of these two factors. Budgets will be set for each segment of program, for the core storage it will occupy and the time it will take to run. These estimates will be fitted together to make the overall picture of the system. They will be quoted in the Program Specifications, and the programmer will constantly watch that his work is not likely to exceed the budget. Any indication that it will, must be communicated to management immediately.

THE USE OF SIMULATION

The design of a complex real-time system usually requires the use of *queuing theory* or *simulation*. Whether the use of simulation is warranted in the design will depend upon the complexity of the system and the accuracy with which the throughput and program sizes are known. In a complex system with queuing problems and multi-programming, the use of simulation will certainly be needed to monitor the design progress because the system is too complex to analyze by arithmetical methods or by queuing theory—especially when this is not in the hands of an expert.

Simulation is a useful tool to check the design continuously. It makes it possible to build a model of the working system, or perhaps a succession of models of parts of the system. These models can then be adjusted easily and endlessly. As the estimates for individual programs become better, these can be built into the model so that it steadily becomes more closely representative of the truth. Different volumes of throughput can be fed to the model so that its capacity is measured. Its behavior under various circumstances can be investigated.

Simulation models of this type can also be of great value in helping to decide between alternative methods of operation. Arguments will arise in a healthy system as to the merits of different programming techniques. Different file configurations will be possible. There may be arguments in favor of different arrangements of lines, terminals and channels.

Simulation languages have been devised to enable persons relatively inexperienced in the use of simulation to build models of this type easily. One of these in common use is IBM's Gordon Simulator. The user of this and other simulator languages first describes his system by means of a block diagram which indicates how transactions pass through the system. The speeds of various facilities are indicated along with the time the transactions spend in parts of the system, the storage capacity, and so on. In the diagram different blocks describe various actions or characteristics of the system and indicate what alternate types of action can occur. The person running the model specifies the transaction types and the load they place upon the system. He is then able to measure the lengths of queues in the system, response times, percentage utilization of facilities, and so on. He can vary the load and observe what happens.

A similar sort of model using this language can be written, for example, to describe the behavior of traffic in congested city streets. The traffic flow can be varied and the traffic jams that occur can be observed. It could have been discovered that the building of an underpass in London would result in greater traffic congestion in Piccadilly than ever before. Alternative routes could have been investigated. In a similar way the cause of congestion in a real-time system can be investigated by means of a relatively simple model. A model of this type will enable a Control Group who are monitoring the implementation progress to fully understand what is going on.

It is a good idea to have a central Control Group monitoring the development of the system. This could be the Control Group described in Chapter 35 for reading and approving the specifications of the system and changes that are made in the specifications. Moreover, this Control Group would recheck the estimates of the system at the scheduled intervals and operate simulation models, describing how the system is likely to perform when all the bits and pieces are put together. It would maintain the budgetary control of core and processor time utilization. The same Control Group would also use a tool such as PERT for detecting any paths in the programming progress that may become critical and cause a hold-up.

Only by means of such tight monitoring can management be sure that it is steering a course that will lead to success.

40

TEN ESSENTIALS FOR MANAGEMENT OF REAL-TIME PROGRAMMING

As its conclusion this book summarizes what the author considers to be the ten most essential points for success in the managing of the programming of a real-time computer system.

1. Plan the Implementation Schedule in Detail

Because the programs are so interdependent, the schedule should be planned in detail from the start, preferably with a technique such as PERT to make sure that all items are ready when needed. This should have a tight management follow-up of any indicated delays. Specifications and coding of Supervisory Routines, Support Programs, macro-instructions, and so on, should then be ready by the time other programming effort needs them. A monthly PERT computer run will pinpoint any slippage and show up new critical paths. Management should insist that key dates throughout the schedule are met.

Objective (almost mathematical) progress reporting is necessary to achieve this.

2. Use Budgetary Control of Core Storage and Processing Time

So that the multiple programming effort does not run the system out of core or time, budgets for these should be set for each program. Any indication that a budget will be exceeded will give rise to a reevaluation.

3. Monitor the Implementation Progress Closely

Estimates for all the critical factors in the system design should be revised periodically. The check times should be planned in the schedule. Any creeping inflation which may make the system unworkable should be detected as early as possible. On a complex system this may involve writing of simulation models of the system. These will present an increasingly more accurate picture of the system's behavior as more programming detail becomes known.

4. Stress the Importance of Teamwork in Programming

The programmers must work together as a team; each must know how his own contribution fits into the system as a whole and understand the interactions between his work and the work of others. Programmers must appreciate that the ease with which the system fits together is more important than individual brilliance.

Probably no single factor is going to have more effect on the success of the system than the recruiting of the best possible programming team.

5. Write Good Specifications and Documentation

The programs and data must be accurately specified in a manner that is designed to control the interactions between the work of different people. Necessary changes to Specifications should be approved and equally well documented. A mechanism must be set up for notifying programmers and other persons whom these changes affect. The final programs must be well written up so that they can be used and modified by other people.

6. One Overall Control Group is Essential

A Control Group is required, with a knowledge of the complete system, for approving Specifications and changes to Specifications. This Control Group should monitor the progress of the system and maintain the budgets for core and time. It should arrange for a centralized source of data for testing and should keep account of the testing progress.

It is important that there should be one overall Control Group and one overall manager. Management should not be split, as has sometimes been the case.

7. Use Model-by-Model System Build-up

It is necessary to control changes that are requested, both by outside personnel and management and by the programmers themselves, by saving modifications for a subsequent "model" of the system. In this way the system should be built up model-by-model, each model being *frozen* when its programming is under way. The first model or models may be prototypes, not fully operational systems. Design feedback from each model will be used to improve the performance of the next.

The system may be divided into sub-systems, and each of these may have separate models, and possibly prototypes. For example, there may be different models of the Supervisory System.

8. *Plan the Handling of All Component Failures and Errors*

Any component may fail, and a rich variety of errors are possible. These must all be thought about and the question must be answered, "What will the system do when they occur?" In particular, file reconstruction procedures must be planned in case an accident should damage the files. This factor must be considered at the outset as it will affect both hardware and programs.

9. *Plan What Happens if the Load or Complexity Increases*

The system capacity is less easy to expand than with a conventional system. However, the load may increase, new functions may be added, or the present functions may require more facilities than were anticipated. It is prudent to plan for such future expansions with the thought that they may occur suddenly. In some systems the load became much greater than planned almost immediately after cut-over because people liked the system and made more use of it than was anticipated.

10. *Plan Program and System Testing from the Start*

Program and system testing can be one of the biggest headaches of a real-time system. It requires detailed planning and often much extra program writing. It often needs modification of the Supervisory Programs. It is essential that it is thought about from the outset in the design of a system. It cannot be separated in any of its phases from the specification writing or maintenance of the programs.

It is necessary to plan, especially for testing, extra programming requirements, extra hardware requirements and extra implementation time. Program and system testing in a complex application can take as long as the specification writing and coding.

GLOSSARY

The terms used in real-time applications differ considerably from one system to another, and from one computer manufacturer to another. The terminology in this book has been consistent throughout, in order to avoid confusion. The technical terms used are defined below.

Analysis Block. This is a relocatable segment of the computer storage in which data are stored which can later be used to analyze the performance of the system. These may be program testing data or statistical data. There may be an Analysis Block for each transaction in the system during program testing. When the transaction leaves the system this block is dumped on tape or onto a file. The Analysis Block may be chained to the Message Reference Block.

Analysis Mode. This is a mode of operation in which the performance of the system is monitored by special programs for subsequent analysis. When the system is running in Analysis Mode, program testing data or statistical data may be automatically recorded.

Any-Sequence Queue. This is a group of items in the system waiting for the attention of the processor. They are organized in such a way that items may be removed from the group regardless of the sequence in which they entered it.

Application Program. The working programs in a system may be classed as Application Programs and Supervisory Programs. The Application Programs are the main data-processing programs. They contain no input/output coding except in the form of macro-instructions which transfer control to the Supervisory Programs.

Automatic Recovery Program. This is a program which enables a system to carry on its function when a piece of equipment has failed. It may bring into play duplex circuitry or a standby computer, or it may switch to a mode of degraded operation.

Block-Chaining. A block of data in core is associated with another block so that an item or queue of items may occupy more than one block. The linkage between the blocks may be by programming or, on some machines, it may be automatic.

Central Scanning Loop. The nucleus of a set of Supervisory Programs is a loop of instructions which determines what work is to be done next. When one item of work is completed, control will be transferred to the Central Scanning Loop which will scan requests for processing to determine the next item to be processed. When no item requires the attention of the computer, it may cycle idly in this loop. Alternatively, it may go into a WAIT state which can be interrupted if the need arises.

Chaining (in file addressing). When a randomizing technique is being used for file addressing, a file address may be created which does not in fact contain the item that is being sought. The location sought will instead give another file address in which the item may be stored. This second address also may not contain the item but may refer the computer to a third address, and so on.

Channel Scheduler. A list of requests for input/output operations on a channel are executed in a desirable sequence by a Channel Scheduler Program. When one operation on a channel is completed, the Channel Scheduler Program initiates the next on the list.

Channel Waiting Queue. This is a group of items in the system waiting for the attention of the Channel Scheduler Program.

Close-down, orderly. If the system is forced to stop it should execute an orderly close-down, if possible. This ensures that a restart can be made in an orderly fashion and that no messages are lost. All records are updated that should be updated, and no records are accidentally updated a second time when the restart is made. All incoming and outgoing transmissions are completed, and an administrative message is sent to the terminals to notify the operators of the close-down.

Close-down, disorderly. This may occur when the system stops because of an equipment error which prevents it from doing an orderly close-down. When this occurs special precautions are needed to ensure that no messages are lost and that no records are updated twice.

Contention. This is a method of line control in which the terminals request to transmit. If the channel in question is free, transmission goes ahead; if it is not free the terminal will have to wait until it becomes free. The queue of contention requests may be built up by the computer, and this can either be in a prearranged sequence or in the sequence in which the requests are made.

Debug Macro-instruction. A macro-instruction placed in a program which records certain data or programs or other facts that are subsequently used for program testing analysis.

Degree of Multi-programming. Where several transactions are being handled in parallel by the systems in a multi-programming fashion, the degree of multi-programming refers to the number of these transactions.

Departure Time. When a segment of an Application Program is completed and control is returned to the Supervisory Programs, the time at which this happens is referred to as the Departure Time.

Diagnostic Programs. These are used to check equipment malfunctions and to pinpoint faulty components. They may be used by the computer engineer or be called in by the Supervisory Programs automatically.

Diagnostics, Unit. These are used on a conventional computer to detect faults in the various units. Separate unit diagnostics will check such items as arithmetic circuitry, transfer instructions, each input/output unit, and so on.

Diagnostics, System. Rather than checking one individual component, system diagnostics utilize the whole system in a manner similar to its operational running. Programs resembling the operational programs will be used rather than systematic programs that run logical patterns. These will normally detect overall system malfunctions but will not isolate faulty components.

Duplexing. The use of duplicate computers, files or circuitry, so that in the event of one component failing an alternative one can enable the system to carry on its work.

Dynamic Core Allocation. The allocation of storage in a computer in such a way that at one time a piece of work may occupy one part of storage and at another time it may occupy another, depending on the circumstances. It is used to give a more efficient utilization of core when multi-programming takes place.

Dynamic Scheduling. The decision which piece of work to do next is made by the computer from moment to moment, depending upon the circumstances. In conventional applications the computer has a fixed and preset schedule. This is often not so in a real-time system, where the schedule is determined as the transactions arrive and work proceeds.

Entry Time. When control is transferred from the Supervisory Programs to an Application Program, the time at which this transfer is made is referred to as Entry Time.

Errors, intermittent. Equipment errors which occur intermittently but not constantly. These are difficult to reproduce, and diagnostics may not detect such faults because they may not occur when the diagnostic is being run.

Errors, solid. Equipment errors which always occur when a particular piece of equipment is used. They are repeatable and therefore relatively easy to detect.

Errors, transient. A type of error which occurs only once and cannot be made to repeat itself.

Exit Macro-instruction. This is the last macro-instruction of each and every Application Program. It causes the blocks of storage used by that program to be released, including the Message Reference Block, so that the other programs may use them. If necessary, conditions associated with the transaction in question are reset.

Fall-back Procedures. When the equipment develops a fault the programs operate in such a way as to circumvent this fault. This may or may not give a degraded service. Procedures necessary for fall-back may include those to switch over to an alternative computer or file, to change file addresses, to send output to a typewriter instead of a printer, and so on.

Fall-back, double. Fall-back in which two separate equipment failures have to be contended with.

Fail softly. When a piece of equipment fails, the programs let the system fall back to a degraded mode of operation rather than let it fail catastrophically and give no response to its users.

File Addressing. A data or a file record have a key which uniquely identifies those data. Given this key, the programs must locate the address of a file record associated with these data. There are a variety of techniques for converting such a key into a machine file address.

File Packing Density. A ratio of amount of space (in words or characters) on a file, available for storing data to the total amount of data that are stored in the file.

File Reconstruction Procedures. There is a remote possibility that vital data on the files will be accidentally destroyed by an equipment failure, or a program or operator error. The means of reconstructing the file must be devised should such an unfortunate circumstance occur. Vital data must be dumped onto tape or some other media, and programs must be written so that the file may be reconstructed from these data if necessary.

Initializer Routine. When a message enters the system certain functions must be performed upon it before the Application Programs begin processing it. These functions are checking for errors in the message, erasing backspace characters, analyzing the action code, and so on. They may be performed by an Initializer Routine.

Input/Output Control Program. That part of the Supervisory Programs which executes and controls all input and output operations.

Interrupt. Various external events, such as the arrival of a new message or the completion of an input/output operation, may interrupt the program that is presently in progress. This means that the central processing unit leaves this program, stores any working data that it needs to continue the program at a later time, and executes a different program which deals with the cause of the interrupt. After the cause of the interrupt has been dealt with, control will return to the original program that was interrupted.

Interrupt Control Routine. When an interrupt occurs this routine may be entered. It may take action such as storing the working details of the program that was interrupted so that control may be returned to it, and analyzing the cause of the interrupt to decide what action should be taken.

Interrupt Logging. When program testing or monitoring the behavior of the system, the interrupts that occur may be logged. An interrupt occuring at an unpredictable time during the execution of a program may possibly cause a program error. It is therefore important during testing to know what type of interrupt occurred.

Interrupt Log Word. An indication of what interrupt occurred during the running of each segment of program may be made in an Interrupt Log Word. As each interrupt occurs a bit is set in this word, characteristic of that type of interrupt. The Interrupt Log Word is written onto tape or some other medium for later analysis.

Interrupt Priority Table. For machines which do not handle interrupts in a fully automatic manner this table may list the sequence in which interrupt indicators should be tested.

Introspective Program. A program which monitors its own behavior. It may record program testing or statistical data in an Analysis Block.

List. This word means the same as Queue. It refers to a group of items in the system waiting for the attention of the processor. The number of items in the list will vary from time to time. Normally queues are "dynamic", which means that they consist of storage areas which can be anywhere within part of the core and which are chained together by means of words in each area, containing addresses of consecutive areas in the queue.

Load Sharing. Two computers which normally form a duplexed pair may share the load of the system during peak periods. During non-peak periods one of the two computers can handle the entire load with the other one acting as the standby.

Macro Exerciser. A means of testing the Supervisory Programs and other macro-instructions. The macro-instruction routines are made to operate repeatedly with varying conditions in an attempt to discover any program errors.

Macro-Instruction. One line of program code which generates a program routine rather than one program instruction.

Main Scheduling Routine. The nucleus of a set of Supervisory Programs is a loop of instructions which determines what is to be done next when one item of work is completed. Control will be transferred to the Central Scanning Loop which will scan requests for processing to determine the next item to be processed. When no item requires the attention of the computer, the computer may cycle idly in this loop. Alternatively it may go into a "wait" state which can be interrupted if the need arises.

Master and Slave Computers. Where two or more computers are working jointly, one of these is sometimes a master computer and the others are slaves. The master can interrupt the slaves and send data to them when it needs to. When data pass from the slaves to the master it will be at the master's request.

Mean Time to Failure. The average length of time for which the system, or a component of the system, works without fault.

Mean Time to Repair. When the system, or a component of the system, develops a fault, this is the average time taken to correct the fault.

Memory Protection. This is a hardware device which prevents a program from entering areas of memory that are beyond certain boundaries. It is useful in a multi-programmed system. Different programs in that system will be confined within different boundaries, and thus cannot do damage to each other.

Message Reference Block. When more than one message in the system is being processed in parallel, an area of storage is allocated to each message and remains uniquely associated with that message for the duration of its stay in the computer. This is called the Message Reference Block. It will normally contain the message and data associated with it that are required for its processing. In most systems it contains an area of working storage uniquely reserved for that message.

Multiplexor. A device which uses several communication channels at the same time, transmitting and receiving messages and controlling the communication lines. This device itself may or may not be a stored-program computer. It will always be attached to a stored-program computer.

Multi-priority Queue. This is a group of items in the system waiting for the attention of the processor. The items have different priorities and form in effect a number of queues of different priority from which items may be extracted on a first-come-first-served basis.

Multi-processing. Multi-processing means that more than one computer is used in the processing of one transaction.

Multi-programming. Multi-programming means that more than one item is in one computer, with the items being processed in parallel.

Multi-thread Processing. A thread refers to a sequence of events or programs which are needed for the complete processing of a message. In some systems all of these programs or events will be completed before work begins on a new message. This is referred to as single-thread processing. In other systems a thread for one message may be broken while a thread for another message continues. In this way several threads may be handled in parallel. This is referred to as multi-thread processing.

New Input Queue. This is a group of new messages which have arrived in the system and which are waiting for the computer to begin processing. The New Input Queue will be scanned, along with the Work-In-Progress Queue and possible other queues, by the Main Scheduling Routine.

Next-Available-Block Register. This is a facility on a line control computer which automatically allocates storage to new characters arriving on the communication lines. When one block of core is filled, the next characters go automatically to the next block. The address of the next block is contained in a register referred to as the Next-Available-Block Register. The available blocks of storage are all chained together. When one block from a chain of available blocks is assigned, the address of the next block is automatically stored in the register.

On-Line. An on-line system may be defined as one in which the input data enter the computer directly from their point of origin and/or output data are transmitted directly to where they are used. The intermediate stages such as punching data into cards or paper tape, writing magnetic tape, or off-line printing, are largely avoided.

Overflow Areas in a File. When randomizing is used for file addressing, the addresses generated refer to pockets where one or more file records are stored. The pocket may however already be full, having a different item stored in it. In this case the item in question must be stored in an overflow location in the file which is chained to the location first found.

Overloads. The rate of input to some real-time systems will vary from one moment to another. At times a momentary overload may occur because all the communications lines transmit data to the computer at once, and the computer is not fast enough to process this sudden flood of messages. There are various types of emergency action possible for dealing with this type of overload.

Overload Simulator. It is necessary to program test the system under overload conditions. However, it is usually undesirable to use for such a test as many messages as would be needed to produce a genuine overflow. Therefore, the system is modified in some artificial way to produce a condition which makes the programs behave as they would during an overload, but which does not actually need this number of transactions.

Output Queue. This is a group of output messages which have been produced by the system and which are waiting for the Output Scheduler to transmit them down the communication lines.

Pilot Model. This is a model of the system used for program testing purposes which is less complex than the complete model, e.g., the files used on a pilot model may contain a much smaller number of records than the operational files.

Pilot Tape. This is a tape used for loading the files. It contains all the data used on the pilot model.

Pockets (in file addressing). When randomizing is used for file addressing, this technique locates a small area in the file in which one or more records are kept. This area is referred to as a pocket. It is usually economical to have a small number of records in a pocket. A pocket may, for example, correspond to one track on a disk file containing perhaps 20 records.

Polling. This is a means of controlling communication lines. The communication control device will send signals to a terminal saying, "Terminal A. Have you anything to send?" if not, "Terminal B. Have you anything to send?" and so on. Polling is an alternative to contention. It makes sure that no terminal is kept waiting for a long time as could conceivably happen with a contention network.

Polling List. The polling signals will usually be sent under program control. The program will have in core a list for each channel which tells the sequence in which the terminals are to be polled.

Priority Error Dump. In some systems equipment errors, or program errors, cause an interrupt which makes the system execute a priority program. This priority program may dump onto tape, or other media, areas of core storage or other information which enables programmers or engineers to assess the cause of the error.

Priority Routine. When an interrupt occurs the program in use at that time will be left and a different program will be executed to deal with interrupt. This new program is sometimes referred to as a Priority Routine.

Program Relocation. This means that programs can operate in different locations in core. In most systems Application Programs are in segments which may be read into different locations of core and operated from these locations. This can be achieved by programming or by a circuitry device. Normally, special circuitry is needed for program relocation.

Pseudo File Address. The Application Program, when giving an address for obtaining a record from the files, may not give an actual machine address but a false address which is converted by the Supervisory Programs into an actual machine address. The reason for this is that the actual machine address may change from one time to another because different file units may be used as part of a duplexing or fall-back process.

Push-down Queue. This is a group of items or areas in the system chained together and organized in such a way that the last item to be attached to the group is the first one to be withdrawn from it, giving a last-in-first-out priority.

Queue. This is a group of items in the system waiting for the attention of the processor. Normally, queues are "dynamic" which means that they consist of storage areas which can be anywhere within part of the core, and which are chained together by means of words in each area, containing addresses of consecutive areas in the queue.

Random-access Files. These are storage media holding a large amount of information in such a way that any item may be read or written at random with a short access time, i.e., usually less than one second. Example of random-access files are disk storages, drums, and magnetic tape or strip files.

Randomizing (for file addressing). A means by which a record may be located in a large random-access file, given a key set of characters which immediately identifies this record. The key is converted into a random number by means of an algorithm, and the random number is converted into the machine address of a pocket where the item may be stored. If the item is not stored in that pocket, the pocket will contain the address of an overflow pocket which should be examined in the search for the item.

Real-time. A real-time computer system may be defined as one that controls an environment by receiving data, processing them and returning the results sufficiently quickly to affect the functioning of the environment at that time.

Reasonableness Checks. Tests made on information reaching a real-time system or being transmitted from it to ensure that the data in question lie within a given reasonable range.

Recovery from Fall-back. When the system has switched to a fall-back mode of operation and the cause of the fall-back has been removed, the system must be restored to its former condition. This is referred to as Recovery from Fall-back. The recovery process may involve updating information on the files to produce two duplicate copies of the file.

Relocatable Programs. A relocatable program is one that can operate from different locations in core. In most systems Application Programs are in segments which may be read into different locations of core and operated from these locations. This can be achieved by programming or a circuitry device. Normally, special circuitry is needed for program relocation.

Resident Executive. That part of the Supervisory Programs which must remain permanently in core, i.e., this is not to be stored on the files, to be called in when required, as are other parts of the Supervisory Programs.

Response Time. This is the time the system takes to react to a given input. If a message is keyed into a terminal by an operator and the reply from the computer, when it comes, is typed at the same terminal, response times may be defined as the time interval between the operator pressing the last key and the terminal typing the first letter of the reply. For different types of terminal, response time may be defined similarly. It is the interval between an event and the system's response to the event.

Saturation Testing. Program testing with a large bulk of messages intended to bring to light those errors which will only occur very infrequently and which may be triggered by rare coincidences such as two different messages arriving at the same time.

Seek. A mechanical movement involved in locating a record in a random-access file. This may, for example, be the movement of an arm and head mechanism that is necessary before a read instruction can be given to read data in a certain location on the file.

Self-checking Numbers. Numbers which contain redundant information so that an error in them, caused, for example, by noise on a transmission line, may be detected. A number may, for example, contain two additional digits which are produced from the other digits in the number by means of an arithmetical process. If these two digits are not correct it will indicate that the number has in some way been garbled. The two additional digits may be checked by the computer as a safeguard against this.

Sequential Queue. This is a group of items in the system waiting for the attention of the processor, and organized in such a way that the first item to gain attention will be the first one placed in the group, i.e., priority first-in-first-out.

Set-up Services. When a message enters the system certain functions must be performed upon it before the Application Program begins processing it. These functions are checking for errors in the message, erasing back-space characters, analyzing the action code, and so on. These are referred to as Set-up Services.

Simulation. This is a word which is sometimes confusing as it has three entirely different meanings, namely:

Simulation (for Design and Monitoring). This is a technique whereby a model of the working system can be built in the form of a computer program. Special computer languages are available for producing this model. A complete system may be described by a succession of different models. These models can then be adjusted easily and endlessly, and the system that is being designed or monitored can be experimented with to test the effect of any proposed changes. The simulation model is a program that is run on a computer separate from the system that is being designed.

Simulation of Input Devices. This is a program testing aid. For various reasons it is undesirable to use actual lines and terminals for some of the program testing. Therefore, magnetic tape or other media may be used and read in by a special program which makes the data appear as if they came from actual lines and terminals. Simulation in this sense is the replacement of one set of equipment by another set of equipment and programs, so that the behavior is similar.

Simulation of Supervisory Programs. This is used for program testing purposes when the actual Supervisory Programs are not yet available. A comparitively simple program to bridge the gap is used instead. This type of simulation is the replacement of one set of programs by another set which imitates it.

Status Maps. Tables which give the status of various programs, devices or input/output operations.

Supervisory Programs. Those computer programs designed to coordinate service and augment the machine components of the system, and coordinate and service Application Programs. They handle work scheduling, input/output operations, error actions, and other functions.

Supervisory System. The complete set of Supervisory Programs used on a given system.

Support Programs. The ultimate operational system consists of Supervisory Programs and Application Programs. However, a third set of programs are needed to install the system, including diagnostics, testing aids, data generator programs, terminal simulators, and so on. These are referred to as Support Programs.

Switchover. When a failure occurs in the equipment a switch may occur to an alternative component. This may be, for example, an alternative file unit, an alternative communication line or an alternative computer. The switchover process may be automatic under program control or it may be manual.

Single-thread Processing. See Multi-thread Processing.

System Utilization Loggers. A device, frequently a program, designed to gather statistics about the operation of the system. These may, for example, indicate how many messages the system is handling at a given time and how much processing time remains available.

Terminals. The means by which data are entered into the system and by which the decisions of the system are communicated to the environment it affects. A wide variety of terminal devices have been built, including teleprinters, special keyboards, light displays, cathode tubes, thermocouples, pressure gauges and other instrumentation, radar units, telephones, and so on.

Test Supervisor Program. The Supervisory Program used solely for testing purposes. It may read the input to the test at appropriate moments and log the output from the test. It may be controlled by a timing device.

Transfer Vector. This is a means of transferring control from one relocatable program to another. This cannot be done by a simple branch or transfer, instruction because the location of the program to which the control is being transferred is not known at the time of writing the programs. The Transfer Vector is a table which may contain a list of transfer or branch instructions, enabling transfers to be made to the entry points of the various programs in core. This table must be updated when new programs are brought into core.

Uncommited Storage List. When dynamic storage allocation is used, those blocks of storage which are not at a given moment allocated will be chained together. When a block is needed for a specific purpose it will be taken from this chain of blocks. The chain of blocks is referred to as the Uncommitted Storage List.

Violation Subroutines. Subroutines which are executed when the input to the system does not conform to specific criteria, e.g., a gauge reading may not lie within certain limits, or it may have changed too much since the last time it was read, or an operator may have transmitted an invalid message, and so on.

WAIT, Macro-instruction. When an Application Program is processing a message and a request is given which causes a delay so that no further processing can continue, e.g., an input/output request, a WAIT Macro-instruction is given. This causes control to be transferred to a Supervisory Program. Processing continues on other messages, but it will continue on this message only when the cause of the delay has been removed and the processor is ready to continue work on this message. This type of Macro-instruction is needed for Multi-thread Processing.

Watchdog Timer. This is a timer which is set by the program. It interrupts the program after a given period of time, e.g., one second. This will prevent the system from going into an endless loop due to a program error, or becoming idle because of an equipment fault. The Watchdog timer may sound a horn if such a fault is detected.

Work-In-Progress queue. This is a queue of items on which processing has been started and interrupted. These items are waiting for the computer to complete their processing.

INDEX